IDENTITY, IDEOLOGY AND CONFLICT

Ideologies and identities are central to the organisation of political life and political conflict, yet most empirical studies tend to obscure their significance. This failure to take the politics of identity seriously is no mere oversight; it arises from an absence of an adequate theory and method. This study draws on both social theory and psychological (especially psychoanalytic) theory in an attempt to overcome these lacunae. First, it develops a novel theory and method for the analysis of ideology and identity. It does so by addressing the structuration process through which unconscious rules integral to the organisation of political subjectivities and political and social relations are drawn upon in the making of political conflict. Second, it develops a detailed analysis of the politics of identity in Northern Ireland through focusing upon Unionist ideology and Unionist identities in crisis. The political conflict within Unionism is analysed through a consideration of the variety of unconscious rules drawn upon by political actors and citizens in the making of Northern Ireland's history of the present.

IDENTITY, IDEOLOGY AND CONFLICT

The structuration of politics in Northern Ireland

JOHN DANIEL CASH

CAMBRIDGE
UNIVERSITY PRESS

Published by the Press Syndicate of the University of Cambridge
The Pitt Building, Trumpington Street, Cambridge CB2 IRP
40 West 20th Street, New York, NY 10011-4211, USA
10 Stamford Road, Oakleigh, Melbourne 3166, Australia

First published 1996

Printed in Great Britain at the University Press, Cambridge

A catalogue record for this book is available from the British Library

Library of Congress cataloguing in publication data
Cash, John Daniel.
Identity, ideology and conflict: the structuration of politics in Northern Ireland
p. cm.
Includes bibliographical references.
ISBN 0 521 55052 1 (hc)
1. Northern Ireland – Politics and government – 1969–
I. Title.
DA990.U46C36 1996
320.9416'01'9 – dc20 95-41395 cip

ISBN 0 521 55052 1 hardback

CE

This book is dedicated to my mother and in memory of my father

Contents

Acknowledgements

This study was conceived in the United States while I was a graduate student at Yale University, its complexities were explored and experienced during eighteen months of fieldwork in Northern Ireland and, finally, it was written in Australia, where I currently work at the University of Melbourne and where, as an undergraduate, I first began to think about identity, ideology and politics and the integration of psychoanalysis and social theory. To spread out the conduct of such a study over three such disparate locations, as I have done, is to multiply one's reliance upon the assistance and encouragement of others by at least a factor of nine! It is these multiple others whom I wish to acknowledge here.

At the University of Melbourne, where I studied as an undergraduate and where I currently teach, I had the good fortune to first encounter the late Alan Davies in my undergraduate years. It is his example of commitment to originality and seriousness of thought which I have tried to follow in my subsequent work. As well, it is his special interest in psychoanalytic and psychosocial studies which helped establish my own interest in this field. In my final undergraduate year I studied with Graham Little and have continued to learn from him to this day. I wish to acknowledge the profound effect which the curious brilliance of his teaching has had upon me. Fran Hattam, Vicky Hattam, Graeme Garrett, Angus McIntyre and James Walter joined me in an exuberant exploration of all things psychoanalytic at around this time and I assure them that I still savour it all.

At Yale University I had the good fortune to work with Robert Lane, Bill Foltz, Robert Lifton and Stanley Greenberg. In their different ways each of them assisted me in finding a way to link an interest in social, political and psychological theories to the analysis of significant political processes. At Yale I also met Ian Shapiro who, from our first encounter, has been my sternest of intellectual critics as well as the most generous of my intellectual companions. I thank him for the seriousness with which he has always responded to my work.

In Northern Ireland, at the University of Ulster in Coleraine, I was extended the most generous of welcomes both by the Department of Social Anthropology and Sociology and by the, then, fledgling Centre for the Study of Conflict. John Darby, Nick Dodge and Dale Sanders, along with their families, made my two lengthy visits, and my recent short visit, both intellectually rewarding and socially convivial. I thank them for their friendship and their guidance. While in Northern Ireland I conducted a series of interviews with thirty members of the two principal Unionist parties: the Official (Ulster) Unionist Party, and the Democratic Unionist Party. I thank these individuals for the kindness they extended to me. I suspect that many of them would disagree with the interpretation I develop in this study, although I am certain that some would not. To all of them I extend the hope that, in its inevitably minuscule way, this study may contribute to the type of understanding which can help make a positive difference in Northern Ireland.

In research of this kind the scholar is inevitably reliant on the assistance of skilled librarians. I wish to thank the staff who assisted me at the Linenhall Library in Belfast, at the Ballymena Public Library and at the British Library, both at Colindale and at the British Museum.

At the University of Melbourne I have had the great pleasure of working closely with Michael Dutton and the intense grouping of committed and brilliant students whom we often have had the good fortune to share. This affinity of intellectual curiosity and ethical commitments, and the community of interest which it supports, has been both a solace and a joy to me. I have also been privileged to teach and subsequently work with two unusually talented scholars, Anthony Elliott and Kwok Wei Leng. To learn while teaching and teach while learning and to have the support and encouragement of those whose intellectual interests you have helped form is to receive a remarkable gift.

Several others have also taken an interest in this research. They include Guinever Threlkeld, Judith Brett, Norma Grieve, Phillip Darby, Leslie Holmes, Peter Collins, Anthony Kitchener, Anthony Moran, Albert Paolini, Kirsty Major, Tony Phillips, John Jirik and

Eric Timewell. I greatly appreciate their many kindnesses. John Haslam, my editor at Cambridge University Press, has offered both strong encouragement and a keen critical appraisal since he first received the typescript. I greatly appreciate the manner in which he has helped bring this project to completion. The two anonymous reviewers provided me with many helpful suggestions which I have been pleased to incorporate. Sheila Kane, my copyeditor, has performed delicate surgery on the text; in the process improving its coherence while teaching me a great deal about the manner in which I write.

At various stages in the conduct of this research I received financial support from the University of Melbourne Travelling Scholarship Fund and the Council on International and Area Studies, Yale University. I am very grateful for this assistance.

Finally, my wife, Gabrielle, and our two children, Finn and Conall, have loved me, indulged me and distracted me. I thank them for all of it.

PART I

Theory with an empirical intent: theories of ideology, subjectivity and intersubjectivity

Introduction: Theory with an empirical intent

> For if much of service has been got by following Occam's law to the effect that 'entities should not be *multiplied* beyond necessity', equally much of disservice has arisen through ignoring a contrary law, which we could phrase correspondingly: 'entities should not be *reduced* beyond necessity'.
>
> (Kenneth Burke, *A Grammar of Motives*, emphasis in original)

Ideologies are complex and dynamic formations which are at once cognitive, affective and conative in character. They both construct and evaluate the political and social field and they motivate behaviour within it. That such is the case is particularly apparent at moments of stress or crisis; at least if one observes the crisis from the privileged perspective of an alien. For instance, to live in the United States during the period of the occupation of the US Embassy in Teheran was to experience, both within the public domain and broadly within the private domain, the pervasive capacity of an ideological process to structure the thoughts, feelings and behavioural orientations of a whole society (these were perhaps best expressed in the popular aphorism of the time, 'We should nuke downtown Teheran'). Similarly, to live in Britain during the Falklands/Malvinas episode was to witness the narrowing and focusing of the 'civic culture' around one sanctioned construction of reality. In both cases, at least in my own experience, the cognitive rigidity and emotional valence of these ideological forms was quite palpable. Except within narrow conclaves it was difficult to speak or indeed think in a reflective and critical manner about the complexities of such issues. The conceptual ground was so narrowed and so emotionally charged that to tug at its boundaries was to risk, at least, the occasioning of discomfort or insult to those individuals, that is to say the vast majority, who recognised these ideologies as in some sense their own.

3

The above characterisations are somewhat idle reflections which are intended merely to suggest, or recall, for the reader some prominent features of ideologies. However even as such they go beyond the conventional academic notions of ideology. For they recognise that ideologies are dynamic structures which have affective as well as cognitive dimensions, and that they at once touch both individuals and whole social formations.

This study endeavours to develop a theory of ideology (and identity) which is adequate to such a complex, dynamic and potent object. Thus it eschews approaches which regard ideology as merely a derivative or reflection of economic or social processes. Similarly it regards approaches which concentrate solely on the psychological characteristics of individuals or groups as unduly limiting and restrictive. It intends to replace such partial perspectives with a more adequate theory of ideology, one which recognises the centrality of ideology to both the constitution of subjectivity and the structuration of political and social relations. The study takes as its point of departure the apparent anomaly of the persistence and regeneration of ideologies of ethnicity in the modern world. It focuses on Northern Ireland as one particularly striking example of this apparent anomaly.

Ideologies of ethnicity, whether they assume racial, regional, religious or other forms, are striking features of the contemporary world. Wherever they occur these ideologies touch intimately upon the constitution of political subjectivity; forming, at least potentially, a central aspect of individual identity. At the same time, they are also a central cultural form for the organisation of political and social life. Hence, at once, they touch both individuals and whole social formations, and they do so in palpable ways. A further feature of such ideologies, one which is characteristically discounted, is that they are marked by emotion.

Prevalent theories of ideology are unable adequately to grasp these features. Characteristically, prevalent theories privilege either the individual or the social and then derive the features of the suppressed part (the social or the individual) from the features of that part which they have privileged. In other words, they tend to fall prey to either psychological or economic or social reductionism. Whenever this reductionism occurs it obscures the complex character of ideology. This complex character of ideology lies exactly in its inclusion of the subjective and the social as thoroughly interrelated;

as two sides of the same process. Prevalent theories also tend to discount the emotional component of ideologies and they have difficulty in relating ideology to the organisation of social and political relations. The theory developed in this study attempts to overcome these various limitations.

The very persistence or regeneration of ideologies of ethnicity in the modern world is something of a mystery to our commonsense understanding. We tend to assume, particularly with regard to Western societies, that growth, progress, modernisation, industrialisation, capitalism (or what you will), should eradicate such primordial identifications and sentiments. If sectarianism and other such ideologies of ethnicity are traditional, indeed irrational, then surely they must wither and die! Yet the contemporary world, East and West, North and South, First, Second and Third, provides clear evidence that ideologies of ethnicity are prevalent and persistent. Indeed they seem to be proliferating.[1] How could this be?

This 'ethnic revival' presents a profound challenge to more than our commonsense understanding of how the world should be ordered. It confounds all those theories of growth, modernisation or development which have their basis in the Enlightenment tradition and which retain their faith in the power of reason; including the case where reason has been transubstantiated into proletarian class consciousness. Consequently, the incapacity of so much contemporary theory to adequately explain the persistence and regeneration of ideologies of ethnicity in the modern world, although substantial in itself, is best recognised as one instance of a far broader range of anomalies and lacunae within the major traditions of political and sociological theory; all having their basis in the failure of this theory adequately to grasp the centrality of ideology to the constitution of both political subjectivities and social and political relations. From this perspective it is a profound irony that the past thirty years, which were so confidently expected to exemplify a brave new world beyond ideology, should have witnessed an ideological explosion.[2] Feminism and the other liberation movements, the conservation, anti-nuclear and green movements, fundamentalist religions of various types and a host of other passionately upheld and non-negotiable single issue movements; all of these, along with ideologies of ethnicity, nation

---

[1] See A. D. Smith, *The Ethnic Revival in the Modern World* (Cambridge University Press, 1981), passim.

[2] See D. Bell, *The End of Ideology* (New York: Free Press, 1960), passim.

and race, have become central to an ever more unmanageable political order. The rational administration of politics within convergent and consensual political cultures seems further away than ever, as do those other certainties regarding the emergence and consolidation of ideologies of class consciousness. All such certainties have been confounded by the multifarious complexity of political life and the centrality of ideology to its constitution.

As we can see, the failure of prevailing theories to comprehend the persistence and regeneration of ideologies of ethnicity calls their general assumptions about ideology radically into question. This failure constitutes the opening, the persistent gap between explanans and explanandum, from which I hope to develop a more adequate theory of ideology. At its most general, then, this study is concerned to develop a theory of ideology which specifies both the character of ideology and the character of its relationship to other political and social processes. This leads it to pose a group of questions of which the most central are the following. How is an ideological formation structured, and what are its rules of structuration? How is an ideology reproduced and transformed? How does an ideology operate to organise subjectivities and the field of intersubjective relations? How does crisis affect an ideological formation? What are the mechanisms of articulation between ideological and other political processes? How do class processes enter into the determination of an ideological formation?

The final question concerning the significance of class processes is, of course, a perennial one within political and social theory. Usually it is taken up in an economistic manner by both advocates and opponents. That is to say, ideology is usually regarded as epiphenomenal, as merely the reflection, at the level of consciousness, of economic or class processes. Ideology is regarded as a transparent medium or register with no structure of its own. It is merely a derivative effect of something whose structuring principle is other and elsewhere. As such it is denied any constitutive or determinative role within the political process. The point of the whole group of questions outlined above is to establish a somewhat novel problematic which should allow a thorough-going break with such a limiting and misleading approach. In responding to the group of questions which constitute this problematic I will not be content with programmatic statements which remain at a high level of abstraction. Rather I take it as central to any theory and method concerned with the analysis of ideology that it be both conceptually sophisticated and able to support a systematic and detailed examination of a particular ideology. Moreover it must be able to integrate and move between these levels of analysis in a consistent manner. Hence, one litmus test for the adequacy of any theory of ideology is its ability to be applied to the analysis of particular cases. The benefits of such a requirement are manifold. In particular the discipline which it imposes should generate both conceptual clarification (a rare commodity in this domain) and a more comprehensive understanding of ideology in its various aspects. This should facilitate the replacement of mechanistic and instrumentalist conceptions of ideology by a conception which recognises both its centrality and its contingency.

My intention in this study is to develop an approach which takes seriously the centrality of ideology and identity to the structuration of political life. I attempt to do so in two interrelated ways. First, in part 1 I attempt to develop a somewhat novel theory of ideology, one which recognises ideology as a structure of signification, communication and subjection which is central to the organisation of both subjectivity and social and political relations. This theory is developed by drawing critically upon four traditions within contemporary social theory (namely structuralism, post-structuralism, structuration theory and the theory of communicative action) and by looking closely at the ways in which each has appropriated psychological theory (in particular psychoanalysis, but also cognitive-developmental theory). These various theories are drawn upon and then selectively drawn together, and not merely reproduced, in an attempt to specify the manner in which ideological formations operate. To achieve this I opt for a revised theory of structuration, one which places the unconscious rules of structuration at the centre of its account. Second, having elaborated this somewhat novel theory of ideology, in part 2 I draw upon this theory to analyse the case of Unionist ideology in Northern Ireland. First of all, I analyse the major forms of Unionist ideology, elaborating the characteristics of each. Then, building upon this, I develop an account of some central aspects of the political process in Northern Ireland; in particular those aspects involving the conflict for hegemony between these major, and distinct, forms of Unionist ideology. When my discussion calls for it I also develop an analysis of some principal features of Nationalist and Republican ideologies. The leading empirical question which organises this study is the following:

in what manner has Unionist ideology operated in Northern Ireland to 'reproduce' that society as a 'divided' society? My contention is that only by taking ideology (and identity) seriously are we likely to offer an adequate answer to this question. Along the way we will notice that those answers to this question which, in Kenneth Burke's phrase, have 'reduced [entities] beyond necessity' are seriously misleading.[3]

This study can be described as an attempt to develop social and political theory with an empirical intent. In part 1 the discussion, first of all, develops a novel theory of ideology and then, in chapters 4 and 5, it specifies the manner in which such a theory may be drawn into empirical research. This latter step is the crucial dimension of this study, as it is here that the strengths of the sophisticated theory of ideology are extended to the analysis of empirical evidence, hopefully in a manner which preserves these strengths. As I claim below, it is at this point, the extension of theory to empirical analysis, that most studies falter, often falling into the very reductionist moves which they have castigated or overlooked in their theoretical sections. In part 2 this extension of sophisticated theory into empirical analysis is carried a step further when I focus explicitly on the issue of the role of Unionist ideology in Northern Ireland. The intention here is to demonstrate the strengths of the theory and methods of analysis established in part 1 by developing an account of the structuration of Unionist ideology during the, by now, lengthy crisis of the past thirty years. After establishing some preliminaries in chapter 6, in the succeeding chapters I develop an analysis of Unionist ideology as it has moved from a position of relative hegemony to a position of relative crisis. The evidence used in these chapters is drawn from the public political discourse. It includes political statements and speeches, as recorded in the regional and local press and as recorded in the magazine and pamphlet literature of the various political groupings. By focusing on the unconscious rules of structuration of Unionist ideology I attempt to offer a detailed explanation of the splintering which has occurred within Unionism since the 1960s and an explanation of the particular forms which this (splintered) ideology has taken. These chapters offer a novel approach to the processes through which non-negotiable, uncompromising forms of political subjectivity are endemically,

---

[3]   K. Burke, *A Grammar of Motives* (New York: Prentice Hall, 1945).

though not automatically, reproduced within a crisis-ridden ideological formation. The period of the 1960s and early 1970s is read as an attempt by various actors and movements to institutionalise a novel set of rules. Within Unionism the failure of this enterprise led to an internal splitting of what, previously, had been a relatively united movement. Certain exclusivist, triumphalist and denigrating rules, which had always been a part of Unionism, were now drawn upon in the creation of a new set of political and paramilitary groupings which set about recolonising the ideological field so that it more fully met their own preferred notions of identity, authority and the proper pattern of social and political relations. The intention in these chapters is to analyse this dynamic political process within Unionism, so as to highlight the manner in which this process may be more adequately conceptualised as a conflict over which rules of ideology should dominate the institutional and public space. The related intention is to explore the ways in which a more adequate understanding of the character of the political subjectivities at play in Northern Ireland can offer a better understanding of the restrictions and distortions which endemically mark and limit attempts to institutionalise different, more 'liberal' identities and patterns of relationship. It is claimed that this approach offers new insights into the relationship between political subjectivities and the scope and limits of political action. Finally, in the concluding chapter I make use of the approach developed throughout this book to offer a preliminary analysis of the current situation in Northern Ireland subsequent to the cease-fire and publication of the British and Irish governments' 'Framework Document'.

TWO CONVENTIONAL APPROACHES TO THE STUDY OF IDEOLOGY

As an initial step, two broad types of approach to the study of ideology, one sociological and the other psychological, may be distinguished. The first comprehends ideology as a more or less immediate effect of social, or economic, processes. It involves numerous variations on the one set theme: individuals as the mere bearers or carriers of ideological systems. In this approach an analysis of ideology is seen to require a consideration of class processes, or modernising processes or whatever the particular sociological theory in use specifies as the determinant social process. Such an approach has major limitations. Principally, it is unable to enter the ideological discourse itself and to treat ideology as an autonomous or relatively autonomous structure with its own determinate rules of structuration. Rather it falls prey to what may be termed an equivalence fallacy.[4] It regards the ideological formation as a thoroughly plastic medium which operates in more or less immediate and perfect synchrony with whichever social process is understood as the determinant of its character. The rules of process characteristic of the social field are merely extended to the ideological field unquestioningly. This extension – the assumption of an equivalence between the rules of process of the social field and the rules of process of the ideological field – is seriously misleading.

Modernisation theory is one of the social theories which highlights this failing.[5] This theory sees the emergence of a modernised ideological formation as the inevitable outcome of the modernisation of social relations. Being unconcerned with the internal rules of structuration of the ideological formation itself, it must choose, or oscillate, between being reductionist and being idealist and descriptive. That is, the cultural norms of modernity are regarded either as the direct effect of social processes or as mere givens which, once implanted, continue to inhere. The case of Northern Ireland, in which the modernisation of economic and social relations coexists with, and appears to have generated, primordial identities and ideologies, confounds such a happy ignorance of the character of ideology. As, indeed, does the more general 'ethnic revival' within the modern world.

A second approach to the study of ideology operates, principally, at the psychological level and comprehends ideology as the complex construction generated by an interaction between an ideological formation, usually described as a culture, and the personality system of the individual under examination. Rather than working with abstract and schematic descriptions of this or that ideological system, such a psychological approach characteristically concerns itself, initially, with detailed and expansive accounts of the thoughts and feelings of particular individuals as elicited, usually, through a series of interviews. An immediate effect of such an approach is the substitution of extremely rich and complex evidence in place of the somewhat arid schematisations characteristic of the sociological

[4]   See chapter 1 for a more detailed discussion of this proposed equivalence fallacy.
[5]   See chapter 1 for a more detailed discussion of modernisation theory.

approach. A first corollary of this is the necessity for the development of methods of analysis which recognise the complex integrity of such evidence. A second corollary is that ideologies themselves, and not their putative social determinants, become the primary objects of attention.

If the above may be counted as advantages of the psychological approach, in its conventional form it also has serious limitations, both inherently and in practice. By bracketing any concern with the intersubjective character of ideologies, and by focusing on the individual psychological determinants of a subject's system of values, beliefs and feelings regarding the political order, many other aspects of ideologies are excluded from systematic consideration. In particular, as Geertz pointed out some twenty-five years ago, the ideological system itself, rather than its psychological (or social) determinants, is excluded from analysis.[6]

Both the virtues and limitations of such an approach can be seen in Robert Lane's work on ideology. In *Political Ideology* , *Political Thinking and Consciousness* and *Political Man,* Lane uses (or reflects upon their use in *Political Man*) intensive interviews with a relatively small group of subjects as the source of ideological evidence.[7] He then proceeds in two directions simultaneously, attempting to establish both the 'core belief system' and the idiosyncratic transformations worked upon this by the personality system. Lane's work is exemplary in that it moves (as is too seldom the case with the political psychological approach), on the basis of a considered evaluation of evidence gathered from intensive interviewing, from the individual to the social. However even Lane's exemplary work remains caught within the limitations of its paradigmatic approach. Due to a privileging of socialisation processes above other (social) processes, ideological formations are recognised as a determinant within the political process only insofar as they are internalised. Although the social and the cultural are included within the scope of such an approach, they are only incorporated insofar as they derive from and return to the individual actor, or groupings of such actors. In particular, the effect of such an approach is to radically diminish the role of ideology as the discursive field which is recursively involved in

---

[6] See C. Geertz, 'Ideology as a Cultural System', reprinted in *The Interpretation of Cultures* (New York: Basic Books, 1973).

[7] R. E. Lane, *Political Ideology* (New York: Free Press, 1962), *Political Thinking and Consciousness* (Chicago: Markham, 1969) and *Political Man* (New York: Free Press, 1972).

the organisation of *both* intersubjective relations and individual subjectivities.

In this study I propose a third approach to the study of ideology, one which, at least in intention, appropriates the virtues of both the sociological and psychological approaches whilst overcoming their limitations. It does so by directing its attention to the ideological formation itself, observing the variety of its forms both synchronically and diachronically, and finally attempting an explanation of ideological transformations within a crisis-prone society over time. In order to do so, as I have already outlined, it appropriates and reworks some aspects of social theory, psychoanalytic theory and cognitive-developmental theory.

NORTHERN IRELAND AS A CASE STUDY

Northern Ireland has been selected as a case study as it has consistently confounded the prevailing theories of ideology. During the nineteenth century Belfast was the most rapidly growing in population, and one of the most rapidly industrialising, of all cities in the United Kingdom. In this same period the city experienced significant sectarian riots in 1856, 1864, 1872, 1880, 1886, and 1898. Furthermore these riots increased in their intensity as the nineteenth century progressed.[8] Throughout the twentieth century such conflict has persisted and since 1968 Northern Ireland has experienced recurrent sectarian conflict.

Despite such a dismal track record, in 1969 we find Terence O'Neill, the champion of a non-sectarian liberalism and of a new deal for Catholics in Northern Ireland, at the very moment of his defeat and retirement as prime minister, reflecting in the following vein:

The basic fear of the Protestants in Northern Ireland is that they will be outbred by the Roman Catholics. It is as simple as that. It is frightfully hard to explain to a Protestant that if you give Roman Catholics a good job and a good house they will live like Protestants, because they will see neighbours with cars and TV sets. They will refuse to have eighteen children, but if the Roman Catholic is jobless and lives in a most ghastly hovel he will rear eighteen children on national assistance. It is impossible to explain this to a militant Protestant, because he is so keen to deny civil rights to his Roman

---

[8]   See I. Budge and C. O'Leary, *Belfast: Approach to Crisis* (London: Macmillan, 1973), pp. 28, 75.

Catholic neighbours. He cannot understand, in fact, that if you treat Roman Catholics with due consideration and kindness they will live like Protestants in spite of the authoritarian nature of their church.[9]

This bears some consideration, for whilst reiterating a faith in the therapeutic virtues of modernisation – a good job, a good house, a car and a television set – in its very terms it reproduces the ideology of ethnicity it is intending to displace. This is apparent from the seemingly unproblematic classification of persons as Roman Catholic or Protestant, to the reiteration, either directly or in the form of a simple reversal, of themes of Catholic fecundity, irresponsibility, laziness, wilful poverty and mindless subjection to priest and church. O'Neill's statement typically has been regarded as an indicator of his personal failings, of his 'sublime paternalist arrogance'[10] or of his 'stilted vision'.[11] To personalise in this way is to miss the point. For the fascinating aspect of all this is that O'Neill did not habitually construct the political and social reality of Northern Ireland in such sectarian terms. As a survey of his political speeches, even during elections and at Twelfth of July demonstrations, and of his writings reveals, such a statement was remarkably unusual for O'Neill. Why then, at a moment of Unionist crisis in 1969, did O'Neill promote the virtues of modernisation in such sectarian terms? What had happened to the Unionist ideological formation to render such a mode of address appropriate, indeed perhaps even necessary, for communication between Unionists? To put this more generally: how does the structure of an ideology change as it moves between moments of hegemony and moments of crisis? At such critical moments, which type of ideological rule tends to dominate, and why?

To answer such questions we require an enhanced capacity to analyse and categorise ideological processes. We need to be able, first of all, to notice transformations as they occur, and, secondly, to offer some detailed account of the forms these transformations take. At present such a capacity does not exist in any adequate form. Consequently quite central aspects of the ways in which ideologies operate are simply not seen, resulting in confusion and incoherence of often quite mammoth proportions. By recognising that ideologies may change in their structure (or rules for the organisation of both

---

[9] Quoted in A. C. Hepburn, *The Conflict of Nationality in Modern Ireland* (London, Edward Arnold, 1980), p. 182.

[10] M. Farrell, *Northern Ireland: The Orange State* (London: Pluto Press, 1980), p. 256.

[11] Hepburn, *The Conflict of Nationality*, p. 182.

intersubjectivity and subjectivity) and not solely in terms of their content, and by developing a theory of ideology and some related methods of analysis consonant with such a recognition, I hope to be able to provide a more thorough and detailed analysis of the forms an ideology may take, both synchronically and diachronically. Further, building upon this, I hope to establish the implications of such (newly observed) ideological forms for political organisation and political conflict.

This approach is developed in response to an implicit and distorting assumption common to otherwise diverse theories of political and ideological processes, namely the assumption that the construction and evaluation of reality proceeds according to one uniform and unchanging mode of reasoning. This assumption is quite unacceptable and misleading. As everyday notions of polarisation, the psychoanalytic concept of regression and a great body of social psychological research make clear, reasoning processes and procedures for information processing and the construction of reality vary with relation to the threatening or stressful aspects of the environment. As Lazarus puts it, summarising a comprehensive survey of the research on threat and coping:

There appears to be a relationship between the degree of threat and the tendency of the individual to employ more primitive, desperate, or regressive types of defences. More adaptive and reality-oriented forms of coping are most likely when the threat is comparatively mild; under severe threat, pathological extremes become more prominent.[12]

Janis, when studying the effect of 'reflective fear' upon 'discriminative' decision making, observed a similar phenomenon. Moderate levels of fear produce high vigilance and careful discrimination. However 'when reflective fear reaches a very high level there is an increase in indiscriminative vigilance reactions, manifested by reduced mental efficiency and a predominance of regressive thought processes'.[13]

This distinction between the regressive effects of high vulnerability and the vigilance effects of moderate vulnerability is highly suggestive for the analysis of a dominant ideology as it moves between positions

[12]   R. Lazarus, *Psychological Stress and the Coping Process* (New York: McGraw Hill, 1966), p. 150 (emphasis in original).

[13]   I. Janis, 'Psychological Effects of Warnings' in G. Baker and D. Chapman (eds.), *Man and Society in Disaster* (New York: Basic Books, 1962), p. 67. See also I. Janis and L. Mann, *Decision-Making* (New York: Free Press, 1977), passim.

of hegemony and positions of crisis. By extending the implications of this analysis of individual and group psychological processes to the study of an ideological formation we may be better able to comprehend its internal complexity and its variability. However, such an extension is not as straightforward as it may at first appear. It requires a novel conception of ideology and a novel conception of the articulation between ideology and other political and social processes. It is to such matters that I now turn.

CHAPTER I

Competing paradigms in the study of intergroup relations

In Northern Ireland a row has broken out between Nationalists and Unionists over a decision to change the name of Londonderry city council to Derry City Council. The row over the name of Londonderry, *which has been brewing for over 300 years*, came to a head when the Northern Ireland secretary Mr James Prior gave his approval for the change which had been proposed by the council's Roman Catholic majority. Representatives of the city's Protestant community, who prefer the name Londonderry, walked out of the city council in protest and they are threatening to boycott all future meetings.

(News About Britain, BBC World Service, 25 January 1984)

Political and social relations in Northern Ireland have been marked and organised by the categories of Protestant and (Roman) Catholic since the sixteenth and seventeenth centuries. This phenomenon has led many observers, with more or less sophistication, to develop an explanation of the current pattern of political and social relations in Northern Ireland which highlights the apparent continuity of the present with the past. Such an approach, which we can term the pluralism paradigm, places culture, or ideology, and its institutionalisation at the centre of the account.[1]

The great virtue of pluralism theory is its capacity to encompass the complex phenomenology of ethnic or racial identity.[2] It begins

---

[1] In this chapter I discuss three principal paradigms which are drawn upon in the study of intergroup relations and find each of them wanting in various respects. In my opinion the best brief discussion of these three 'schools' (as he calls them) is offered by Stanley Greenberg in his, now, classic *Race and State in Capitalist Development* (New Haven and London: Yale University Press, 1980).

[2] To avoid any possible confusion I would stress that pluralism theory, as first developed by Furnivall, and as extended and formalised by Kuper and Smith, and others, is quite distinct from pluralist democratic theory as developed by Robert Dahl and others. Pluralism theory is concerned with the analysis of divided or plural societies in which the overlapping and cross-cutting allegiances characteristic of modern democracies are conspicuously absent. It is concerned, then, with the political organisation and interaction

by accepting the reality of such phenomena as primordial identifications, cultural distinctiveness and ideologies of racial or ethnic difference; and it directs attention to their institutionalisation through differential incorporation and cultural reproduction. Its great failure is that it does not reach beyond description and taxonomy towards an adequate causal explanation of ideological and other processes. It observes the reproduction of plural society but cannot adequately explain this. This becomes apparent as soon as the issue of change or transformation arises. Pluralism theory is unable to address, in a systematic way, transformations within an ideology of ethnicity. It is so committed to the notion of persistence that it is likely to discount change, treating it as merely the repetition of traditional themes.[3]

The pluralism paradigm is prevalent in many explanations of the social and political process in Northern Ireland. For instance, it informs most of the research by political scientists, by anthropologists and by historians, although it is not always explicitly designated as such. In this implicit form it also informs most journalistic accounts. Perhaps most significantly, it is adhered to by virtually all Northern Irish inhabitants for at least some of the time, though not always with great consistency. None of this should come as a surprise as there is an obvious sense in which it is the natural attribution appropriate to the ways in which social reality presents itself in Northern Ireland. However, despite its surface plausibility, the pluralism paradigm can capture neither the complexity nor the dynamic character of ideology. For instance we will observe later that Unionist ideology is not solely ethnic or plural in form, but far more complex than this, including at least liberal and dehumanising forms as well. Moreover as the shift between plural (or corporate, as I will term them) forms and liberal forms makes clear, it is a dynamic structure which does not merely repeat the plural theme ad infinitum. To emphasise continuity in a manner which tends to ignore potential or actual change is to risk an unduly static account of political and social

of corporate groupings and identities. Leo Kuper gives a useful in extremis definition as follows: 'The plural society, in its extreme form, is characterized by a superimposition of inequalities. The same sections are dominant or subordinate, favoured or discriminated against, in the political structure, in the economy, in opportunities for education, in human rights, in access to amenity. And issues of conflict also tend to be superimposed along the same lines of cleavage and inequality.' L. Kuper, *Genocide* (Penguin Books: Harmondsworth, 1981), p. 58.

3   See, for example, L. Kuper, *Race, Class and Power: ideology and revolutionary change in plural societies* (London: Duckworth, 1974).

relations. It is to raise culture, or ideology, to the level of serious consideration, but to freeze it fast into a tradition which perseveres through its very institutionalisation. Consequently, with pluralism theory we have a restricted and limiting form of taking ideology seriously.

Other groups of observers have never taken ideologies of ethnicity (e.g. Protestant or Catholic identity) at all seriously. Armed with a sure knowledge of the logics of capitalism or modernisation they have recognised such ascriptive, pre-capitalist forms of identity as a mere residue, the no-longer vital labels from a pre-history which modernity has rendered redundant. Indeed, for the modernisation paradigm such labels are mere epiphenomena whose sole social and political function is, in the short term, to disguise or confuse the brave new rational world which takes birth with the 'end of ideology'.

Virtually all nineteenth-century political and social theory was agreed as to the likely impact of processes of industrialisation and modernisation. There would be a thoroughgoing transformation of the norms, values and constraints informing social organisation. Individuals and collectivities would be freed from the narrow and ascriptive claims of tradition. Universalistic criteria would come to inform all aspects of social organisation. Rationality would conquer and prevail. Central to this would be the dissolution of ethnic or tribal cultures and their replacement by more rational, market-oriented or class-oriented ones. Ideologies of ethnicity would become obsolete.

Of course the above is a rather bald schematisation. As such it highlights what we can now recognise as the apocalyptic naïvety, in this regard, of such major theorists as Marx, Durkheim and Weber. For all their sophistication the assumption of a thoroughgoing cultural transformation was deeply embedded in all aspects of their work. Indeed it became the progressive or liberal commonsense of the age. As Parkin, for instance, has noted:

It was widely felt that the homogenizing influence of the modern industrial state would be too powerful to allow the survival of those traditionalistic and narrow 'tribal' loyalties that flourished under agrarian systems. This is one of the assumptions that bourgeois social theory shared in common with Marxism.[4]

---

[4]   F. Parkin, *Marxism and Class Theory* (London: Tavistock, 1979), p. 31.

Moreover we are ourselves hardly immune from such assumptions. They exercise a profound influence over social and political thought, and 'commonsense', even today, despite what has been recognised as the 'ethnic revival'. Indeed, under the rubric of modernisation theory, they inform the major, though declining, tradition of explanation regarding the effects of 'development' upon forms of ideology and forms of political and social organisation.

The Marxist variant of the modernisation paradigm has also taken its social toll in Northern Ireland, playing havoc with the programmes of would-be Labour groupings and the left wing of the Republican movement. This variant regards working-class solidarity and the emergence of class consciousness as the necessary and natural effect of capitalist industrialisation. At the core of this theory lies what may be termed an 'economistic' assumption; i.e. the assumption of a direct, reflective connection between class position and the contents of consciousness. Faced with the evident data concerning the persistence of an all-class Unionist bloc since the middle of the nineteenth century, this theory must resort to the totally unsatisfactory 'solution' of positing a false consciousness which has been sedulously and artificially maintained by a bourgeois elite condescending to beat the Orange drum. The liberal variant of this paradigm makes a similar move by resorting to the concept of prejudice; which is taken to be a set of irrational beliefs (the distinguishing characteristic of bigoted and intransigent individuals) which have no social basis.

In both variants such concepts are used as the residual category which rescues the paradigm in the face of an overwhelming amount of contrary evidence. This is achieved by abstracting the residual concept from the social process and regarding its object, prejudice or false consciousness, as an artificial impediment to the 'natural' imperatives of modernisation. Clearly this paradigm is unsatisfactory in its application to Northern Ireland. Given that the slogan 'Remember 1690' can function, 300 years later, as a potent political rallying cry, such a paradigm is radically called into question.

At the psychological level both the modernisation and pluralism paradigms commit what I would term an 'equivalence fallacy'. They assume that there is an equivalence between those dimensions of the social structure which are regarded as salient and those dimensions which are considered to be reflectively internalised by the individual. So the modernisation paradigm sees the individual as a microcosm of the rational, universalist culture which it observes, and the pluralism paradigm sees the individual as a microcosm of the traditional and ascriptive culture which it highlights. When stated in this way it is clear that this fallacy derives from a set of extremely narrow and unjustified assumptions about both ideology and rationality, both of which are treated as derivative repositories of the social.

One response to the manifest inadequacies of the modernisation paradigm is a broad body of research which may be designated as neo-Marxist. This neo-Marxist paradigm, in its first moment (as exemplified, for instance, in the work of Farrell on Northern Ireland and Saul and Greenberg on South Africa) draws its method of analysis from an economistic reading of Marx's political writings; principally from *The Eighteenth Brumaire* and *The Class Struggles in France*.[5] This paradigm relies upon a distinction between the broad interests of capital in general and the particular interests of specific class fractions. In effect the various class fractions are treated as so many unitary class subjects which calculate their interest, according to an instrumental rationality, or a utilitarian mode of calculation, in terms of the needs, capacities, opportunities and vulnerabilities attached to their economic position. Ideologies, both formally and substantively, are denied any degree of autonomy. As epiphenomena they play no determinative or constitutive role in the intergroup relations process, nor in the prevailing pattern of domination.

In a second moment, influenced by the work of Althusser and Poulantzas and the rediscovery of Gramsci, this approach places the state and ideology at the centre of the explanatory account. However, as the work of Bew, Gibbon and Patterson on Northern Ireland (or the work of John Saul on South Africa) makes clear, this formal recognition of the need to conceptualise ideology as a relatively autonomous formation is not realised at the level of empirical application. For instance, in the case of Bew, Gibbon and Patterson they quickly fall back into labelling ideology as mere 'rhetoric', despite their adoption of an Althusserian approach.[6]

[5]   See, for example, Greenberg, *Race and State*. In more recent work Greenberg has moved to a sophisticated version of what I go on to describe as the second moment of neo-Marxism. See his *Legitimating the Illegitimate: state, markets and resistance in South Africa* (Berkeley: University of California Press, 1987). See also M. Farrell, *Northern Ireland: The Orange State* (London: Pluto Press, 1980) and G. Arrighi and J. Saul, *Essays in the Political Economy of Africa* (New York: Monthly Review Press, 1981).

[6]   See P. Bew, P. Gibbon and H. Patterson, *The State in Northern Ireland: 1921–1972* (Manchester: Manchester University Press, 1979).

In his work on Southern Africa John Saul encompasses both moments of the neo-Marxist paradigm, as sketched above, and offers a clear example of the failure of the second moment to realise the relative autonomy of ideology. For this reason I shall comment on his work in some detail. In his early work, which is otherwise exemplary in a positive sense, the approach to the analysis of ideology is crudely economistic. Various class fractions are identified (e.g. international capital, national manufacturing capital, white working class etc.), their particular, essentially economic, interests are specified and their ideology is regarded as an epiphenomenal derivative or expression of such interests.[7] What we might term a 'fractional-capital logic' approach is employed. The great virtue of this approach is that it operates at the level of the social formation and, consequently, is able to capture a good deal of the complexity of class processes. Its limitation is its conception of ideology. It would seem to have been a recognition of this very limitation which accounts for Saul's movement to the second moment of the neo-Marxist paradigm. In an article on 'the dialectic of class and tribe', drawing particularly on the work of Laclau, he locates the problem of the first moment of the neo-Marxist paradigm in its failure to recognise the relative autonomy of ideology, and proposes an approach intended to remedy this.[8] Consequently it is particularly interesting to examine his subsequent work on South Africa and to consider the ways in which this recognition of the relative autonomy of ideology informs a piece of empirical research.[9] Writing in 1981, Saul and his co-author Gelb characterise the institutionalisation of apartheid in South Africa as a Nationalist Party project to reform economic and social relations to the benefit of Afrikaner capital and the white working class. They continue:

But whose class interests did this solution serve? Most overtly, no doubt, those of the main elements the Nationalist Party had grouped together into its winning coalition: the Afrikaner petty bourgeoisie, agrarian capital, the white working class ...

Not that the Nationalists' project even then can be interpreted as being merely the sum of such class interests. As hinted above the nature of its

---

[7]   See, for example, Arrighi and Saul, *Essays in the Political Economy of Africa*.
[8]   This article is reprinted in J. Saul, *The State and Revolution in Eastern Africa* (New York: Monthly Review Press, 1986), chapter 14.
[9]   J. Saul and S. Gelb, *The Crisis in South Africa* (New York and London: Monthly Review Press, 1981).

racist and exclusivist-ethnic (Afrikaner nationalist) preoccupations lent this project much of its fire, its political focus and clout, its 'extremism'. Nonetheless, having done full justice to the complex interplay of class, racial, and national assertions which was present here, one may still doubt whether the outcome was really so very far out of line with the basic interests of the most developed (and essentially non-Afrikaner) sectors of capital.[10]

Moving to the debate over reform the text continues (some 25 pages later)

Once again, any too neat a reduction of the reform debate either to a straightforward manifestation of the 'logic of capital' or to an epipheno-menon of class alliances can tend to obscure our understanding of the precise nature of the incoherence which marks the dominant classes' response to crisis. We must return to some of the elements introduced at the outset of the chapter.

The reference here is not chiefly to those (relatively autonomous) ideological guarantors of the populist alliance – racism and Afrikaner nationalism – which framed the hard response to capitalist crisis after 1948, even if these are perhaps now more seriously in contradiction with capitalism's economic calculations than once they were. Rather the primary reference is to the political logic which we saw, in part, to underlie these variables, a 'logic' which now focuses the fear that reform is really a Pandora's box.

... One great strength of the verkrampte/HNP position lies here (i.e. with the political logic of the situation) more perhaps than in any appeals to residual atavisms which might otherwise be thought to be their most important stocks-in-trade.[11]

The first of these quotations regards ideology as a 'preoccupation' which lends 'fire, political focus and clout, and "extremism"' to the class interests of certain fractions. These class interests are themselves regarded as subordinate elements whose field of operation is effec-tively restricted or governed by the basic interests of the 'most developed (and essentially non-Afrikaner) sectors of capital'. As a consequence, such subordinate class interests are, after all, not 'so very far out of line with the basic interests of the most developed ... sectors of capital'. Fractional-capital logic is collapsed into capital logic. Further, the relationship between the various class interests is conceptualised as extra-ideological. That is, ideology plays no constitutive role in the determination or calculation of interest. It merely expresses these interests, sometimes adding a dash of fire and

---

[10]   Ibid., p. 41.   [11]   Ibid., p. 66.

brimstone. And even this expressive function is redundant; ideology is effectively epiphenomenal.

Still gesturing against this very practice, in the second quotation Saul and Gelb ritually acknowledge the relative autonomy of ideology. Yet in the next moment they treat this same ideology as external to political calculation. They end by sliding ideology into the concept of 'residual atavisms'. Here the notion of ideology as relatively autonomous collapses into a notion of ideology as largely irrelevant. Indeed these quotations are clear examples of this. Firstly ideology is treated as irrelevant to capital logic. Secondly it is treated as irrelevant to 'political logic'. Its field of operation is progressively narrowed towards the irrational and ephemeral; which is taken to be such solely because it is allowed no place in the 'logics' of neo-Marxism.

All this occurs despite clear gestures and intentions to the contrary. I suggest that it occurs because Saul and other neo-Marxists have no adequate means of analysing a particular ideological formation as a relatively autonomous structure. Hence at the empirical level we characteristically find the attribution of 'heat' and other irrational or illogical properties (in contrast to capital and political logic) to ideology. This may occur despite the contrary intentions of the author. A major aspect of this failing (though not the only one) is the neo-Marxist anxiety in the face of the manifest psychological properties of ideology. So, for instance, in his discussion of the dialectic of class and tribe Saul explicitly rejects any possible role for psychological theory in the analysis of ideology; he denies that ideology has significant psychological properties.[12] This denial is repeated, explicitly or implicitly, by virtually all other neo-Marxists, not without symptomatic consequences of the kind outlined above.

As this example illustrates, the assumptions about rationality implicit in the neo-Marxist paradigm are normative assumptions drawn ultimately from utilitarianism. This is one of the reasons why the logic of interests can proceed outside of ideology. What we are really offered is a formal analytic model of calculation (usually not explicitly developed) for decision making within an interest structure which has already determined (prior to the calculation) the scope of choice and the values attached to any particular option. This begs the question of ideology at a fundamental level. For unless it is

---

[12] Saul, *The State and Revolution in Eastern Africa*, chapter 14.

recognised that interests are themselves calculations within the terms of an ideological discourse, i.e. that they are constituted though not exhausted by ideology, it is illegitimate to claim that the relative autonomy of ideology is being respected.

The implications of the above discussion of John Saul's work on ideology extend beyond the scope of the neo-Marxist paradigm to all approaches in which ideology is given a central position at the level of theory but is then inadequately handled at the level of empirical analysis. Saul's work serves as one good, and characteristic, example of the very general problem which I addressed in my introduction; the difficulty of successfully developing theory with an empirical intent and then extending this theory to the analysis of empirical evidence.

The various failings of the three paradigms that I have discussed point to the need to think again. In chapters 2 and 3 I will begin this process by looking closely at a number of different conceptualisations of ideology. To this end I will turn to some aspects of contemporary social theory, in particular the work of Anthony Giddens and Jurgen Habermas, as a resource for specifying a more adequate theory and method for the analysis of ideological processes.

CHAPTER 2

Conceptualising ideology

Both interest theory and strain theory go directly from source analysis to consequence analysis without ever seriously examining ideologies as systems of interacting symbols, as patterns of interworking meanings.

Clifford Geertz, 'Ideology as a Cultural System'[1]

In this chapter I will develop two main themes. First, by briefly reviewing the history of various conceptualisations of ideology I will attempt to demonstrate that ideology is a pre-eminently psychosocial concept; i.e. a concept which is at once concerned with the interplay of both social and psychic processes. I will demonstrate that, typically, particular theorists tend to emphasise one or the other half of this dichotomy and, thereafter, to derive the repressed half as a mere reflection. A close look at the history of the concept highlights the ways in which this repressed half, as I am calling it, tends to return in the interstices and the blind spots of the particular theory. Second, by looking to structuralist and post-structuralist theory, on the one hand, and to the theory of communicative action, on the other, I will try to establish that even a psychosocial conceptualisation of ideology, as this term is conventionally understood, is inadequate on at least two counts. These are the persistence of a philosophy of the subject in the core assumptions of conventional psychosocial research and the related failure to understand ideology as an institutionalised, cultural form with its own rules of structuration. Such a recognition is essential to any theory of ideology which hopes to escape what I have previously termed the equivalence fallacy.

Ideology is a prime example of an 'essentially contested concept', that is to say its very definition is perennially in contention. As David

---

[1]   C. Geertz, 'Ideology as a Cultural System', in *The Interpretation of Cultures* (New York: Basic Books, 1973).

McLellan has recently noted, this feature renders the concept of ideology 'elusive' for the very reason that it 'asks about the bases and validity of our most fundamental ideas'.[2] As McLellan's phrasing suggests, differing responses to questions concerning the bases of ideology and to questions concerning its veridical nature have been central to the career of this concept. In what follows I will briefly describe this career from a different, though not unrelated, perspective. As already indicated, I will begin this discussion by focusing on ideology as a pre-eminently psychosocial concept. At the same time I will attempt to retain the notion that ideology, adequately conceived, is a principal form and location of political and social power.

Consider some equivalents for the term ideology which have been suggested by Robert Lane: attitude, belief system, character, codes, creeds, culture, dogma, ethos, idea systems, ideals, identity, image, knowledge, mind, myth, opinion, personality, spirit, values and utopia.[3] What is so striking about these terms is that, as we read along the chain, they switch emphasis between the individual and the sociocultural in an apparent effort to hold the two together. I suggest that this is not merely accidental; ideology is a concept which inherits the disciplinary divisions between sociology and psychology whilst holding out the promise of overcoming these divisions. Herein lies its powerful attraction; ideology is a concept which is both central and contested due to its complexity of reference and its multidisciplinary character, rather than despite these features. The concept of ideology holds out the promise of an explanation as to how the individual and the social interpenetrate, of how we come to be actors or subjects with particular, personal characteristics which, at the same time, have a basis in the pattern of political and social relations.

CLASSICAL CONCEPTIONS OF IDEOLOGY

The term ideology was coined by Antoine Destutt De Tracy, a philosophe around the time of the French Revolution. Indeed De Tracy wrote some of his *Elements of Ideology* whilst awaiting the guillotine, and was only spared, by a matter of barely two days, due to the Thermidorian Reaction. For De Tracy and his associate

---

[2] David McLellan, *Ideology* (Bristol: Open University Press, 1986), p. 1.

[3] Robert E. Lane, 'Patterns of Political Belief', in J. Knutson ed., *Handbook of Political Psychology* (San Francisco: Jossey-Bass, 1973), pp. 83–4. This set is drawn from a longer list provided by Lane.

Pierre Cabanis, ideology was a term which designated the science of both rational thought and the rational ordering of society. Thus it carried forward the intentions of the Enlightenment. The term ideology (the science of ideas) was chosen ahead of a competing term, psychology, because the latter, derived as it is from the Greek word psyche, denoting soul or spirit, was thought to have too many metaphysical connotations. It was exactly this type of idealism and superstition which the new science of ideology promised to dispel. Cabanis, who is often described as the founder of physiological psychology, claimed that before the new science of ideology 'there was no precise notion of the way we deal with the external world, nor of the material nature of our ideas, nor of the series of operations by which the sense-organs and the brain receives impressions of external objects and transforms them into sensations and perceptions'.[4]

De Tracy shared Cabanis' physiological concerns but, influenced by his reading of Locke, concentrated more specifically on the relations between human ideas and sensations. As he put it, 'thinking is only sensing, and all our ideas are only diverse sensations, whose differences and combinations it is only a matter of untangling'.[5] Thus, for instance, to judge is merely to combine and compare various sensations. A major impediment to this untangling of sensations was natural language, which De Tracy and Cabanis regarded as unduly imprecise. Although individual sensations were veridical they were also 'in [themselves] absolutely internal and non-transmittable'.[6] In the social act of transmission through language these veridical sensations were corrupted. A new, precise and uniform language purged of all metaphysics was thus essential. In these respects the ideologists anticipated twentieth-century behaviourism.[7]

Given the political setting, one consequence of the new science of

---

[4]   Cabanis, anticipating at once Mary Shelley's *Frankenstein* and 'the Nazi doctors', himself took advantage of the revolution (eventually he had to flee to escape imprisonment) to conduct experiments on the 'feelings, or lack of feelings, of subjects following decapitation by the guillotine'. He concluded this research, 'thus the scientific materialistic answer to the question whether beheaded people still sense and think was; no'. See Michael Billig's *Ideology and Social Psychology* (Oxford: Blackwell, 1982), p. 8.

[5]   A. Destutt De Tracy, *Elemens d'idéologie* (Paris, Madame Levi, 1827), vol. III. Translated by and quoted in Billig, *Ideology* p. 25. This and the following quotes from De Tracy are Billig's translations and are taken from his *Ideology*. Throughout this brief discussion of the ideologues I rely heavily on Billig's account.

[6]   De Tracy, *Elemens*, vol. III. Quoted in Billig, *Ideology*, p. 18.

[7]   For example, B. F. Skinner's *Beyond Freedom and Dignity* (New York: Knopf, 1971).

ideas was a thoroughgoing anti-clericalism. Thus the ideologues
challenged the concept of God because it lacked corresponding
sensations. They also launched themselves into public policy formation. In the decade immediately following the Thermidorian Reaction in 1794 they served as members of the Senate and applied their
new science to the reform of education. Thus in 1795 the 'Law on the
Organization of Public Instruction' was passed. This embodied the
new rational principles of the ideologues and, amongst other things,
used the new term 'social science'. It also devoted a section of the
new Institut National to 'moral and political science'.

Napoleon, at first an enthusiastic supporter of the ideologues,
became disenchanted soon after his elevation to emperor. The
ideologues lacked the appropriate priorities for the new order of the
empire. To boot, they were far too impractical, and retained a
commitment to pure research. 'Off with their heads' was the cry
again, though this time they were merely demoted to the back
benches of the Senate, where they were thoroughly isolated from any
further policy role. Napoleon described them as 'windbags' who
knew nothing of the realities of power and who were 'always
distrusting authority'. He asserted that 'we must lay the blame for all
the ills that our fair France has suffered on ideology, that shadowy
metaphysics which subtly searches for first causes on which to base
the legislation of peoples, rather than making use of laws known to
the human heart'.[8]

In the various dichotomies which organise this first conceptualisation of ideology much of its later history is pre-figured. Thus we see
distinctions being upheld between thought and language, between
thought and feeling, between reality and misrecognition, between
science and superstition and between the psychological and the
social. Later conceptualisations of ideology could be usefully ordered
as so many variations on the arrangement of these dichotomous
terms. What we also see is the connection between power and
knowledge as an infant social science strikes an unhappy bargain
with the Napoleonic state.

The contemporary currency of the term 'ideology' is mainly
attributable to the influence of Karl Marx and to the succeeding
generations of Marxists. Marx picked up on Napoleon's negative
inflection of the term. Thus in *The German Ideology* Marx, along with

---

[8]   Quoted in Billig, *Ideology*, p. 12.

Engels, developed the materialist conception of history by playing out some implications of the dichotomous distinction between ideas and ideology on the one hand and sensuous human activity or practice on the other. Historical materialism (as it came to be known) does not begin with a focus upon consciousness but with a focus upon the production and reproduction of material life. In their material activity human beings also produce their conceptions of the world. However through historical change these conceptions come to represent and preserve class interests, more specifically ruling-class interests. They do so by, at once, reflecting and distorting class interests. Thus, for Marx, ideology comes to mean any cultural form or system of representation, or any form of consciousness which, at once, captures and distorts class interests, making them appear as universal interests which are the natural attributes of a properly ordered society. Religion is one example of this, liberal political economy is another. Much of this is quite evident in the famous camera obscura metaphor from *The German Ideology* and in the related discussion of ideologies as 'forms of consciousness' which have 'no history, no development'. As Marx and Engels put it:

Morality, religion, metaphysics, all the rest of ideology and their corresponding forms of consciousness, thus no longer retain the semblance of independence. They have no history, no development; but men, developing their material production and their material intercourse, alter, along with this their real existence, their thinking and the products of their thinking.[9]

By the time he wrote *Capital* Marx had modified his conception of ideology. We can see this in his characterisation of the market as an ideological category. Before the market everyone is equal, insofar as everyone may enter into exchange relations. Before the market none of our particular qualities are of account, neither race, religion nor any other ascriptive criterion has any significance. All that counts is our capacity to complete the exchange; usually, though not necessarily, with money, the universal equivalent. In this sense the market is universal; it acknowledges no disqualification other than the inability to complete an exchange of equivalents. Hence in the labour market the worker exchanges labour-power for wages. Neither party is constrained by anything other than his or her own free-will. As Marx puts it: 'They contract as free agents and the agreement they come to is but the form in which they give legal expression to their common

[9] K. Marx and F. Engels, *The German Ideology* (New York: International Publishers, 1970) p. 47.

will.'[10] They are equal 'because each enters into relation with the
other, as with a simple owner of commodities, and they exchange
equivalent for equivalent'.[11] Moreover they only dispose of that
which is their own and they look only to themselves (unwittingly
following the principle of the invisible hand). In Marx's understanding the market is real but partial; it is a phenomenal form
which registers but disguises the real human relations which underlie
the capitalist society. We see a part and take it for the whole; more
particularly we see freedom and equality in the market and thus fail
to see the inequality and exploitation which characterise the relations
of production. The market is real but partial and as such it disguises
the exploitative relations of production upon which it is based.

This latter notion of ideology bears some similarity to that
advanced by Althusser, who, drawing upon psychoanalytic theory,
characterises ideology as an imaginary relationship of individuals to
their real conditions of existence.[12] In both cases ideology is not
illusory, in the sense of being false. Rather it is illusory, or imaginary,
in that only one particular or phenomenal form of reality is seen. For
Marx this form is generated by the forces of production, for
Althusser, and this is a significant difference, this form is the universal
form of recognising oneself as a human subject. In both cases the
'real', recognised only by science, is disguised or covered over.
Moreover, in capitalist and pre-capitalist societies, this disguise
operates in a manner which protects sectional, class interests.

With Lenin ideology loses its negative connotation and takes on a
positive one. Lenin writes of the socialist revolution as, in part, a
struggle for the hegemony of socialist ideology, as 'an unremitting
and most merciless ideological and political struggle against bourgeois liberalism'. In this conception ideology also takes on a clear
psychological component. The 'life and death struggle' for socialism
is understood as one which requires 'tenacity, discipline and a single
inflexible will' and which calls for 'tenacity, self sacrifice and
heroism'. It relies upon, and can only be secured by, the birth of a
new anthropological type, 'socialist man'.[13]

[10] K. Marx, *Capital*, vol. i, pt. 2. This translation is by David McLellan in his *Karl Marx, Selected Writings* (Oxford: Oxford University Press, 1977), p. 455.
[11] Ibid.
[12] L. Althusser, 'Ideology and The Ideological State Apparatuses', in *Lenin and Philosophy* (New York and London: Monthly Review Press, 1971).
[13] These quotes from Lenin are taken from *Left-Wing Communism, An Infantile Disorder*, as quoted in Billig, *Ideology*, p. 53.

This notion of building a new socialist character (socialist man) to fight for the new order bears all the marks of the French ideologues. Moreover Lenin shares their psychological assumptions. He, too, relies upon a 'reflection' theory of knowledge. As he put it in *Materialism and Empirio-Criticism*, 'the mind is secondary, a function of the brain, a reflection of the external world. The senses give us faithful images of things and thus sensations are a true copy of ... objective reality. The sole source of our knowledge is sensation'.[14] Again we see ideology being represented as the repository of a truth which promises to wipe away the half-truths and deceptions of an exploitative social order. However if this science-ideology dichotomy is one of Lenin's themes, the other theme concerns the coincidence of knowledge and power. To oppose capitalism is to oppose capitalist ideology. This opposition must do more than negate, it must substitute an alternative ideology which is grounded in the science of Marxism. If all ideologies are equal, in that they all incorporate positive norms and values and in that they all must compete in the battle for hegemony, one ideology is more than equal in that it has a scientific basis.

With Gramsci this Leninist conception of ideology, and of hegemony, is strengthened. Ideology becomes both the site and the stake of class struggle, and this struggle is understood as one regarding moral and intellectual, as well as political hegemony. Gramsci understands that this struggle has no inevitable or privileged outcome. Rather it is a contingent process which is enacted through the practices of social actors as they go about their everyday routines. It is, then, a struggle at the level of commonsense understandings and evaluations of what is proper, what is ideal and what is possible. Gramsci identifies culture and language, both repositories and media of everyday communication, as the new field of ideology.

If, in the Soviet Union, a new 'socialist man' was in the process of being planned and produced as the material repository of socialist ideology, in Western Europe another new anthropological type was thought to be nascent. In the period following the First World War and the revolution in Russia, the certainties of the new science of dialectical materialism were sorely challenged by the failure of the socialist revolution on its home turf of Western Europe. In the advanced capitalist societies the transition to socialism was eagerly

[14] V. I. Lenin, *Materialism and Empirio-Criticism*, (Peking: Foreign Languages Press, 1972), p. 95.

awaited by Marxist activists and theorists alike. Its failure to keep its appointment with history gave rise to a paradigm crisis within Marxism. This was heightened by the success of fascism, especially in Germany and Italy. The birth of the new 'socialist man' was keenly anticipated throughout the whole of Europe. However, in Western Europe a quite different anthropological type was to be discerned: the authoritarian personality. In place of the socialist virtues this new creature was the repository of the vices of an advanced monopoly capitalism requiring obedience rather than initiative and consumption ahead of production. This new character type was the true product and container of capitalist ideology in its modern, monopoly form.

Although something of a parody, the above does sketch in the contours of the crisis within Marxism in the years following the First World War, and the types of consideration which gave rise to both critical theory and Gramsci's speculations on hegemony.[15] In both cases ideology, characterised as the 'cement' which binds a society together despite rational, class-based divisions, is understood as the novel factor which, previously, had been inadequately theorised.[16] In both cases an undue emphasis upon the economy, indeed a tendency towards economism, is understood as the source of a radical misreading of contemporary history. A generation later, this time in France, Althusser was to repeat this step away from economism in the attempt to develop a better conceptualisation of ideology, and for much the same reasons. Between them these traditions within Marxism cover the broad outlines of a turn towards what I regard as a more adequate conceptualisation of ideology. In what follows in this chapter I will attempt to both delineate and establish the virtues of such an approach. I will also point to some limitations. I will proceed by looking closely at four exemplary texts: Erich Fromm's 'Method and Function of an Analytic Social Psychology', Louis Althusser's 'Ideology and Ideological State Apparatuses', Anthony

---

[15] For a detailed discussion of these matters see Martin Jay, *Marxism and Totality* (Berkeley: University of California Press, 1984). So as to avoid any confusion, I should state that Gramsci never posited a character type as the repository of ideology. Rather, and this is his great contribution, he shifted to a new understanding of ideology as 'commonsense'. The preceding paragraph is written with an eye turned towards critical theory.

[16] Gramsci's use of cement as a metaphor for ideology is well known. It is, perhaps, less well known that Fromm used the same metaphor at about the same time, almost certainly without any awareness of Gramsci's usage. See E. Fromm, 'The Method and Function of an Analytic Social Psychology', in A. Arato and E. Gebhardt, eds., *The Essential Frankfurt School Reader* (New York: Urizen Books, 1978).

Giddens' *The Constitution of Society* and Jurgen Habermas' *Knowledge and Human Interests.*[17]

By contrasting Fromm's text with the following three mentioned above, I will try to bring out some features of a paradigm shift in the manner in which psychoanalysis has been read into social theory; a shift from the philosophy of consciousness and its unitary, centred subject to a theory of decentred subjectivity organised, and subject to reorganisation, within structures of language or communication. I will suggest that psychoanalysis was always itself a party to this paradigm shift, but that the socialisation reading of psychoanalysis into social theory delivered up an irrationalist version of the philosophy of consciousness; i.e. the philosophy of consciousness was read back into psychoanalysis inappropriately. In this way I hope to indicate that psychoanalysis is able to provide a theory of what I term doubly decentred subjectivity and its organisation within culture, one which provides us with the basis for an adequate theory of ideology and subjectivity.

IDEOLOGY, CHARACTER AND THE UNCONSCIOUS

In its first and still most pervasive form the appropriation of psycho-analysis by social theory took the form of a socialisation theory of a social learning type. This reading was so powerful that it still looks like the 'obvious' reading of psychoanalysis for the purpose of incorporating subjectivity into a theory of social and political rela-tions. However this was always a radical misreading of Freud. We can start to see some of the features of this socialisation reading by looking at Erich Fromm's 'The Method and Function of an Analytic Social Psychology', which I regard as a classic statement of the socialisation version of the appropriation of psychoanalysis by social theory.

Fromm begins with a masterful *coup de main* which, at once, carries psychoanalysis into the heartland of the then current Marxism. 'Psychoanalysis is a materialistic science which should be classed among the natural sciences.'[18] Whilst appearing to solve the problem of orthodoxy, by this move Fromm cuts himself off from the radical potential of psychoanalysis. Thus he continues:

---

[17] Fromm, 'Method and Function'; Althusser, 'Ideology'; A. Giddens, *The Constitution of Society* (Cambridge: Polity Press, 1984); J. Habermas, *Knowledge and Human Interests*, trans. J. Shapiro (Boston: Beacon Press, 1971).

[18] Fromm, 'Method and Function', p. 478.

In certain fundamental respects, the instinctual apparatus itself is a biological given; but it is highly modifiable. The role of primary formative factors goes to the economic conditions. The family is the formative influence on the individual's psyche. The task of (analytic) social psychology is to explain the shared, socially relevant, psychic attitudes and ideologies – and their unconscious roots in particular – in terms of the influence of economic conditions on libido strivings.[19]

And in a summary statement on the pivotal role of the family: 'The family is the medium through which the society or the social class stamps its specific structure on the child, and hence on the adult. The family is the psychological agency of society.'[20]

In this approach psychological dispositions and action orientations are understood as the internal stamp and register of a dynamic externality, the political economy. Fromm sets out to historicise or sociologise 'psychical reality' at the cost of more or less eliminating it. Psychical reality disappears into the mere reflection of the socio-logical logic which is organising the inquiry. This is a characteristic failing of the socialisation form of the appropriation of psycho-analysis by social theory. What we are offered is a psychoanalytically modified social learning theory which posits a unidirectional causal process which in this instance begins at the level of the economy, is registered, in a reflective manner, within the family structure and is then 'stamped' upon the child and 'hence' the adult. The psychological dimension of this process is carried through the sexual drives 'which [as characterised by Freud] can be postponed, repressed, sublimated and interchanged, (and) are much more elastic and flexible than the instincts for self-preservation'.[21]

Fromm draws on this malleability of the sexual drives to establish his historicist argument regarding the manner in which changing economic conditions produce altered family structures, which in turn give rise to a general, trait-like, libidinal structure; in this instance the authoritarian type. However, it seems to me that in the process he delivers up a pre-psychoanalytic notion of libidinal structure or social character, or at least a notion which misses the force of Freud's position. We can, perhaps, best see this if we draw the contrast with Freud's understanding of the adult heterosexual couple.

In this regard consider Freud's *Three Essays on the Theory of Sexuality*. Beginning with the exotic inversions and perversions Freud notices the same pattern to neurotic phantasies and, then, to typical child-

[19]   Ibid., p. 486.   [20]   Ibid., p. 483.   [21]   Ibid., p. 480.

hood behaviour. In this way he breaks down any neat dichotomy between the normal and the perverse as we are all caught within this massively extended notion of sexuality. We all experience polymorphous perversity in childhood, and those of us who arrive at genital sexuality preserve aspects of this perverse, yet normal, history in the very constitution of our sexed subjectivity. Thus, according to Freud, we become a subject by becoming a sexed subject and we do this through the development of a libidinal organisation which arises from the various and multiple component instincts and from the various phantasies and the various histories attached to each of these component instincts as they become more or less integrated into a particular libidinal structure.

As a consequence of this understanding Freud does not treat the adult heterosexual couple as stereotypically 'normal' and then regard this trait of 'psychological maturity' as the one determinant of sexual behaviour. Rather, Freud sees the heterosexual couple as two individuals, each with a history which not only went into shaping their libidinal structure but which also remains available. Thus they each may keep 'dipping back' into polymorphous perversity; each of them retains the dynamic of the component instincts. Their 'normality', properly understood, is evident in this very capacity for an organised and sanctioned access to polymorphous perversity. They re-experience polymorphous perversity from the position of an organised genital sexuality.[22]

Fromm's analysis of what he terms libidinal structures is quite at odds with Freud's position on sexuality. Fromm's insistence on libidinal structures as trait-like, freezes the dynamic aspect of the Freudian position. For Fromm the multiple forms of subjectivity which we experience from infancy as we become sexed adult subjects are seen as merely the pre-history of the dominant character structure. Once established this character structure is set and determines the general action orientation. Recall the quote: 'stamps its specific structure on the child, and hence on the adult'. In this understanding all other forms of subjectivity or personality are erased, that is to say, power, history, the dynamic unconscious and psychical reality are all erased.

---

[22] See S. Freud, *Three Essays on the Theory of Sexuality* in *The Standard Edition of the Complete Psychological Works of Sigmund Freud* (London: Hogarth Press, 1962), hereafter *SE*, translated by J. Strachey, vol. VI, p. 130. While my example relates to an adult heterosexual couple, clearly a similar statement may be made regarding an adult homosexual couple.

The advantage of this, for Fromm and others who take this position, is one of specificity, but this advantage is achieved at a huge cost. If the sado-masochistic libidinal structure, or the authoritarian personality as it was later termed, is the characteristic product of a particular society, then that datum can be fed into the social analysis in a way which treats it as a trait of that particular society – that is, a very particular content can be ascribed to the libidinal organisation of a particular society. In this manner historical specificity is achieved, but only by assuming that personality or subjectivity has a fixed, trait-like character and that this character is a general feature of the modal personality structure attributed to the particular society. However, by making these assumptions, at once complexity, diversity and any capacity for change through action is lost. At this point we have a cause for real concern. For this is a one-dimensional type of thinking – it comes perilously close to stereotyping – the very fault which the Frankfurt School was concerned to diagnose and eradicate.

In his discussion of what he regards as a failing of psychoanalysts, a failing which he does not regard as inherent to psychoanalysis, Fromm suggests that practising psychoanalysts analogise rather than analyse when it comes to discussions of social relations; that is, they treat social types as analogous to neurotics. In particular they ascribe a universal oedipal complex to all social types on the basis of this false analogy:

In doing this, they overlooked a point of view that is fundamental even to psychoanalytic individual psychology. They forgot the fact that neurosis – (whether a neurotic symptom or a neurotic character trait) – results from the abnormal individual's faulty adaptation of his instinctual drives to the reality around him; most people in a society, i.e. the 'healthy' people, do possess this ability to adapt. Thus phenomena studied in social (or mass) psychology cannot be explained by analogy with neurotic phenomena. They should be understood as the result of the adaptation of the instinctual apparatus to the social reality.[23]

This said, Fromm, in practice, treats the normal as 'neurotic' as he defines this; that is he commits the very error which he accuses other psychoanalysts of having perpetrated. With Fromm the trait of authoritarianism is given such a privileged position as the character type for monopoly capitalism that the dynamic, multifaceted char-acter of the individual (the polymorphous perversity under one

[23]   Fromm, 'The Method and Function', p. 485.

description) is denied. In so doing he throws out more than the bath-water.

How is power conceptualised by Fromm? How does it operate to determine character? Again the answer is provided by that notion of 'stamping a specific structure on the child and hence on the adult'. Power is located in the logics of the political economy and works its psychological effects within the crucible of the family as the incursion of external forces. Fromm recognises the libidinal as malleable within limits and thus effectively regards the psychological space as one of amplification; the instincts add on an intensity to the cool logic of the political economy.

I have focused on Fromm's early work with the Frankfurt School because I believe that, even today, this approach, broadly under-stood, remains the predominant reading of psychoanalysis into social theory. In particular, this paradigmatic approach tends to reassert itself when the move is made to empirical research.[24] We can see this even in such an unlikely case as Louis Althusser. Althusser's theory of ideology marks a significant break with the apparently historicist and clearly subject-centred analysis of the Frankfurt School tradition. However, as we will see, due to an inadequate specification of his conceptualisation of ideology Althusser falls into the 'socialisation trap'; when he turns to offering some brief empirical illustrations the socialisation paradigm reasserts itself.

ALTHUSSER AND THE THOROUGHLY DECENTRED SUBJECT

Writing in the mid-sixties, faced with the failure of Marxism and of the European communist parties to deliver the revolution, Althusser developed a structuralist Marxism which, in its most interesting and influential aspects, developed a novel theory of how societies, principally contemporary Western capitalist societies, reproduced themselves. Central to this theory was a notion of ideology as 'a new reality'. It was not force and the coercive repression of the state which reproduced a system of class exploitation, rather this was principally achieved by ideology, which operated through interpel-lating or constructing individuals as the willing subjects of the system of exploitation which assigns to them their very subjectivity. These subjects, far from being agents, are understood as the mere effects of

---

[24] Consider Joel Kovel's *Age of Desire* (New York: Pantheon Books, 1981), as just one example of this.

ideological practices, which are themselves located within what are awkwardly termed ideological state apparatuses. That is to say, these subjects are radically and thoroughly decentred, being a mere, although far from insignificant, effect of the institutionalised practices of ideology. However, these same subjects imagine themselves to be coherent, unitary agents capable of forming the world to their (rational) will. The rational, centred subject of humanism, liberal commonsense, psychology (and most forms of political science), is actually an imaginary, ideological construction. It is through his incorporation of Lacanian psychoanalysis that Althusser is able to theorise this thoroughly decentred subject and to develop an account of its constitution through the process of interpellation; a process modelled on the Lacanian mirror-phase.

We can focus on both the strengths and limitations of Althusser's novel conception by asking the question: how does ideology operate (according to Althusser)? In the second section of his seminal article 'Ideology and the Ideological State Apparatuses', Althusser develops his four theses about ideology in general; that it is 'eternal' ('exactly like the unconscious'), that it is imaginary, that it is material and that it operates through interpellation or calling. This last, 'Ideology interpellates individuals as subjects', Althusser terms his 'central thesis'.

Let me comment on two of these theses. In claiming that 'ideology is the imaginary relation of individuals to their real conditions of existence' Althusser draws on Lacanian theory to reconceptualise the character of ideology as illusory or imaginary, but not thereby without real effects.[25] For Lacan, to be a subject is to be caught within a play of signification whilst imagining that you (or I) are more than the mere effect of this play, whilst imagining that you have some human essence, be this reason, prejudice or a combination of both, which gives some weight or persistence to the 'I' that you take yourself to be. The analogy with Coleridge's classic account of how a play or poem works may help to explain this. For Coleridge 'the willing suspension of disbelief for the time being' is essential to our understanding of the play (or poem) as a field of action, intention and meaning. Unless we suspend our disbelief about the artifice of the play we will not be able to enter into the imaginary set of social relations and subjectivities which it constructs and sets in motion. It

---

[25]   See, for instance, Jacques Lacan, *Ecrits: A Selection* translated by A. Sheridan (London: Tavistock, 1977), especially chapter 1.

will be a performance without meaning or significance, a mere set of behaviours and sounds. Similarly, for Althusser, to be a subject capable of going on in the day to day routines through which society is reproduced we already must have 'suspended our disbelief' regarding the real incoherence of the unconscious processes which actually underlie our centred, coherent 'I'. This 'suspension of disbelief' is a necessary 'developmental' moment which, for Lacan and Althusser, occurs in the mirror phase when the infant, as an unintegrated and often conflicting array of passions and bodily capacities, sees its image as a coherent gestalt and then takes itself to be that image. This identification with the specular image introduces a new psychical instance, the ego or 'I'. However, unlike in some developmental theories, this rudimentary 'I' and its fancied bodily coherence is imaginary, an anticipation of a psychic coherence which, with the subsequent entry into language, is to be forever deferred. It is through this operation that we form, unconsciously at the mirror phase, a specular 'I' which we take to be coherent and persistent. With the entry into language and the symbolic order this 'I' becomes a floating signifier which performs two operations at once. First, it actually takes on the significations or meanings which the social institutions, the ideological state apparatuses in Althusser's terms, ascribe to it. The process of interpellation tells the 'I' the characteristics which it has for the moment. Second, whilst its actual characteristics are declared by the ideological state apparatuses, the 'I', through the 'suspension of disbelief' already achieved in the mirror phase, imagines that these characteristics are its very own properties, its essence. These two operations together constitute the imaginary character of ideology.

The manner in which I have presented the last part of this exposition is intended to suggest the potential richness of Althusser's reworking of the concept of ideology. However Althusser himself fails to capture this potential. I will attempt to explain some major features of this limitation by discussing Althusser's central thesis before turning to some of his own examples of the operation of ideology.

Let me begin with an example from Frank Burton's study of Northern Ireland, which is based on ethnographic field-work in Belfast. To analyse his ethnographic material Burton developed a concept of 'telling' the difference between Protestant and Catholic. This process of 'telling' the difference is central to the daily social interactions which occur outside the 'safe' environment of family, friends and the immediate neighbourhood. Hence the riding of public buses is a particular everyday routine where the process of 'telling' is constantly in operation. In Belfast, at least during the period of Burton's research in the 1970s, there was a complicated pattern to riding on buses. Burton, who was living in a Catholic household in a Catholic neighbourhood, got on the wrong bus at one stage and this is what happened:

I was sharing a bus with some Protestant youths who could be identified as Protestant because they sang, when we passed a Catholic church: 'I tell you what I think/That's Celtic stink/'Cos I'm a Rangers fan.' They took great interest in those passengers who were getting off near a Catholic area I was visiting. As I got off several of these adolescents stuck their heads out of the windows and shouted. 'Let's see who the fenians are, get a good look at them', and then directly to me: 'You fenian bastard'. The appropriate adrenal response on my own part brought home the significance of the bus stop.[26]

Althusser's central thesis that 'ideology interpellates individuals as subjects' is usefully illustrated by this instance. According to this theory of ideology, interpellations like the one experienced by Burton happen all the time, though typically not so dramatically. All the institutions we live within work broadly in this way; they tell us we are this, that and the other, i.e. they tell us what we are; whilst all the time (and this is the ideological effect) leading us to believe that what we are is what we have decided to be. At the core of this ideological effect is the belief (based on our everyday experience) that each of us is a centred subject, an 'I', which consists (i.e. has a consistency) and persists across space and time. However this is a misrecognition of the actuality. The 'I' which each of us takes to be ourself is actually the imaginary effect of the various social institutions which act upon us through ideology. Actually, each and every one of us is a thoroughly decentred subject which, as a specific subject, has no consistency and no persistence through social time and space. Insofar as we do consist and persist we do so as the mere effect of the consistency and persistence of the ideological state apparatuses. It is *they* which determine the 'subjective' characteristics of each and every one of *us*. However, this imaginary relation of individuals to their real conditions of existence is not insignificant. Rather, as the

[26]   Frank Burton, *The Politics of Legitimacy* (London: Routledge, 1978), p. 37.

'new reality', ideology is the central mechanism through which the reproduction of societies is achieved.

Burton's experience of interpellation makes it clear that we can be called in a variety of forms. His identification, for that moment, as Irish Catholic is clearly not a class interpellation, nor could it readily be reduced to one. Only a moment's reflection is necessary to make it apparent that ideologies can, and characteristically do, interpellate us according to gender, nationality, race, religion, voluntary associations and, even outside Belfast, support of football team, amongst many other possibilities. Our interpellation as a form of labour-power, or as capitalist, is only one other such possibility. However, due to a residual economistic reductionism within his structuralist Marxism, Althusser is unable to adequately handle any but class interpellations. Of course he can admit the occurrence of non-class interpellations as mere phenomena, but he then must reduce these to a class belonging. Ian Craib has described this residual failing in the following terms:

When they turn to the political and ideological levels Althusser and his followers deal not with underlying structures but with surface institutions only. A more fruitful logical way in which to develop the Althusserian approach would be to attempt to analyse the underlying structures of the political and ideological levels, with their respective causal mechanisms, and identify the way in which they in turn act upon the economic level. This has not happened.[27]

Althusser's principal limitation is that the complexity of ideology cannot be realised because it is always interpreted through a grid which is only concerned with ideology's functional role in the reproduction of labour power and the relations of production. He is not interested in the fullness or plenitude of these interpellated subjectivities, and the potential multiplicity of such subjectivities which this entails. Rather he is only interested in the significance of such subjectivities for the reproduction of class relations. Hence their plenitude, the multiplicity of significations which they might entail, is denied by reducing any specific subjectivity to being just another variation on the one set theme of class subjectivity. Thus Althusser recognises the relative autonomy of ideology but is unable to realise it. It is in this limitation of Althusser's theory of ideology that we can glimpse the ghost of the philosophy of the subject within the new machine of thoroughly decentred subjectivity. Consider the following

[27] Ian Craib, *Modern Social Theory* (Sussex: Harvester, 1984), p. 139.

examples of interpellation which Althusser provides in the first
section of his essay on 'Ideology and the Ideological State Apparatuses' :

> The communications apparatus (operates) by *cramming* every citizen with
> daily doses of nationalism, chauvinism, liberalism, moralism, etc., by means
> of the press, the radio and television ...
>
> It [the school] takes children from every class at infant-school age, and
> then for years, the years in which the child is most *vulnerable, squeezed*
> between the family State apparatus and the educational State apparatus, it
> *drums* into them, whether it uses new or old methods, a certain amount of
> know how wrapped in the ruling ideology.[28]

It is those three verbs to describe the interpellation process, along
with the notion of the child as 'vulnerable' that I want to draw
attention to. Here we have an example of the return of the repressed
at the moment that empirical application is even thought of; the
structuralist theory of ideology developed in psychoanalytic terms
falls back immediately upon a crude social learning version of a
socialisation theory.

There are other difficulties with Althusser's theory; principally its
suppression of time and its reductionist tendency regarding the class
belonging of all ideology and all subjectivity. In subsequent work
within this tradition some of these difficulties have been more or less
overcome. Althusser does, at the theoretical level, make a radical
break with any philosophy of consciousness. Further, this tradition
has produced a lot of interesting empirical research, such as the
classic *Policing the Crisis*.[29] However, this tradition of research is less
than satisfactory both in its conceptualisation of subjectivity and in
its capacity to specify ideological rules for the structuration of social
and political relations. In particular, by depriving his thoroughly
decentred subject of any capacity for agency and of any capacity for
a partial penetration of the conditions of his or her subjection, either
as an individual or as a member of a group, Althusser covers over a
central source of the dynamism of the decentred subject. It is, in
part, due to this that his theory of ideology and subjectivity is so
relentlessly, and unduly, deterministic.

[28] Althusser, 'Ideology', pp. 154-5.
[29] Stuart Hall, C. Critcher, J. Clarke and B. Roberts, *Policing The Crisis: mugging, the state and law and order* (London: Macmillan, 1978).

HABERMAS AND (DISTORTED) COMMUNICATIVE RATIONALITIES

The Enlightenment project construed reason as the guarantor of human emancipation. Instantiated within science, technology, industry and 'human relations', reason deemed itself to be a transformative force. It would wipe away both the dismal facts of necessity and scarcity and the mind-numbing restrictions and distortions of prejudice and tradition. In its various modern instantiations as science and technique it would preside over the birth of the rational society and the rational subject.

Writing of what they termed the 'dialectic of enlightenment' in the 1940s, Horkheimer and Adorno, two of the original figures of the Frankfurt School, assessed this promise of enlightenment quite differently.[30] The dreadful spectacles of a bureaucratically administered genocide and a technically sophisticated 'war machine' led them to postulate the 'demise of the Enlightenment' and a 'reversion to barbarism'. In their analysis such 'spectacles' were not merely an historical accident; rather they were the underside of the Enlightenment project itself, one of its intrinsic and inevitable properties. This malevolent property of the Enlightenment project could be traced directly to the instantiation and broad expansion of an instrumental, utilitarian rationality concerned solely with the manipulation and control of nature and society. So pervasive was this instrumental rationality that it had become the dominant reality principle of the modern era, marginalising all other forms of reason and relatedness as it pursued its 'rake's progress' towards domination and despair. Hence the massive extension of instrumental rationality characteristic of the modern era gave rise to a 'disenchantment of the world'. Reason, which had promised so much freedom and happiness and so much liberation from both scarcity and superstition, instead found its apotheosis in the emergence of fascism; a principle and practice of oppression and domination which is more or less mirrored in contemporary Western societies.

As we have already seen, Fromm, with Adorno and, later, Marcuse drew on psychoanalytic theory to develop this analysis of the dialectic of enlightenment. Ideology was the major concept through which they joined together the social and the individual

---

[30] See Theodor Adorno and Max Horkheimer, *Dialectic of Enlightenment* (London: Verso, 1979).

aspects of this dialectic of enlightenment; the family being the principal ideological agency.

In *Knowledge and Human Interests* Habermas carries forward this concern with the dialectic of enlightenment in a new and expanded way. In his approach psychoanalysis offers a model and explanation of how ideologies operate as distorted communication, and of how they might be replaced by communicative rationality. Habermas argues that the human species has three cognitive (or knowledge-constitutive) interests. These are the technical, the practical and the emancipatory. The technical interest follows, or arises from, the fact that human societies are tool-using. The practical interest arises from the fact that human societies communicate through the use of language and have an interest in this communication as such, i.e. in itself: that is to say, communication is an anthropologically rooted interest *per se*. There is a third interest in, as Held puts it, 'the human capacity to be self-reflective and self-determining, to act rationally. As a result of it knowledge is generated which enhances autonomy and responsibility; hence it is an emancipatory interest.'[31]

These three interests give rise to the conditions for the possibility of three sciences, the empirical-analytic, the historical-hermeneutic and the critical. The empirical-analytic sciences are concerned with discovering the causes of regular law-like phenomena; e.g. what happens to a gas when it is heated. This can be understood as a subject-object relationship (though not adequately if taken up in a positivist form). The hermeneutic sciences are concerned with a subject-subject relationship. Their interest is not to discern causes but to interpret meanings and, through doing so, to enable, or facilitate, communication and understanding.

Such particular and critical sciences as Marxism and psycho-analysis need to span the divide between the empirical-analytic and the hermeneutic sciences. They need to do the spanning of this divide because they are concerned with human individuals, or human societies, which are capable of reason, but never (at least until now) entirely free. So, in the terms I have just introduced, at once they are concerned with the relation between object and subject and, at the same moment, with the relation between subject and subject. Thus, regarding the object–subject relation, they are concerned with the way in which objective or reified social proper-

[31] David Held, *Introduction To Critical Theory* (London: Hutchinson, 1980), p. 318.

ties, whether these be economic, cultural or whatever, determine subjective experience and subjectivity itself. Regarding the subject–subject relation, in this case they are concerned with the way in which subjects, who are capable of self-reflection concerning their motives and reasons for action, can construct social relations which meet the prescriptive requirements of their motives and reasons. They are, then, concerned with the possibility of constructing a rational society through human cooperation.

Properly understood the intention of such particular sciences as Marxism and psychoanalysis is to increase the realm of freedom, to replace object–subject relations by subject–subject relations. This can be achieved through human reflection upon and penetration of (and eventually the transformation of) those causal relations which suppress freedom (i.e. both individual neurosis and (unnecessary) ideological distortions). However this cannot be achieved by a merely contemplative rationality. Something more is called for. Psychoanalysis offers the most successful example of this 'something more'.

Let me pose a question: what is the source or location of these causal relations which suppress freedom? The short answer: at the social level they are ideologies and institutions which operate to suppress freedom, just as psychopathological symptoms do in the case of individual neurosis. The longer answer: Habermas' account of distorted communication produced by ideologies and their institutions is organised around a contrast between Marx and Freud. Habermas says of Marx that although he 'established the science of man in the form of critique and not as a natural science, he continually tended to classify it with the natural sciences'.[32] Marx's emphasis upon the labour process and the laws of its development as a closed process led him to understand history as operating behind the backs of human agents. This productivist reductionism constructs the human species as merely the observer of causal processes outside its control. However, through ideology, which at once mirrors and distorts this class process, even observation is restricted. All this arises from Marx's failure to see that the emancipatory interest, with which he was concerned, presupposes both a technical and a practical interest and thus two domains of labour and interaction.

In *The Future of an Illusion* and elsewhere, Freud sees this and thus

32   Habermas, *Knowledge and Human Interests*, p. 276.

does not collapse ideologies or illusions back onto the production process. Human interaction is organised through institutions which have arisen as the result of the repression of needs which cannot be gratified or satisfied.[33] Thus they encode distortions and limitations or restrictions within their cultures or norms. They organise distorted communications, they repress rationality and freedom. They are the equivalent of symptoms. Consequently, at the same time they are the medium of power. The forms they take on act to shape and organise the manner in which generalisable interests are suppressed. However these ideologies, and the power which they exercise, can be changed. With increased technical control more needs can be satisfied, some repressions can be lifted, some distortion of communication can be dispelled. If humanity makes its history through work it also makes it through interaction. Both can be transformed.

It is Habermas' rewriting of psychoanalytic theory as a theory of distorted communication which enables him to develop this account of ideology. Schematically, psychoanalysis offers a model of two related processes, and these can be specified at two levels. At the level of the individual, psychoanalysis offers a model of how psychical life can be distorted, trapping individuals into systems of thought and feeling which oppress and harm them, and against which their rational capacities offer little effective defence. Psychoanalysis demonstrates that the defences, or the defence mechanisms, are anything but rational; rather they become part of that object-like other place, that 'it' or id, or more correctly that unconscious, which produces the distortion and harm. Against them mere rationality is a fragile support.

Secondly, psychoanalysis also offers an account of how these harmful distorting psychical processes can be overcome, of how the individual can reclaim his or her personal history and, through so doing, dissipate the harmful psychic distortions. It offers a model of effective liberation.

An analogous model is applicable at the social level. First, on the analogy of individual neurosis, psychoanalysis offers a model of how cultures or ideologies, themselves compromise formations of a defensive character, operate to distort social relations, thus, as at the level of individuals, trapping subjects into systems of thought and feeling which oppress and harm them, and against which their

---

[33]   Freud, *The Future of an Illusion, SE* vol. XXI.

rational capacities offer little effective defence. The difference is that, at the level of the individual, we are typically dealing with delusory formations, i.e. delusions which are in contradiction with reality, which are inevitably false and can never be any different. However, at the social level we are typically dealing with illusory formations, i.e. illusions, such as Freud's example of religion. There is nothing necessarily and ineradicably false about illusions; over time they may be 'achieved'. The feature of societies is that they do change over long historical periods (both Freud and Habermas have an evolutionary notion of change in mind). Thus the illusions of one generation, illusions which ensnare subjects in (alienating) modes of thought and feeling which, in turn, distort intersubjective communication and turn social relations into relations of authority, power and coercion, these illusions, which might be necessary for one generation, may become an unnecessary cultural relic to a later generation because the desires which fuel them have been actually achieved; i.e. there is no longer any need to repress the desires which, previously, only the illusion could satisfy because now social conditions can allow the individual to satisfy these desires in actuality. In this manner Habermas appropriates psychoanalysis both as a theory which explains how cultural forms operate ideologically as media of authority, power and coercion and, in the same movement, as a theory which explains how historical change may give rise to emancipatory potentials.

What is involved here? We can begin to answer this by putting the question: how are neurotic symptoms formed? We are all born with very generalised libidinal and aggressive drives which seek immediate gratification. These drives are the psychical representatives of our biological constitution. As such they come to take particular form as ideas accompanied by a quota of affect (i.e. ideas with a particular intensity of feeling attached). Many of these ideas are unacceptable as such to our consciousness, because they contradict our preferred image of ourselves, or they contradict social prohibitions which we have internalised, or both. Although unacceptable as such to our consciousness, normally they can be reworked in various ways and, thus, find an acceptable expression; though at the cost of a severe distortion. (In dreams this is what happens with each and every one of us; our dream-thoughts, accompanied by their particular intensity of feeling, disguise themselves to avoid censorship, and, in a compromised form, achieve expression and realisation in a phantasy form.)

For some people this conflict between the unconscious and the censoring agencies of the mind will give rise to symptoms. Symptom formation occurs as follows, according to Habermas. Caught between the pressures of the drives and the dangers and restrictions of reality the ego must find a means of defending itself against those wishes or needs which cannot gain satisfaction. It does so, characteristically, through a process which Habermas compares with excommunication. An aspect of language is censored and thus purged from the public set of meanings. This aspect of language continues to speak, but cannot be understood. It cannot be raised within the process of communicative action. Rather, it is privatised and thus its meaning is distorted.[34] However this private language retains some connection with public communication and through this the defensive process can be reversed through a depth hermeneutics; in the process dissolving a cause into a reason which is grasped and thus loses its powers to distort.

A second question: what is the patient's relation to the symptom? For the analysand the symptom is experienced as something alien which seriously disturbs the patient's ability to get on with his or her life. Symptoms operate as quasi-natural causal processes over which the patient has no control.

A third question: what is the psychoanalyst's relation to the symptom? Although initially experienced as something alien, through listening to the patient's talk and to the patient's resistances to, and resistances within, the talking, the symptoms themselves come to take their place in a chain of meanings and feelings. The symptoms themselves speak and eventually the analyst and the person in analysis come to understand their meanings, in the process turning a cause into a meaning and thereby dissipating its capacity to disturb and distort. Thus, through self-reflection and the reappropriation of one's own history, a cause of illness is turned into a reason for recovery.

For Freud and for Habermas institutions and ideologies (or illusions) are exactly like symptoms. In a compromised or distorted form they contain, and thus give (distorted) expression to, thoughts and feelings which cannot be otherwise realised. These thoughts and

---

[34] The meaning of 'rat' to the Ratman in Freud's classic 'Notes Upon A Case Of Obsessional Neurosis' is a good example of this process; 'rat' operates as a condensation which collapses many separate scenic moments, thoughts and feelings onto the one signifier or idea. See Freud, *SE* vol. x.

feelings may be both life-enhancing and life-destroying. In their ideological and institutionalised form they characteristically escape critique, but they also restrict the capacity for rational re-evaluation. They take on an automatic, obligated form of relatedness to the subjects they organise; they declare the commonsense understandings which are beyond criticism because they are apparently so naturally given; they establish the framework of our practical consciousness which we draw upon routinely, and usually not very consciously, as we manage our actions and interactions within the constellation of institutional settings, such as family, work, school, political group etc., which constitute our social and political world. Because they satisfy, albeit in a compromised form, the desires of subjects, these same subjects come to have an emotional investment in their perpetuation. These emotionally valued ideologies and institutions act in a causal way (i.e. beyond reason) determining the character-istics of the subjects whom they address. These ideologies contain patterned forms of representation and emotion (the compromise formations) which are both beyond critique (like symptoms) and also are emotionally valued by those whom they satisfy (as they provide a secondary gain).

Habermas' appropriation of psychoanalysis by social theory carries psychoanalysis into the paradigm of communicative action and offers a powerful model of what might be termed a psychosocial theory of subjectivity and social and political relations, one which has escaped the philosophy of the subject. However I would identify two principal difficulties with Habermas. First, and I have already indicated this, his notion of communicative rationality risks a certain one-dimensionality, it captures the rational dimension of commu-nicative action at the cost of repressing, or barring off, the desiring, affective, authority-oriented and power-situated dimensions of all communicative action. This is why I would prefer to talk of commu-nicative rationalities in the plural and to raise questions regarding the characteristic forms and deformations of these various rational-ities. Psychoanalytic theory is well suited to such a purpose. A second, not unrelated, difficulty with Habermas, it seems to me, is that we never get much sense from anything he writes of how we might recognise, let alone analyse, the patterned forms of representa-tion and emotion which constitute the various particular patterns of distorted communication. That is, Habermas, even in his later work, does not provide a detailed account of what an ideology, or a pattern of distorted communication, actually entails. In Geertz's term he does not offer anything approaching a 'thick description'. In what follows, especially in chapter 4, I will try to redress this by drawing on psychoanalytic group psychology to develop an analysis of the psychodynamic rules of structuration of a particular ideological formation.

What these various social-theoretical appropriations of psycho-analysis illustrate is a paradigm shift from the philosophy of consciousness, concerned with what Foucault has termed a subjec-tivity which is centred in the self-relation of the knowing subject, to a theory of the decentred subject as developed in differing ways within structuralism and post-structuralism and within a theory of commu-nicative action. (In chapter 3 we will observe a similar move within the theory of structuration.)[35] In passing I have implied that this shift had already been achieved by Freud in his interpretation of dreams, symptoms, jokes and slips. However, the appropriation of psycho-analysis as a socialisation theory tended to restore the philosophy of consciousness; though this time in an irrationalist form. As both Althusser and Habermas serve to demonstrate, an analysis of ideology which relies on psychoanalytic theory can escape the restrictions of a theory of ideology couched in terms of a philosophy of the subject. It is my intention to carry this more adequate conceptualisation of ideology into empirical research. The final theoretical step in this regard is now taken up with regard to the theory of structuration.

[35] For a detailed comparison of communicative as against subject-centred reason see Jurgen Habermas, *The Philosophical Discourse of Modernity*, translated by F. Lawrence (Cambridge, MA: MIT Press, 1987), chapter 11.

CHAPTER 3

The structuration of ideology

> To the extent that ideologies are historically necessary they
> have a validity which is 'psychological'; they 'organise' human
> masses, and create the terrain on which men move, acquire
> consciousness of their position, struggle etc.
>
> (Antonio Gramsci, *The Study of Philosophy*)

The sociological imagination is schizoid in character. In one form it
rests on assumptions which regard the individual as the creator,
generator and controller of the social world within which he or she
moves and acts. It is clearly megalomanic. In another characteristic
form the sociological imagination bears all the marks of paranoia.
Individuals, or subjects, are weak, empty and purposeless except
insofar as they are controlled by the master code, the structure which
interpellates them and tells them what they are, what they must do
and how they must feel, think and act.

We can state the above less tendentiously as follows. Political
and social theory conventionally falls into one of two camps. In
one of these, whether as the methodological individualism of
Weberian or interactionist sociologies, as the philosophy of action
or as neo-classical economics and its political science offspring, the
individual stands at the centre of the explanatory account. His or
her reasons, intentions and actions produce effects and it is the
relationship between the former and the latter which is the
appropriate object of scrutiny. However, the conditions and
institutional settings within which reasoning, intending and acting
take place are systematically obscured, as are their unintended
consequences. In the other of these camps, whether in the guise of
structuralism or of functionalism, social processes occur behind the
backs of individuals and irrespective of their reasons and rationali-
sations. Individuals are regarded as social or cultural dopes who,
at most, are the mere effects and carriers of processes which have

their determining bases in forms, systems or structures which are external to them.

Both of these approaches are unsatisfactory. Where the individual is accentuated they collapse into voluntarism; where the social is emphasised they collapse into a determinism. Such a dualism has many liabilities. Principal amongst these is an incapacity to satisfactorily capture the processual aspects of any sphere of political and social action. For the individualist approach, as in an existentialist novel, action is unconstrained and amounts to a sheer act of will. For the sociological approach, as in the structural Marxism of Louis Althusser, thoughts, feelings, dispositions and actions are the effect of an interpellating Subject or structure which summons mere subjects into being and disperses them within a set of social relations. Within this problematic the possibility of being or doing otherwise is entirely eliminated. Hence the analysis of any political and social practice as a contingent process unfolding through time is rendered redundant.

Some attempts have been made within social theory to overcome this dualism or splitting. Perhaps most significantly, there has been a whole tradition, beginning with the work of Talcott Parsons and, in its more radical form, the work of the Frankfurt school, which has attempted to overcome the split between the individual and the social by developing and building upon a notion of internalisation. This approach has many virtues, but also some significant limitations. Its virtues lie in a concern to capture the complexity of the psychological processes involved in the formation of the subject. However in linking subject and society it concentrates unduly on the central, ontogenetically primary, processes and experiences concerning the constitution of the self; thus weighting any analysis of action too heavily in terms of its primitive antecedents. In its attempt to link subject and society this sociopsychological approach goes far beyond the clear limitations of the two prior positions of methodological individualism and sociological or structural determinism. However its restriction on the mode of articulation between subject and society – internalisation – and the attendant restriction upon the central moments of this articulation – the early years – detract from its overall adequacy.

More recently in social theory a fourth position has been developed: the theory of structuration. This theory attempts to dissolve the split or dualism between theories of action and theories of structure by capturing what it designates as the 'duality of structure'.

Giddens, the principal exponent of this approach, explicates this term as follows:

> By the duality of structure, I mean the essential recursiveness of social life, as constituted in social practices; structure is both medium and outcome of the reproduction of practices. Structure enters simultaneously into the constitution of the agent and social practices, and 'exists' in the generating moments of this constitution.[1]

This notion of structure relies on a distinction between the concepts of system and structure. Social systems are understood as systems of relations and interactions which are reproduced through time and space. They possess structural properties which may be more or less deeply layered into them. These structural properties are the rules which are chronically and persistently drawn upon by individuals in the performance of actions (i.e. as the medium of actions) and, in the same moment, are thereby reconstituted (as an outcome of such actions), perhaps in a modified form. Giddens offers an example drawn from his reading of Saussure:

> When I utter a sentence I draw upon various syntactical rules (sedimented in my practical consciousness of the language) in order to do so. These structural features of the language are the medium whereby I generate the utterance. But in producing a syntactically correct utterance I simultaneously contribute to the reproduction of the language as a whole.[2]

As in this instance of a speech-act, all social practices draw upon and reconstitute structures. Thus they are not merely synchronic or static. Rather they are processes taking place across time and space. These acts or practices are, in Giddens' terminology, instances of structuration. Structuration involves both constraint and enablement. The rules and resources which are drawn upon in social practices limit and shape the possible outcomes, but do not determine them.

This emphasis upon the centrality of rules prompts several questions. What does Giddens mean by the term 'rule'? How would one make use of such a concept in empirical research and to what effect? Does the concept have any particular application in the study of ideology?

The term 'rule' has several connotations. For instance we may

---

[1]   A. Giddens, *Central Problems in Social Theory* (London: Macmillan, 1979), p. 5. See also the cognate, though distinct, position developed by R. Bhaskar in his *The Possibility of Naturalism* (Sussex: Harvester, 1979), and elsewhere.

[2]   A. Giddens, *Profiles and Critiques in Social Theory* (London: Macmillan, 1982), p. 37.

speak of rules as prescriptions which should by obeyed and proscrip-
tions which should not be violated. Or we may speak of doing
something as a rule, such as usually having cup of coffee in the
afternoon. Giddens, however, explicitly sets these and other common
notions aside. In his conception of structuration theory, rules are
akin to algebraic formulae; they are a structuring principle capable
of generating a multitude of particular instantiations. At least this is
how I interpret his intentions. But let us look for a moment at his
exact formulation:

> I mean that it is in the nature of formulae that we can best discover what is
> the most analytically effective sense of 'rule' in social theory. The formula
> $a^n = n^2 + n-1$ is from Wittgenstein's example of number games. One
> person writes down a sequence of numbers; a second works out the formula
> supplying the numbers which follow. What is a formula of this kind and
> what is it to understand one? To understand the formula is not to utter it.
> For someone could utter it and not understand the series; alternatively it is
> possible to understand the series without being able to give verbal
> expression to the formula. Understanding is not a mental process in the
> sense in which the hearing of a tune or a spoken sentence is. It is simply
> being able to apply the formula in the right context and way in order to
> continue the series.[3]

In this account the structures which are drawn upon in the process of
structuration have a virtual existence as formulae which order the
social process. Subjects are understood as knowing the rules if they
can go on in the situation; for instance if they can continue the series
of numbers in Wittgenstein's game. In Giddens' terminology such
'practical consciousness' is an adequate and typical form of knowing
the rules. An implication of this is that social practices reconstitute or
transform the rules chronically, over and over again, through the
multitude of particular actions. Consequently, any social practice
may be analysed both in terms of its content or particular characteristics and in terms of its structural characteristics.

Already it should be clear that in structuration theory the reproduction of social relations is dependent upon the interaction of
human beings as knowledgeable agents. Structures do not operate
behind the backs of individuals as, on some readings, is the case with
Althusser, nor do they think themselves through human subjects
(again, either as speech or as symptom) as in Lacan. Rather, knowledgeable agents interact and, through so doing, re-produce the rules

[3]   A. Giddens, *The Constitution of Society* (Cambridge: Polity Press, 1984), p. 20.

of interaction, and thus re-produce social relations through time and space. Agents are skilled performers with a vast range of repertoires at their command. As such, and insofar as they know the rules of social interaction, they are constantly involved in the structuration process.

The question then arises: in what ways can we, as human agents, be said to know these rules? In what ways do they organise our interactions? To answer these questions Giddens proposes three forms of knowing: discursive consciousness, practical consciousness and the unconscious. Each of these ways of knowing is inherently linked to a particular mode of memory or recall. As he puts it:

discursive and practical consciousness refer to psychological mechanisms of recall, as utilized in contexts af action. Discursive consciousness connotes those forms of recall which the actor is able to express verbally. Practical consciousness involves recall to which the agent has access in the duree of action without being able to express what he or she thereby 'knows'. The unconscious refers to modes of recall to which the agent does not have direct access because there is a negative 'bar' of some kind inhibiting its unmediated incorporation within the reflexive monitoring of conduct and, more particularly, within discursive consciousness. The origins of the 'bar' are of two related sorts. First, since the earliest experiences of the infant, shaping the basic security system whereby anxiety is canalized or controlled, predate differentiated linguistic competence, they are likely to remain thereafter 'outside the bounds' of discursive consciousness. Second, the unconscious contains repressions which inhibit discursive formulation.[4]

Having incorporated a theory of the unconscious into his schema of forms of knowing, Giddens then proceeds to limit its scope as much as possible. By building upon Erik Erikson's work in an admittedly selective way, the unconscious is limited to some fundamental functions of an integrated ego or I, functions having to do, principally, with the capacity for trust, but also with capacities for autonomy and initiative. I want to raise one critical question. Giddens tells us that between them discursive and practical consciousness cover virtually the whole field of social relations; of these, by far the more significant is practical consciousness, our routine, implicit knowledge of how to go on in the day to day activities which constitute our social field. It would seem reasonable, then, to assume that Giddens has no use for psychoanalytic theory. However, as I have just pointed out, this is not the case. To be more precise

---

[4]   Ibid., p. 49.

Giddens uses psychoanalytic theory to ground a concept of ontological security; to be able to go on routinely we need to be capable of trust, autonomy and initiative. Yet miraculously, for Giddens, these capacities, once established in the early years, are insignificant so far as the characteristics of 'normal' social interaction are concerned; for normally interaction does not challenge our core assumptions about trust, autonomy and initiative. These are merely residual. They only take on significance at moments of crisis or, as Giddens terms it, in 'critical situations', i.e. 'in circumstances of radical disjuncture of an unpredictable kind which affect substantial numbers of individuals, situations that threaten or destroy the certitudes of institutionalised routines'.[5] These critical situations lead to psychological regression, the irruption of the unconscious into social life. The striking aspect of all this is that, for Giddens, the irruption of the unconscious operates as a falling out of culture into nature. Defence mechanisms, understood as individual psychological modes of adaptation based in instinctual defensive responses of the human species, operate to preserve the human individual at the cost of desocialisation. This approach to the unconscious and its relation to processes of structuration prompts the following question. Why does Giddens find himself turning to psychoanalysis in order to conceptualise the extraordinary and the critical? Clearly there are many other psychologies which he might have selected. However, like so many other major social theorists of this century, Giddens is drawn to psychoanalysis, though in an ambivalent manner. My own reading of this turning to psychoanalysis, both for Giddens in particular and for social theory more broadly, is that in quite crucial ways the other psychologies, that is the other available theories of subjectivity and rationality, are manifestly inadequate when applied to the study of identities, or subjectivities, and to the study of social and political relations. Unlike psychoanalysis these other psychologies repress our primary modes of being, thinking, feeling and communication. Although repressed in theory, this primary field of being, thought, feeling and communication will not go away; it insists and persists. It can be denied for much of the time, but at the cost of splitting reason from emotion. In this context Giddens serves as an exemplar for the very reason that he does not fully embrace psychoanalytic theory. Rather, and this is what is so instructive or exemplary, he turns to

---

[5] Ibid., p. 61.

psychoanalysis in extremis. He characterises what he terms 'critical situations' as situations marked by an irruption of the unconscious.[6]

Giddens suggests that critical situations carry implications for 'the generality of routine social life'. It is worth pondering what he has in mind. Giddens draws a neat distinction between the routine and the critical situation. As I have already suggested, in the critical situation Giddens understands agents to have fallen out of culture and into nature. That is they fall into, or regress into, a culturally unmediated psychological state in which the primitive defence mechanisms are predominant. It is important to note that these primitive defence mechanisms do not take on specific cultural forms, they specifically do not constitute a set of rules for the structuration of social communication and interaction at moments of crisis. Rather they are, as it were, the natural state of all humans at those moments when reality overwhelms them; and that is all that can be said about them. Later I will propose that a more adequate approach to the place of the unconscious within culture and ideology involves a critical reworking of structuration theory, but not its wholesale rejection. This reworking needs to move beyond the notion of the unconscious as a kind of security blanket and to open up the whole field of the on-going structuration of unconscious processes *within* culture and ideology.

For Giddens, in radical contrast to critical situations, routine situations are organised by the specific rules of structuration which are peculiar to a particular cultural formation. These rules are known at the levels of practical and/or discursive consciousness; i.e. it is these realms of practical and discursive consciousness which are the field of structuration. Giddens notices that to operate as actors within this field of structuration we have to trust the world to be one which meets our basic expectations. Our 'basic security system' (his substitute term for the unconscious) has to be intact. Routinely it is intact and, as such, it guarantees our ontological security, an ontological security which critical situations disrupt.

What we should notice here is that, for Giddens, unlike Freud and Habermas, there is no dynamic relation between the unconscious, on the one hand, and practical and discursive consciousness, on the other. Rather they are alternate modes of knowing which never

---

[6] In this respect there is a close connection with the work of Fred Weinstein and Gerald Platt. See their *Psychoanalytic Sociology* (Baltimore and London: Johns Hopkins University Press, 1973).

interpenetrate. For Giddens the unconscious, understood as the basic security system, is a developmental moment which, once achieved, leaves no residue. At critical moments this achievement can be undone, but routinely it is the mere pre-history of the competent actor.

The core of structuration theory resides in its conceptualisation of the duality of structure, its concomitant emphasis on the centrality of rules and the rule-governed appropriation of resources, and in its emphasis on the 'making of history' by and through the actions of individual subjects; albeit that this process always involves unintended consequences. I regard it as an unfortunate characteristic of Giddens' elaboration of structuration theory that this very broad claim regarding the status of individual action as a necessary, though not sufficient, moment in the recursive process of social reproduction has been conflated with an ethnomethodological emphasis on practical consciousness and the related notion of action as skilful performance.[7] While in no way wishing to disparage the insights afforded by the use of these concepts in empirical research, I would argue that, in Giddens' hands, they have been overextended. In his attempt to counter functionalism and structuralism Giddens has elevated practical consciousness into the principal form of knowing how to go on skilfully in the vast array of routine social practices. As I have already demonstrated, this elevation of practical consciousness, understood as the knowing of how to skilfully go on, has been achieved at the cost of inappropriately reducing the scope and significance of the unconscious forms of knowing. I have pointed out the instability of this conceptual move within Giddens' own theory of structuration. In conceptualising critical situations Giddens is forced to step outside his notion of practical consciousness and to seek a theoretical basis in his drastically reduced notion of the unconscious. This leads him into the somewhat ludicrous position of having elaborated a social theory which, at moments of crisis, collapses into an impoverished theory of human nature, one which has appropriated those very bits of psychoanalytic theory which, taken alone, cannot support the analysis of social processes. As my discussion of Habermas has demonstrated, it is not necessary to read psychoanalysis in this reductionist manner and to marginalise the unconscious accordingly. In what follows it is my intention to develop a

---

[7] See Bhaskar, *The Possibility*, for an example of a structuration theory which does not rely on a concept of practical consciousness.

theory of structuration, restricted to the field of ideology, which places the unconscious at the centre of its concerns; i.e. I will attempt to specify the unconscious rules of structuration of a particular ideological formation.

One gain from this attempt to write theory with an empirical intent, a gain which many may regard as unlikely until it is pointed out, is methodological in character. Any empirical study of complex political and social processes involving millions of individual actors over long periods of time and dispersed across a multiplicity of settings has to look for means or methods of analysis which are capable of discerning regularities across a broad range of dimensions. These considerations have led many researchers to bypass ways and forms of knowing and to focus on behavioural regularities. The theory of structuration, especially where ideological processes are concerned, is of interest because it offers an alternative to any such behaviourism, one which places ways and forms of knowing at the centre of the explanatory account. Although it is certainly possible to elaborate rules of practical consciousness, any extension of an empirical analysis beyond a particular institutional setting quickly meets with the methodological problem of how to adequately organise the multiplicity of particular rules which are at play. This problem lies in the very conceptualisation of practical consciousness. The unconscious, however, when understood as a mode of reasoning or as a structure and not merely as a set of contents, is a concept well suited to this empirical task. Furthermore, when the matter is approached in this way those readers who are suspicious of any notion of an unconscious are able to assess the value of such a concept in relation to the explanation of an empirical case.

Giddens has been rightly criticised for his failure to provide good, developed examples of specific rules for the structuration of specific social systems. In place of this, characteristically Giddens has offered either *ad hoc* examples drawn from the ethnomethodological or anthropological literature or very generalised schemas. In the first case the problem is that, while the examples are interesting and informative, it is difficult to see how their scope could be generalised beyond the particular institutional settings in which they have been observed. In the second case, and this underscores the extent of the first problem, the difficulty is that the broad schematisations which Giddens offers are thoroughly unconvincing as instances of rules which are, in any meaningful sense, 'known' and drawn upon in the process of structuration. For instance Giddens proposes the following as examples of 'structural sets':[8]

private property : money : capital : labor contract : profit
private property : money : capital : labor contract : industrial authority
private property : money : educational advantage : occupational position

As Thompson has wryly noted with regard to these structural sets, 'these features of the capitalist system cannot be treated as so many "rules" that workers follow when they turn up at the factory gates, as if every worker who accepted a job had an implicit (albeit partial) knowledge of Marx's *Capital*'.[9]

As I have already indicated in chapter 2, there is more than one way of reading psychoanalysis into social and political theory. In contemporary theory, under the strong influence of structuralism and post-structuralism, there is a tendency to accept the conceit that the unconscious is not only universal or transhistorical but also that it is always the same; that it lacks any dynamism. Lacan, Althusser and Mitchell, as well as Lévi-Strauss, have advanced this position; though Mitchell does not regard it as inevitable. Indeed, for her, this inevitability is extinguished with the demise of patriarchy.[10] However, even in those cases where the structuralist emphasis on synchrony has been rejected the bad habit of placing the unconscious outside of history, too often, has been retained. Again we see this with Giddens' version of structuration theory.

Giddens is one writer who finds the whole structuralist cum post-structuralist account intolerable. As he has put it, 'structuralism, and post-structuralism also, are dead traditions of thought'.[11] Nevertheless, he retains an asocial and ahistorical notion of the unconscious, though one which is now marginalised to critical situations and stripped of its dynamic complexity. As explained above, in this conception the unconscious is a transhistorical species attribute upon which is grounded the basic capacities for trust,

[8] Giddens, *Central Problems*, p. 104 and *The Constitution*, p. 302.
[9] John B. Thompson, *Studies in the Theory of Ideology* (Cambridge: Polity Press, 1984), p. 164. As Thompson's critique of Giddens overlaps with my own in this regard, I refer the reader to his text for further discussion of the problem I have outlined above. It should be clear that I regard structuration theory as eminently suitable for the development of a theory of ideology, whatever its broader claims may or may not involve.
[10] See J. Mitchell, *Psychoanalysis and Feminism* (New York: Pantheon, 1974); J. Lacan, *Ecrits, A Selection*, translated by Alan Sheridan (London: Tavistock Publications, 1977); C. Lévi-Strauss, *Structural Anthropology*, translated by C. Jacobson and B. G. Schoepf (New York: Basic Books, 1963).
[11] A. Giddens, *Social Theory & Modern Sociology* (Cambridge: Polity Press, 1987), p. 73.

autonomy and initiative which are understood as central to the
capacity of individuals to enter into social interaction. This unconscious is developmentally significant but, for all but critical situations, socially irrelevant. It is part of nature but never part of
culture; hence it is always, already the same. In this last respect it
retains the structuralist conceit, with one important exception. For
Giddens the unconscious, being part of nature rather than culture,
is solely an attribute of individuals.

Habermas, and indeed Fromm before him, have made it clear
that this ahistorical and asocial notion of the unconscious was never
part of Freud's understanding.[12] For Freud the unconscious was
transhistorical and transformable at once; civilisation is that complex
cultural field in which the unconscious is ever present and ever
dynamic. History, which Freud, like Hegel, Marx and Habermas,
understood as an evolutionary process, involves not only social and
technological change but also change in the organisation of the
unconscious within the institutions of culture. Freud and Habermas
are both concerned with the manner in which institutionalised
ideologies (or illusions) can be understood as having an unconscious
component which can and does change across institutional space and
through time, due to the communicative actions of groups and
generations of individual subjects.[13] However, neither Freud nor
Habermas have much to say about the specific forms which these
unconscious processes and patterns of distorted communication take
in particular instances. Consequently it is difficult to move from their
theory of the unconscious to empirical research on particular
ideological formations.

As Gramsci first helped us to see, the field of political conflict is a
field on which ideologies play a central part. The battle for hegemony is principally, though not exclusively, a battle for intellectual
and moral, as well as political, dominance.[14] It is a battle within
discourse over different forms of signification, communication and
subjection. At the same time it is a battle in which all outcomes are
contingent upon human action and in which no particular result is

[12] See E. Fromm, 'The Method and Function of an Analytic Social Psychology' in A. Arato
and O. Gebhardt (eds.), *The Essential Frankfurt School Reader* (New York: Urizon Books,
1978), and J. Habermas, *Knowledge and Human Interests*, translated by J. Shapiro (Boston:
Beacon Press, 1971), chs. 10–12.
[13] See Freud, *The Future of an Illusion*, SE, vol. XXI.
[14] See A. Gramsci, *Selections from Prison Notebooks*, translated by Q. Hoare and G. Nowell
Smith (London: Lawrence and Wishart, 1971).

guaranteed. A structuration theory which concentrates on the unconscious rules drawn upon in this ideological battle for hegemony offers
one way of beginning to specify a core set of rules which are drawn
upon in the organisation of this conflict. Such an emphasis on the
unconscious rather than on practical consciousness is quite compa-
tible with the principal emphases of structuration theory, despite
Giddens' own predilection for the elaboration of these emphases
with an ethnomethodological inflection. The example of Roy Bhaskar's work is telling in this respect. As he has put it: 'It is important to
stress that the reproduction and/or transformation of society, though
for the most part unconsciously achieved, is nevertheless still an
achievement, a skilled accomplishment of active subjects, not a
mechanical consequent of antecedent conditions.'[15]

[15]   Bhaskar, *The Possibility*, p. 46.

CHAPTER 4

Ideology and affect

In psychoanalysis nothing is true except the exaggerations
(Theodor Adorno, *Minima Moralia*)

John Rawls has suggested that '(w)hen fully articulated, any conception of justice expresses a conception of the person, of the relations
between persons, and of the general structure and ends of social
cooperation'.[1] In like manner, when fully articulated, an ideology
expresses a conception of the person, of the relations between persons
and of the general structure and ends of political and social intercourse. However there is a complication in the case of ideologies. As
any ideological formation contains a variety of structural forms, and
thus a variety of conceptions of the person, relationships and social
cooperation, an adequate analysis of an ideological formation involves the specification of these various structural forms and, for each
of them, the specification of the following characteristics:
(1) its conception of the person or subject;
(2) its conception of the proper relations between persons or subjects;
(3) its conception of authority and the proper exercise of power.

To achieve a detailed specification of the structural characteristics
of an ideological formation two methods of analysis will be developed
below, the first drawing on psychoanalytic theory, the second on
cognitive-developmental theory. This analysis will allow a specification of the basic rules of structuration of Unionist politics. Later,
when we come to consider Unionist ideology in detail, we will
observe that similar themes are repeated apparently ad infinitum.
This could lead to a conclusion that the ideology in question is static.
Pluralism arguments, which regard the prevailing situation in

An earlier version of this chapter was published in *Political Psychology*. See J. D. Cash, 'Ideology
and Affect: The Case of Northern Ireland', *Political Psychology*, 10:4 (1989), pp. 703–24.
[1]   J. Rawls, 'A Well-Ordered Society' in *Philosophy, Politics and Society*, eds. P. Laslett and
J. Fishkin (New Haven: Yale University Press, 1979), p. 6.

Northern Ireland as merely the perpetuation into the present of a long-established pattern of political relations, would thus seem empirically vindicated. However, if structural change or variation occurs in the presence of thematic continuity, then the ideological process may be more dynamic than was at first thought; indeed the apparent thematic continuity may well be operating to disguise a more fundamental internal diversity within the ideological formation in question. Unless we are able to observe such structural variations and transformations we may well miss such dynamism and thus be likely to discount the significance of ideological processes. This is the case both diachronically and synchronically. That is, we may fail to notice both that the ideology under observation is varying across time and that at any one time it takes a variety of forms. Ideologies may be far more complex, internally and structurally, than thematic analyses are able to comprehend. Whether this is the case in Northern Ireland and other 'divided societies' is an empirical issue, but such an issue can only be raised when appropriate methods of analysis have been developed.

Any project to establish the rules of an ideological formation raises questions as to the appropriate level of specification. Should we follow Lévi-Strauss and concentrate on specifying the one fundamental structuring principle of all discourse, the dichotomising of the real? Or, in a similar vein, should we follow Freud, Saussure and Lacan and specify the fundamental rules of condensation and displacement, or metaphor and metonymy? The difficulty with such an approach is that the specification of these very general rules regarding the deep structure of ideologies, or of the unconscious, does not allow the specification of internal differentiations within an ideological formation, except as so many variations on the one set of rules. Another possible approach is to focus on the rules governing particular types of situation: parties, violence at soccer matches, funerals, riding of buses and so on.[2] This approach has the opposite difficulty of being too situation bound; it is too specific for our particular purposes. This research calls for an intermediate level of rule specification, one which is able to discern the internal differentiation of an ideological formation, one which facilitates general-

---

[2]   As in the work of Erving Goffman and the work of psychologists such as R. Harre and P. Marsh. See, for instance, E. Goffman, *Frame Analysis* (New York: Harper, 1974), R. Harre and P. F. Secord, *The Explanation of Social Behaviour* (Oxford: Blackwell, 1972), P. Marsh, *The Rules of Disorder* (London: Routledge, 1978).

isation across any number of particular types of situation and one which enables the linkage of a detailed analysis of strips of ideology to the general rule-systems which have been identified. For these reasons, although with some marked differences, I will follow Habermas in focusing upon the determinate set of 'rationality structures' which regulate ideological formations.[3] The principal differences from Habermas are as follows. First, by turning to psychoanalytic group psychology, especially as developed within the Kleinian tradition, I will attempt to specify some core psychody-namic rules which underlie both individual and group identities. By developing psychoanalytic theory in this manner I will be able to pursue, within the analysis of an empirical example, an interest in the place of affects within ideological formations. This concern with affects is central to both the Frankfurt school's conceptualisation of ideology and to Habermas' own extension of this tradition in *Knowledge and Human Interests*. Consequently, by proceeding in this manner I will pursue a direction which Habermas might well have pursued himself following upon the completion of *Knowledge and Human Interests*. However, after his appropriation, in that work, of psychoanalytic theory for the general purpose of demonstrating the characteristics of a self-reflective science and the more specific purpose of developing a theory of ideology elaborated in terms of both labour and interaction, Habermas, while not repudiating his appropriation of psychoanalytic theory, engaged more and more with cognitive-developmental theory. This theory had the advantage of specifying the structural characteristics of different forms of reasoning and different forms of ego and group identity. Thus it allowed the specification of a differentiated set of rule systems. Furthermore, and of especial appeal to Habermas, it cast these differences within an evolutionary framework of ontogenetic and phylogenetic development. Habermas' theoretical and empirical concerns with the development of an adequate theory of communication and the evolution of society called for exactly the degree of specification which cognitive-developmental theory supported. In what follows, I too will take advantage of this specificity of cognitive-developmental theory. However, as already indicated, I have also attempted to complete the implicit agenda of a psychoanalytically derived theory of ideology, one which is capable of observing affects as well as

[3]   See J. Habermas, *Communication and The Evolution of Society*, translated by T. McCarthy (Boston: Beacon Press, 1979), p. 98.

cognitions, and one which was already partly theorised in *Knowledge and Human Interests* but was never specified in a manner which would allow the identification of distinct rule modes.

Building upon the work of Freud, Piaget and Kohlberg, Habermas has observed homologies between the ontogenetic developmental sequence revealed in psychological research and the phylogenetic sequence revealed in historical-cultural research. That is, taking the rules of various forms of reasoning, or 'rationality structures' as the principal focus of his concern, Habermas has observed that the same sets of rules operate at the individual, cultural and institutional levels.[4] The position taken in this study is broadly similar. However, this research indicates a somewhat different pattern from that observed by Habermas. He takes the whole of human history as the object of scrutiny and then periodises this history in terms of the prevalent rationality and group-identity structures.[5] My research suggests that at any one moment, at least for the particular empirical case which I am investigating in detail, the full set of possible variations is present. Over time the concentration of any one rule-system may vary, as may the areas of its domination. That is to say, the extent to which any particular rule-system is institutionalised and routinised is an empirical matter. No evolutionary assumptions need be made.[6] Following Gramsci, Giddens and others, the only assumption I make in this respect is that there always may be a variation across both time and space in the degree of such institutionalisation. The whole process is dynamic. As I have already argued, these variations within the ideological formation are a central aspect of the political process. Clearly, if this is the case, to comprehend this political process we require methods of analysis which reveal the ideological rules of the game. In this and the following chapter I will concentrate on indicating the characteristics of two such methods. A full analysis of the rules of an ideological formation should attend to

[4]   Ibid., p. 98.
[5]   Habermas also discusses world-views and legal and moral systems.
[6]   Habermas finds himself in a delicate position in this respect, given his desire to preserve much of what he has taken from Freud while adopting the somewhat contrary positions developed by Piaget and Kohlberg. This is especially evident with regard to the assumptions regarding regression contained in these two different theories. For psycho-analytic theory regression is a constant possibility, for cognitive-developmental theory regression is presumed to be impossible. Despite Habermas' enthusiastic adoption of cognitive-developmental theory it is important that he retains a concept of regression. This is just one indication of the way in which he reads cognitive-developmental theory through a psychoanalytic lens.

both its affective and its cognitive dimensions. In this chapter I will attempt to develop a method of analysis which supports the analysis of the core psychodynamic rules, rules which are at once cognitive and affective, of an ideological formation. In chapter 5 I will concentrate specifically on the cognitive dimension of an ideological formation; that is, I will concentrate on what Piaget might have termed its 'cognitive unconscious'. Each method has certain advantages and disadvantages which should become apparent as I proceed.

IDEOLOGY AND AFFECT

Ideologies are saturated, indeed suffused, with emotion; emotion informs, shapes and animates them. This is evident even in such a stable and consensual society as Australia, where the day to day business of politics is transacted in an ideological idiom of fear, loathing, hope, despair and desire. No wonder, then, that in such a deeply divided society as Northern Ireland, where conflict has been endemic and the political stakes are unusually high, the passions are quite pervasive. Despite accounts to the contrary, affect-laden ideologies are not merely an ephemeral 'sound and fury' disguising the sharp conflict of material interests. Neither are they a mere residue from an ancient tradition which no longer holds any purchase on the future. Rather they are integral to the constitution and organisation of the contemporary political order of Northern Ireland. They are instantiated in the variety of its institutional settings and reproduced, sometimes with modifications, from moment to moment in the daily routines of its inhabitants. Critically, they will inevitably enter into the very minutiae of the current attempts to make a difference in Northern Ireland.

Amazingly, this affective dimension goes unnoticed and unacknowledged in virtually all theories of ideology. Unable to adequately theorise the presence and persistence of affects, these theories construe them as mere epiphenomena: whilst they add 'heat' and 'colour' to the rational pursuit of interests, they in no way constitute these interests. Strikingly, it is popular accounts of situations such as that prevailing in Northern Ireland which are quick to notice, and indeed highlight, the affective dimension of ideology. It is hardly an exaggeration to suggest that in such popular accounts Northern Ireland is generally characterised as a situation in which two tribal groupings, crazed by ancient enmities which somehow persist despite all latter-day attempts to displace them, confront each other in a fight to the death. Here anger, hatred and aggression stand at the centre of the explanatory account. Of course these affects are regarded as entirely irrational, indeed as 'crazy'. Consequently they are seen as being closed to analysis, just as they are closed to reason and conciliation. Nevertheless, and herein lies the wisdom of the popular accounts, they are seen to be an animating force in the structuring of the political order.

The recent history of the academic study of affects and politics is, thus, quite pertinent. When Alan Davies pointed to 'the neglect of affects' some twenty years ago, his was virtually a lone voice.[7] Of course, as he himself made clear, this voice was not revealing any new truths. Rather it was reiterating, and eventually sophisticating, a problematic of ancient lineage which, from the 1940s onwards, was in almost universal decline. From that time, in political science as in academic psychology and sociology, affects were seen as too recalcitrant, labile and mercurial to constitute a proper object of scientific discourse. No doubt this had its basis in the contemporary hegemony of positivist epistemologies. Only in psychoanalytic theory, which by this time had been cast from the academy, was this interest in affects sustained.

More recently, work in both political science and social psychology has featured a 'newly emerging conventional wisdom' according to which 'social psychology has become too exclusively cognitive and it is time to reexamine the role of affect'.[8] For instance Abelson and others have brought affects under exemplary control through the application of statistical procedures to the analysis of large sample surveys which include a measure for affects. Although, as the authors recognise, the affect measures which they use are rather crude and limited, the results of this research are quite striking. Essentially the research indicates that affective orientation has greater power than semantic or cognitive orientation in predicting political orientation or behaviour (voting as measured by a reliable surrogate measure). It would seem, then, that affects are again becoming a conventional concern of political science. This is just as well for political science as, despite the wish implicit in the end of ideology thesis, a sober look

[7]   A. F. Davies, *Essays in Political Sociology* (Melbourne: Cheshire, 1972), pp. 89–95.
[8]   R. Abelson, D. Kinder, M. Peters and S. Fiske, 'Affective and semantic components in political person perception', *Journal of Personality and Social Psychology*, 42 (1982), pp. 619–30.

at politics across the globe would seem to indicate that the passions remain central to ideology and politics.

The neglect of affects is one striking dimension of a broader failure in social and political theory; one which may be characterised as the failure to take ideology seriously. It will be recalled that Clifford Geertz pointed to this broader problem more than twenty years ago, when he argued for the need to move beyond 'source analysis' and 'consequence analysis' to a concentration upon 'ideologies as systems of interacting symbols, as patterns of interworking meanings'.[9] However it remains the case that, as a rule, academic explanations of particular political and social formations proceed in a manner which marginalises ideology. Interestingly, this is so even in those situations where the authors avow an intention to take ideology seriously and where they both draw upon a theoretical apparatus, and analyse empirical examples, which highlight the need to do so. Thus both John Saul and his associate, writing on South Africa, and Paul Bew and his associates, writing on Northern Ireland, fail to realise their own Althusserian avowals of recognising ideology as a 'new reality'.[10] The former characterise Afrikaner ideology as merely a 'residual atavism' infected by 'heat' and 'extremism', and the latter quickly fall back into the commonplace of characterising Unionist ideology as mere 'rhetoric'. All this occurs despite clear intentions to the contrary. The question arises as to why, even when the need to do so is clearly recognised, it is so difficult to take ideology seriously.

Briefly, the following would seem to be the case. Whilst the theoretical work and the injunctions of Althusser, Habermas, Geertz and others have highlighted the need to attend closely to ideologies, the failure to specify adequate methods for so doing has left this enterprise unrealised. This is especially the case when it comes to the emotional dimensions of ideologies. These are obscured even in the literary method of interpretation proposed by Geertz, the semiological methods employed by some structural and post-structural Marxists, and the psychoanalytic and cognitive-developmental methods drawn upon by Habermas. Thus, even in those few cases where ideology is taken seriously, its affective dimensions still tend to

[9] C. Geertz, *The Interpretation of Cultures* (New York: Basic Books, 1973). The relevant chapter was first published in 1964.
[10] See J. Saul and S. Gelb, *The Crisis in South Africa* (New York and London: Monthly Review Press, 1981); P. Bew, P. Gibbon and H. Patterson, *The State in Northern Ireland: 1921–1972* (Manchester: Manchester University Press, 1979).

be systematically obscured. In this study I attempt to overcome this striking disability of contemporary theories of ideology.

For our purposes ideology may be defined as follows. An ideology is a dynamic and relatively autonomous system of signification, communication and subjection which operates by constructing a social and political order and subjecting individual human beings to cathected positions within this order. (Strictly speaking a structure of signification, communication and subjection is ideological in so far as it performs the above operations.)

Let me briefly elaborate the major elements of this definition. To describe ideology as a system of signification is to indicate the following: firstly that its realm or field is the symbolic; secondly that this symbolic order has structural as well as thematic characteristics. Ideology is more than a set of themes. It is also a structure with determinate modes of organisation and with its own rules of reproduction and transformation.

To suggest that this structure is relatively autonomous is to assert the integrity of these rules of process. It is to recognise ideology as a distinct level of social and political reality. External processes will affect ideology (it is only relatively autonomous) but always according to its own discrete rules of process (herein lies its degree of autonomy). Thus, for instance, the 'modernisation' of the relations of production will not necessarily generate a modernisation of ideological forms. The relationship between the economic and the ideological levels is not such a simple and one-sided affair. Indeed, as the case of Northern Ireland makes apparent, modernisation processes may create an ideological crisis which in turn may generate what appear as 'traditional' themes and forms of ideology.

Ideology operates in the following manner. Firstly it constructs a system of relationships. It states or establishes the various political and social roles, their relationship to each other, the appropriate form of authority and the nature of entitlement. So, for instance, it may construct a system of relationships in which every individual is equally subject to a universal rule of law. Or it may construct a system of relationships in which each human being is first of all regarded as a member of a group – is black or white; Protestant or Catholic; Hindu or Muslim, for example – and in which the groups are differentially entitled and differentially subject to the rule of law.

Having constructed a system of relationships the ideology simultaneously subjects individuals to positions within this system. To use the Althusserian formulation for the moment, 'ideology interpellates individuals as subjects'. That is it 'hails' or tells each individual what he or she is. Hey taxi-driver!, Hey Protestant!, Hey Unionist!, Hey Nationalist!, or whatever.

Thirdly, ideology is a structure of signification which operates according to psychological rules. To raise this consideration is to move far away from the conventional notions of ideology. In particular it involves a marked movement beyond those structuralist and post-structuralist notions which regard the subject as merely an effect and support of the ideological formation. It involves the recognition that the subject is not merely interpellated by an ideology, but rather is an interlocutor, an active party to the discourse.

To see the subject as an interlocutor within the ideological field carries two types of implication for the analysis of ideology. Firstly it involves the recognition that the individual human being brings to the construction of his or her subjectivity a species-specific set of characteristics, including psychological characteristics, which are determinate. That is, they are neither open-ended nor without structure. Consequently any crude notion of an equivalence between the 'socially' salient and that which is internalised, is quite fallacious.

Moreover, the ideological formation itself bears the mark of these species-specific characteristics. It too has determinate forms. Whilst any one human being or generation of human beings enters and is constructed in terms of an established ideological formation, this formation has itself been shaped and constrained (though not wholly determined) by the species-specific characteristics of prior generations. There is a human side, and more particularly a psychological side to all ideology. All ideology is radically mind-dependent.

To regard the subject as an interlocutor is also to recognise that the subject cathects the ideological construction to which he or she has been subjected. That is, the subject invests psychic energy in the object world and in the characteristics of the self which the ideology has constructed. That this should be so is hardly surprising. Being formed in and through these ideological processes, necessarily subjects value the system of signification which tells them both what they are and what their world is.

The implications of this are quite far-reaching and account for the dynamic character of an ideological formation. Any ideological repositioning of subjects in the process of political conflict is never unconflicted and never proceeds as a mere recalling or reinterpellation. Rather it endemically involves challenges to the ontological security of the subject and thus engages the complex field of thought, emotion and interest. In the popular phrase ideological conflict is always 'a battle for the hearts and minds' of subjects, or, as Gramsci would have it, for intellectual and moral, as well as political, hegemony.[11]

As ideologies and the interests which they construct and represent enter periods of crisis there is a tendency for them to take on regressive forms. At the extreme this may involve the dehumanisation of the threatening groups. But there are other positions which also warrant attention, and these are given particular attention below. This regressive, and otherwise defensive, characteristic of ideological formations follows from the cathexis or emotional investment which subjects have in the ideology which constructs both their object world and central aspects of themselves. Conventional notions of ideology fail entirely to take this into account.

Furthermore, as the work of Lazarus, Janis and others suggests, crisis tends to affect moderately vulnerable groups by stimulating more adaptive and sophisticated forms for the construction of political reality.[12] Clearly causal hypotheses of this kind could be developed in a more detailed and elaborate manner. Any such theoretical enterprise relies, first of all, upon the development of an adequate means for distinguishing the internal diversity of an ideological formation and it is this to which I now turn.

IDEOLOGY, SUBJECTIVITY AND THE UNCONSCIOUS

One possible method for the analysis of the affective component of ideology is to conduct a content analysis of affects. To do so requires both a fairly comprehensive list of affects and a reliable means of distinguishing one from another. In *Skills, Outlooks and Passions* Davies

[11] See A. Gramsci, *Selections from Prison Notebooks* (London: Lawrence and Wishart, 1971).
[12] See, for example, I. Janis and L. Mann, *Decision-Making* (New York: Free Press, 1977); R. Lazarus, *Psychological Stress and the Coping Process* (New York: McGraw Hill, 1966).

provides just such a list along with a detailed examination of some central affects and affect-systems.[13] He also provides an example of a content analysis of political affects as expressed in a group of student diaries.

The virtue of such an approach is its capacity to capture the complex phenomenology of an affective structure and to reveal any persistent patterns of association (or exclusion) between one affect and another. Consequently such an approach is able to indicate whether there are any prominent structures of feeling which are central to an ideological formation. Conceivably, affects character-istically form systems or structures which have a determinate rela-tional form and conceivably any particular ideological formation is organised in terms of a limited set of these. A content analysis offers a means of entering such a domain of inquiry.

The limitation of such an approach is that it offers no way of gathering observations under a powerful theoretical description. A content analysis of affects does not theorise the rules of relationship between one affect and another. Neither does it theorise the rules of articulation between the cognitive and affective components of an ideological formation. Consequently it does not discriminate in a manner best suited to capture the qualitative distinctions which a hermeneutic reading of ideologies would suggest.

To achieve this I now turn to psychoanalytic theory in an attempt to develop a cognitive-affective method for the analysis of ideology. In particular I will concentrate on the work of Melanie Klein. There is general agreement within psychoanalytic theory that modes of constructing reality and the mechanisms of defence against anxiety can be arranged along a developmental continuum. Some modes, such as Klein's paranoid-schizoid position, and some defences, such as splitting, projection and omnipotent denial (which characterise the paranoid-schizoid position), are regarded as more primitive than others. However, the various modes and the various defence mechanisms remain available to all human individuals and may become operative. As Hanna Segal has put it (focusing particularly on the defence mechanisms):

No experience in human development is ever cast aside or obliterated; we must remember that in the most normal individual there will be some

[13] A. F. Davies, *Skills, Outlooks and Passions* (Cambridge: Cambridge University Press, 1980), pp. 293ff.

situations which will stir up the earliest anxieties and bring into operation the earliest mechanisms of defence.[14]

To capture this dynamic, potentially regressive, character of the human psyche Klein uses the term 'position', rather than some such term as 'phase' or 'stage', to distinguish between modes of operation. She proposes a developmental sequence in which all individuals pass through a paranoid-schizoid position in the first few months of life to a depressive position and beyond. In the anxiety and affect-laden world of human relationships these positions will frequently recur in the psychological life of the adult. There is reason to believe that they will be particularly prevalent in relation to 'social phenomena'. Jaques has commented on this as follows:

It has often been noted that many social phenomena show a strikingly close correspondence with psychotic processes in individuals . . . My own recent experience has impressed upon me how much institutions are used by their individual members to reinforce individual mechanisms of defence against anxiety, and in particular against recurrence of the early paranoid and depressive anxieties . . .[15]

For present purposes I will briefly characterise the paranoid-schizoid and depressive positions and then outline a method for the interpretation of ideologies which may be derived from this.

In the paranoid-schizoid position the subject constructs a world of part-objects which are either ideal or bad, or alternately one and then the other. This is achieved by the mechanisms of splitting and projection. So, for instance, the mother's breast is split into an ideal breast and a bad breast, i.e. these are constructed as distinct and separate objects. Negative experience and affects are projected into the bad breast and positive experience and affects are projected into the ideal breast. The principal attitudes to these part-objects are an idealisation of the ideal breast and a sadistic wish to punish and destroy the bad breast. The principal affects are, on the one hand, feelings of satiety and bliss and, on the other, persecutory anxiety and feelings of an aggressive and sadistic character. As well as the object, the self may be split and projected in a like manner.

In the depressive position the subject constructs a world of whole objects which may have both positive and negative aspects: i.e.

---

[14] H. Segal, *Introduction to the Work of Melanie Klein* (London: Hogarth Press, 1979), p. 35.

[15] E. Jaques, 'Social Systems as Defence Against Persecutory and Depressive Anxiety', in M. Klein, P. Heimann and R. Money-Kyrle, eds., *New Directions in Psychoanalysis* (London: Tavistock Publications, 1955), p. 478.

objects are at once both good and bad, they are not split. Consequently ambivalence is central to the subject's experience of the object, the same object may be both frustrating and satisfying. Thus the construction of the object is more realistic and is less dominated by the rule of the pleasure principle. The principal affects are feelings of loss and guilt. Whilst some degree of splitting and projection remain available within the depressive position the principal defences are of a different character. They fall into two broad syndromes and may be thought of as constituting the positive and negative poles of the depressive position. Kernberg discusses the positive pole of the depressive position in the following terms:

The predominant defensive operations of the depressive position are reparation, ambivalence, and gratitude. These mechanisms are mutually linked and reinforce each other. Reparation consists in an effort to reduce the guilt over having attacked the good object by trying to repair the damage, express love and gratitude to the object, and preserve it internally and externally. Reparation is the origin of sublimation. Gratitude, originally an expression of the libidinal investment of good objects from the beginning of life on, now also reinforces the love of the object, which is feared to be harmed or damaged by the aggression expressed toward it. Guilt, in other words, reinforces gratitude, and gratitude and reparation reinforce each other and increase the capacity for trusting others and the self's capacity to give and receive love.

Ambivalence is a general expression of emotional growth rather than a specific defense per se; the infant's awareness of love and hate toward the same object fosters a deepening of his understanding about himself and of others. The tolerance of ambivalence implies a predominance of love over hate in relation to whole objects. In more general terms, the integration of love and hate brings about deepening of emotions and emotional growth, deepening self-awareness and capacity for empathic perception of others, and the capacity for further differentiation between objects – thus initiating the differentiation along sexual lines characteristic of triadic oedipal relations.[16]

The negative pole of the depressive position is characterised by Kernberg as the manic defences. These are also directed against the experience of dependence and ambivalence with regard to the object and take the form of control, triumph and contempt. Their purpose is to deny that the object has value and thus to overcome feelings of dependence, of anxiety regarding the loss of the object and of guilt.

[16] O. Kernberg, *Internal World and External Reality* (New York: Jason Aronson, 1980), pp. 30–1.

To make use of Kleinian theory for the analysis of ideology involves a radical transposition. The object of investigation is quite different, as is the type of evidence to be interpreted. Whereas the Kleinian concepts were developed for the analysis of evidence pertaining, primarily, to the personal order, the current approach intends to adapt them to the analysis of ideological data pertaining to the social and political order. Considerable warrant for such a transposition, along with some guidance in how to effect it, is provided by Bion's work on groups (mainly, though not exclusively, small groups) and especially by the work of Jaques, Menzies and Rice on institutions.[17]

For current purposes the central virtue of psychoanalytic theory is its explicit model of the human psyche as a cognitive-affective mental apparatus. This model is both more complex and more adequate than the implicit models embedded in most political and social theory.[18] In place of the usual notions of either a 'blank slate' or a rational utilitarian cogito, psychoanalytic theory, stated in Kleinian terms, regards the human psyche as a complex and conflict-ridden mental apparatus capable of 'rational' calculation, but always subject to paranoid and depressive anxieties and the defensive formations which attend these.[19]

Jaques makes use of this model in what I would describe as his study of distorted communication within institutions. He extends psychoanalytic theory by characterising social institutions and their attendant 'cultural mechanisms' as media for the binding of depressive and paranoid anxieties. As he puts it:

The specific hypothesis I shall consider is that one of the primary cohesive elements binding individuals into institutionalized human association is that of defence against psychotic anxiety. In this sense individuals may be thought of as externalizing those impulses and internal objects that would otherwise give rise to psychotic anxiety, and pooling them in the life of the social institutions in which they associate. This is not to say that the institutions so used thereby become 'psychotic'. But it does imply that we

---

[17] See W. R. Bion, *Experiences in Groups* (London: Tavistock Publications, 1961); Jaques, 'Social Systems'; I. Menzies, 'A Case-Study in the Functioning of Social Systems as a Defence Against Anxiety', in A. Colman and W. H. Bexton, eds., *Group Relations Reader* (California: A. K. Rice Institute, 1975); A. K. Rice, *Productivity and Social Organisation* (London: Tavistock Publications, 1958).

[18] Of course, psychoanalytic theory is regarded as more adequate for this particular object of research, and not as universally so.

[19] This characterisation is stated in Kleinian terms.

would expect to find in group relationships manifestations of unreality, splitting, hostility, suspicion, and other forms of maladaptive behaviour.[20]

In a further move Jaques explains 'intractability' to social change as a resistance to the psychologically disturbing effects of such change. He writes:

And the reasons for the intractability to change of many social stresses and group tensions may be more clearly appreciated if seen as the 'resistances' of groups of people unconsciously clinging to the institutions that they have, because changes in social relationships threaten to disturb existing social defences against psychotic anxiety.[21]

Jaques illustrates these processes in his analysis of a change in methods of payment within one department of a light engineering company: the Glacier Metal Company. A system of piece-rate payment which was in place was felt by all parties to be unsatisfactory. Workers were dissatisfied with a system which created uncertainty as to the amount of their weekly pay packet. Management disliked the complications of rate-fixing and administration which were involved. Hence, under propitious circumstances negotiations began regarding a change to a flat rate of pay. Initially these were conducted by a 'sub-committee composed of the departmental manager, the superintendent, and three workers' representatives'.[22] Despite the propitious circumstances and a general tone of friendliness, 'there was sharp disagreement over specific points'.[23]

One example of Jaques' analysis of this situation will suffice for our purposes. On the basis of his observations as participant observer and consultant, Jaques concludes that the workers were involved in the following defensive procedures:

The workers in the shop had split the managers into good and bad – the good managers being the ones with whom they worked, and the bad being the same managers but in the negotiation situation. They had unconsciously projected their hostile destructive impulses into their elected representatives so that the representatives could deflect, or redirect, these impulses against the bad 'management' with whom negotiations were carried on, while the good objects and impulses could be put into individual real managers in the day-to-day work situation. This splitting of the management into good and bad, and the projective identification with the elected representatives against the bad management served two purposes. At the reality level it allowed the good relations necessary to the work task of the department to be maintained; at the phantasy level it provided a system of social

---

[20] Jaques, 'Social Systems as Defence', p. 479.
[21] Ibid., p. 479. [22] Ibid., pp. 488–9. [23] Ibid., pp. 488–9.

relationships reinforcing individual defences against paranoid and depressive anxiety.

Putting their good impulses into managers in the work situation allowed the workers to reintroject the good relations with management, and hence to preserve an undamaged good object and alleviate depressive anxiety. This depressive anxiety was further avoided by reversion to the paranoid position in the negotiating situation.[24]

In other words the prospect of change generated defensive mechanisms which came to be bound into the social institution of the negotiating sub-committee. Whilst intended as an institution of change, this sub-committee came to function as a system of social relationships which preserved the status quo. It facilitated good relations on the shop-floor, on the basis of mechanisms of splitting, projection and idealisation, at the cost of undermining its own rationale.

Menzies extends the approach developed by Jaques in a later study of the nursing system within a major London hospital. Her principal hypothesis is the following:

Every individual is at risk that objective or psychic events stimulating acute anxiety will lead to partial or complete abandonment of the more mature methods of dealing with anxiety and to regression to the more primitive methods of defense. In our opinion, the intense anxiety evoked by the nursing task has precipitated just such individual regression to primitive types of defense. These have been projected and given objective existence in the social structure and culture of the nursing service, with the result that anxiety is to some extent contained, but that true mastery of anxiety by deep working-through and modification is seriously inhibited.[25]

In this study the often highly stressful tasks associated with the role of nurse are seen as the causes of regression. The resultant primitive forms of organisation are projected into the social structure and culture of the institution. Immediately we should note that whereas Jaques highlights actual and prospective change as the precipitant of regression, Menzies regards a threatening status quo as the precipitant. Clearly, anxiety, whatever its source, is the common element in these two accounts.

Menzies observed the following features of the nursing system. Firstly, to cope with the anxiety, nurses characteristically 'split off aspects of' themselves and projected these 'into other nurses'.[26] Irresponsible aspects were projected into subordinates, stern and

[24]   Ibid., pp. 490–1.   [25]   Ibid., pp. 298–9.   [26]   Ibid., p. 293.

harsh aspects into superiors. This became institutionalised, so that junior nurses actually regarded themselves as irresponsible and often behaved accordingly, and superiors tended to be overly severe. Secondly, a whole set of practices and norms developed which bound or deflected the anxiety, but at a cost. For instance patients tended to be depersonalised, becoming 'the liver in bed 10' or 'the Pneumonia in bed 15'.[27] Other institutionalised practices and norms identified by Menzies include 'detachment and denial of feelings', 'the attempt to eliminate decisions by ritual task-performance' and 'avoidance of change'.[28]

There are three aspects of the construction of a social defence system which I would highlight for current purposes. Firstly, projection is a central mechanism of defence which contributes to distortions in both the construction of political and social reality, and in communication. Menzies makes this point in the following manner:

The nurse projects infantile phantasy situations into current work situations and experiences the objective situations as a mixture of objective reality and phantasy. She then re-experiences painfully and vividly in relation to current objective reality many of the feelings appropriate to the phantasies.[29]

Secondly, the various defence mechanisms contribute to the formation of the social defence system. This includes what I would describe as cultural or ideological encoding. That is, systems of signification, which are both cognitive and affective in character, incorporate or encode the paranoid-schizoid and depressive positions, along with their characteristic defences and affects. This produces intersubjective significatory systems which have encoded within them discrete, and primitive, modes of constructing and evaluating reality.

Thirdly, these significatory systems, once established, operate (to put this in terms of the theory of ideology outlined above) by subjecting individuals (and groups of individuals) to cathected positions within them. As Menzies puts it:

(S)tudent nurses, by becoming members of the nursing service, are required to incorporate and use primitive psychic defenses, at least in those areas of their life-space which directly concern their work ... Unrealistic or pathological anxiety cannot be differentiated from realistic anxiety arising from real dangers.[30]

These studies by Jaques and Menzies involve the application of

[27] Ibid., p. 289.   [28] Ibid., passim.   [29] Ibid., p. 286.   [30] Ibid., pp. 306–7.

psychoanalytic theory, and more specifically Kleinian theory, to social institutions and their cultures; and they highlight certain aspects of such a usage of psychoanalytic theory which is well suited to the interpretation of ideologies. These may be stated as follows:

1 Individual human beings bring species-specific psychological characteristics to all subject-object exchanges (the individual as interlocutor rather than as interpellee). These include a capacity for both 'rationality' and rationalisation; a capacity for sophisticated mental operations and reality testing which is, however, always subject to regressive deformations.

2 Systems of signification encode cognitive-affective positions for the construction and evaluation of social reality. These are integral to (or secreted by), though analytically distinct from, their cognate institutional forms.

3 As they enter an institution individuals fall subject to the cognitive-affective position(s) which the institution's ideology encodes.

4 Crisis and its attendant anxiety, whether induced by imminent or actual change or by a stressful and anxiety-ridden prevailing reality, will tend to generate regressive transformations within a system of signification. Crucially, these regressive transformations do not occur solely at the level of the individual. Rather, contrary to the usual assumption, these more primitive cognitive-affective forms are themselves institutionalised. As structures of feeling they have an ideological and cultural provenance and operate to organise both subjectivity and interaction.

The chief limitation of these studies for the analysis of institutional cultures, and of ideologies more generally, is their reliance on the consultant's interpretations of group process as the principal source of data and as the principal method for distinguishing paranoid-schizoid from depressive constructions and feelings. The following attempts to overcome this limitation.

THE PSYCHODYNAMIC POSITIONS

Building upon Kleinian theory, three psychodynamic positions within an ideological formation can now be distinguished:

1 the dehumanising position
2 the persecutory position
3 the ambivalent position

The dehumanising position is marked by the presence of the paranoid-schizoid position in its most primitive form. The political order is split into an idealised all-good group and a persecutory and hated all-bad group (or groups). Persons are seen solely as members of such groups; that is they are constituted and exhausted by such membership. Moreover persons are constructed as less than fully human: as animal-like or thing-like in the case of the all-bad group, as beyond human complexity in the case of the all-good group. In this regard they are the exact equivalent, at the ideological level, of the part-objects which predominate in the paranoid-schizoid position. As such they are experienced either as persecutory, and thus they become the object of sadistic aggression, or as sublime, and thus beyond criticism for so long as they do not frustrate the wishes of the subject. There is a fusion between the subject and the ideal objects and a thoroughgoing exclusion of the bad objects. The other is, in effect, a screen upon which the subject projects his or her phantasies. Thus interaction is construed as a conflict between good and evil. The actual, specific qualities of the other, and of the subject, are obliterated under the full sway of the pleasure principle. Authority is entirely instrumental (and thus is indistinguishable from coercive power) and is achieved by the venting of aggression upon the hated and inhuman persecutors. The object of authority is the destruction of the persecutors, symbolically and actually.

Consider the following three examples drawn from the Unionist ideological formation, each of which illustrates aspects of the dehumanising position. In passing I note that students of intergroup conflict are depressingly familiar with this kind of material.

A: John Hume the 'rebel' saint from the Bogside, told a mass rally of his brother rioters in Londonderry, that some of his constituents who have been interned are to go on a hunger strike.

This is the best news we have had for a long time ... just think over 300 'rebel' animal funerals ... O'Kane the undertaker must be rubbing his hands, and thinking it's an ill wind that does not do some good. We Loyalists wish them a long and steady fast ... and we only hope that they won't give up so don't disappoint us ... you 'rebel' scum. (*Loyalist News*, August 1971)

In example A the political order is composed of 'Loyalists' on the one hand and a brotherhood of rioters and rebels on the other. Catholics or Nationalists who have been interned (i.e. imprisoned without trial proceedings) are imaged as 'rebel animals' or as 'rebel scum'. Throughout, the passage conveys a pervasive sense of sadistic and unremitting hatred ('a long and steady fast'). It contains a clear and undisguised wish for the death of the internees. Indeed this prospect is the source of the exuberance which informs the passage. At no point is there any ambivalence regarding the internees' situation. Rather they are solely imaged as animals or scum and in both instances a direct connection is made with their preferred-dead status. Nor is the hatred of this passage confined to the internees. The references to the funerals (which connote at least the involvement and grief of extended families and in such a case as death by hunger-strike would involve, more or less, the whole Nationalist community) and to the stock figure O'Kane the undertaker make it clear that the object of their sadism is the Catholic/Nationalist community as a whole. In all these respects the dehumanising position is marked by a primitive form of the paranoid-schizoid position.

B: *Sewer Rats*
The workers in a factory in Flax Street are complaining of a vile stench which is coming from adjacent man-holes leading into the sewers. In addition to the offensive effuvia [sic] hordes of blue-bottles are also in evidence. The theory that the horrible odour is caused by defunct sewer rats is quite tenable, the same rats being of the two legged variety. It seems most reprehensible that the IRA vermin should dispose of their deceased brethren in the public sewers, thereby endangering the health of human beings. The Belfast Corporation bin-lorries could easily be hi-jacked and the carrion removed to the nearest tip head sans ceremony or remark.
(*Loyalist News*, December 1972)

This extract is patently dehumanising. It realises this effect in two related ways. First, it places the signifier 'IRA' within a significatory chain which includes 'blue-bottles', 'sewer rats', 'vermin', 'carrion' and, by implication, rubbish. Secondly it explicitly contrasts all the above with 'human beings'. The passage is animated by the sadistic pleasure which it takes in this symbolic disposal ('dispose') of the 'IRA'.

C: Ulster people are the earth's salt ... the northern counties of Ireland and their people are very, very special indeed. The Ulster Protestant is a strong, robust character, with a fierce loyalty to his friends ... His thoughts run only in 'straight lines'. He has a guileless innocence ... with a built-in honesty ... The Ulster Protestant has no time for double dealing, shady dealing, hypocrisy and weakness. He despises traitors, political puppets, ecumenical jellyfish, opportunists, liars, crooks, apologists and snivellers ...
(*Protestant Telegraph*, 16 January 1971)

Again the example is quite transparent. The political order is split between an idealised and 'guileless' Ulster Protestant whose 'thoughts run only in "straight lines"' and a despised ('despises') significatory chain of 'traitors, political puppets, ecumenical jelly fish', etc.

The persecutory position, which is the most common and least understood position within the Unionist ideological formation, is also marked by the presence of the paranoid-schizoid position, transposed to the construction of the political and social order. It too involves a world of part-objects, though these do not take such a thoroughly primitive form as in the dehumanising position.

Kleinian theory contains two related, but distinct, notions of part-objects. As Segal has put this: 'the object is a part-object, both in the sense of being not a person but an anatomical part, and in the sense of being split into ideal and persecutory objects'.[31] Whilst part-objects in both of these senses are central to the paranoid-schizoid position, they undergo some transformation as they enter the realm of ideological discourse.

Regarding part-objects in the first sense, neither of the ideological positions currently under discussion contains images which explicitly signify anatomical parts or products, e.g. breasts or faeces. In this respect, as a rule, signification within ideological discourse varies from the type of signification which often characterises psychoanalytic sessions. The major difference between the dehumanising and persecutory positions concerns the manner in which this signification of human beings as less than fully human is achieved.

In the dehumanising position the metonymic process characteristic of the paranoid-schizoid position (wherein the person is represented by the part) is replaced by a metaphoric process. For instance in the 'Sewer Rats' example discussed above, an internal persecutory object (perhaps an internalised bad breast or faeces) joins with the phantasied persecutory elements of the political order and together these find signification through the images of 'sewer rats' etc. Hence in the dehumanising position we expect to find, as a rule, dehumanising metaphors substituting for the dehumanising metonymies of the paranoid-schizoid position.

Of course, as indicated above, the dehumanising position is also marked by the splitting processes which Segal refers to in her second

---

[31] Segal, *Introduction to the Work of Melanie Klein*, pp. 123–4.

sense of part-objects. With one important exception, it shares this
with the persecutory position. This latter ideological position also
splits the political and social order into good and evil and sees
interaction as the conflict of these two forces and authority as the
suppression of evil by all means including force. However the
persecutory position, *vis-à-vis* the dehumanising position, is not so
rigidly trapped by the need to split and keep entirely separate the
good and bad aspects of the political and social order. Although only
a mild modification, in the persecutory position there is a capacity to
split the object of anxiety (the Nationalist or Roman Catholic
community or the UK government, for instance) so as to preserve a
positive image of the reference group. Thus there is a capacity to see
some members of the government as good, some Catholics as well
intentioned. However these constructions of the threatening reference group are, unlike their negative counterpart, curiously devoid
of content. The 'good' Roman Catholic or Westminster politicians
never enter the construction of the social order other than as
exceptions. Indeed we might say that they function as the exceptions
which prove the rule of the pleasure principle. For they never act in
this construction of reality. They lack differentiation and they lack
integration. Lacking differentiation, they are seen as having no
particular attributes beyond being 'good' or non-threatening.
Lacking integration, they have no role in the processes of political
and social action.

These two features suggest the particular manner in which the
persecutory position is marked by the presence of part-objects in
Segal's first sense. In contrast with the dehumanising position, in the
persecutory position persons are not explicitly dehumanised. They
are signified as less than fully human, not by the use of appropriate
metaphors, but by being construed in an iconic or emblematic form
as mere ciphers of the split world of good and bad objects. They lack
any individuality or integration into sequences of social and political
action. Thus, in part, the presence of the persecutory position, and
especially its differentiation from the dehumanising position, is
noticeable by the absence of complexity in the construction of
persons. Consider the following from an interview with 'Elizabeth',
an active member of a local Unionist party:[32]

32   Drawn from an interview conducted by the author in 1981. The italicised sections are
     questions addressed to the interview subject by the author. This convention is followed,
     below, in the interview with 'James'.

D: *What would you say lies at the basis of the conflict in Northern Ireland? Fundamentally what is it all about?*
Well in my opinion the Church of Rome is behind it and their greed for power – that's what I would have thought started it all. Though they would say they weren't backing the IRA, I think that you would find if you study it that they do back the IRA in Northern Ireland, very much and they won't condemn them. Well, I'm going back through studying the Bible. Above all else it's a greed for power. I think if you follow all throughout the world where there's troubles, you'll always find a Roman Catholic priest coming up somewhere. He's always in the background, but I think it's just the greed for power.
Is it then fundamentally a religious conflict?
Yes it is.
What is that conflict about?
Well I believe the Church of Rome are just greedy for power. That's how I see it, they just want the power no matter where they are. Where I grew up we were the only Protestant family in the area when I was young. It was all Catholics around us and we were very friendly with our Catholic neighbours. At the same time I wouldn't go back and live in the same area now.
Do you have any fears or concerns regarding the future of the Unionist community in Northern Ireland?
Not particularly, no; but then that would be a religious belief. The Lord has always kept this country in Ireland. I don't think this country would ever go into the South of Ireland. I believe Ian Paisley has been raised in this day to lead the country as a leader. God always provides His man for the day.

In this extract the conflict in Northern Ireland is regarded solely as the result of the machinations of 'the Church of Rome'. This is understood as one part of a world-wide conspiracy: 'all throughout the world where there are troubles, you'll always find a Roman Catholic priest coming up somewhere'. The motivating force of these priestly machinations is 'greed for power'.

Catholics are constructed in an iconic form. Initially the interviewee speaks only of the Church of Rome and the IRA in Northern Ireland, but when discussing the friendly Catholic neighbours of childhood she slips, without any qualification, into extending the significatory chain to include these same former Catholic neighbours. When questioned directly concerning her fears or concerns regarding the future, she states that she has none and goes on to express an unqualified faith in the God-given, manifest destiny of the Protestants in Ireland. Ian Paisley is seen as the agent of this destiny.

This extract is structured by the persecutory position in the following ways. First, there is a splitting of the political and social order into an all good and an all bad group. Interaction is constructed as the conflict of these opposed forces and authority as the supremacy, by force if necessary, of one over the other. Persons are not dehumanised through the use of denigrating metaphors. Rather, as already suggested, they are constructed in an iconic form. Catholics have no characteristics (and no internal diversity) apart from those uniform characteristics which they acquire through their association with the forces of evil. That the Catholic families with which she associated in childhood were friendly is recognised and acknowledged. But this remains an unassimilated perception as it neither enters nor modifies the structural characteristics of the persecutory position. Ian Paisley also is constructed in an iconic form as the mere emblem and cipher of the manifest destiny of the forces of good.

The passage is also remarkable for its absences. Being motivated by the greed for power of the Church of Rome, the conflict is understood as having no social or political basis in Northern Ireland. It is visited upon the society by some deus ex machina, so to speak. Further, as already hinted, political actors lack any motivation; they are merely the passive agents of the persecutory or idealised phantasy objects. Clearly for this ideological position there is no possibility of negotiation or compromise, as the negative reference group lacks any attributes which would allow or encourage such activities.

The affective content of this example is organised and structured according to the rules of construction of the persecutory position. The animating affects are (in the first two long paragraphs) persecutory anxiety and (in the final paragraph) omnipotent confidence. The sole attributed affect throughout the passage is greed. The only admitted affect is, again, confidence of an omnipotent kind.

In the first paragraph a feeling of suspicion is registered. (For the moment the character of this affect is being stated in a minimal manner.) The 'Church of Rome', despite its denials, is intimately linked with the IRA and is 'behind' the conflict in Northern Ireland. The only evidence advanced in support of this contention is the claim that 'they won't condemn them'. Presumably reference is here being made to the Roman Catholic hierarchy in Ireland and their failure to excommunicate and otherwise deny any sympathy or concern for the members of the various Republican paramilitary organisations. Clearly these and other characteristics of the Catholic Church in Ireland may well provide a basis in reality for a feeling of suspicion. (No doubt there are other, perhaps more appropriate, responses to these characteristics of the Catholic Church, but that is another matter.) It is the particular form this affect takes which extends it beyond appropriate suspicion and into persecutory anxiety.

There are some significant oversights, or absences, in the statement. Implicitly it discounts the various counter-claims regarding a supposed 'backing' of the IRA by the Catholic Church which, from time to time, have been made by the Catholic clergy. There is no indication here, or throughout the interview, that these claims have been considered and rejected. Rather they have been discounted ab initio, on account of their source. Indeed they are turned into an indicator of the devious character of the 'enemy'. Similarly the statement ignores any diversity of opinion within the Catholic Church and any independence of attitude within all or part of the laity. All of these are constructed as one unitary persecutor (see the second long paragraph for the reference to the Catholic laity). It also ignores the vast ideological and institutional distance between the Catholic Church in Ireland and the various Republican paramilitary organisations.

It is important to note that the quite slight evidence which serves as a basis for this feeling of suspicion, as well as being privileged above any other evidence, is linked to world history in toto. At this point the Bible becomes the source of revealed historical truth ('Well I'm going back through studying the Bible,' etc.).

It is not any one of these aspects in isolation but rather their structural integration which turns what may first appear as justified suspicion into a full-blown persecutory anxiety. This can be seen in the combination of the unalloyed character of the suspicion with the global and undifferentiated character of its reference.

The third long paragraph is animated by a feeling of confidence. As already suggested, this confidence has an omnipotent quality:

Not particularly, no; but then that would be a religious belief. The Lord has always kept this country in Ireland. I don't think this country would ever go into the South of Ireland. I believe Ian Paisley has been raised in this day to lead the country as a leader. God always provides His man for the day.

This omnipotent quality is a characteristic of the paranoid-schizoid position and may be found in both the dehumanising and persecutory positions of ideology. In this extract it functions as a defence against persecutory anxiety. That is, it constitutes an omnipotent denial of the power of the Church of Rome, etc. despite its supposed, otherwise diabolical, character and the attributed prior universal success of its world-wide machinations. Clearly there is no logical consistency between this statement and those made earlier. There is, however, the psychological consistency of the persecutory position. Finally, the attributed affect of greed is common to the paranoid-schizoid position and its ideological derivatives. In this account it is projected into the reference group object, only to return and persecute the subject.

The ambivalent position of ideology is marked by the presence of the depressive position. It constructs a world of whole objects in both of the senses considered above. Firstly, there is no dehumanisation of other human beings in either of the ways which characterise, respectively, the dehumanising and persecutory positions. Secondly, objects, whether they be individuals, groups or the total political and social formation, are construed as complex and multifaceted. It is from this that the ambivalence arises. Rather than being split and projected in ways characteristic of the dehumanising and persecutory positions, the reference objects are seen as whole objects which retain both their positive and their negative aspects. Thus the capacity for reality testing, *vis-à-vis* the prior positions, is greatly enhanced.

The principal affects of the ambivalent position are feelings of dependence on the object, of anxiety regarding loss of the object (or 'loss-anxiety' as I will sometimes abbreviate it), and feelings of guilt and of responsibility regarding the object. The principal defences are reparation and ambivalence itself. However, modified and qualified versions of the defences of splitting and projection may also play a part in the defensive processes of this position. Consider the following statement made by 'James':[33]

E: I would like to see restored the old ideals of what you might call decent traditional Unionism. But Paisley's brand of Unionism is this fiery politics, he appeals to the gut instincts of the, well in many cases, some of the least desirable members of the community and that's why it's so easy for him to stir up hatred and fear. He plays on the fears, but in many ways I fear that traditional Unionism, vaguely decent Unionism, is going under.

[33]   Drawn from an interview conducted by the author in 1981.

What are the characteristics of traditional Unionism?
Well the characteristics of traditional Unionism are, the one thing that is most important to Unionists, I suppose, is the Throne, the Queen and the link with Britain. The problem nowadays is that while that respect is still there and while that desire and that longing is still there, there has arisen a lack of respect for governments, for parliament and, again, this is especially a DUP (Democratic Unionist Party) inspired thing ... I would see the difference between my idea of Unionism and Paisley's idea of Unionism as this. Paisley wants a Protestant parliament for a Protestant people, and his ideas are all based on his hatred of Roman Catholicism. With me, and I hope, I like to think about the Official Unionist Party, it's not the same. We don't base things on religion, or not so much anyway. I don't, and I would hope the rest of the party didn't either. And that's the difference. The people who support Paisley would talk about Prods and Micks. I would talk about ordinary decent people and terrorists. And I think that's the difference.

In this passage (as in the interview more generally) the political order is construed as a complex and multifaceted reality; i.e. as a whole object in the psychoanalytic sense. Hence the categories Protestant and Roman Catholic do not operate to split the world into good and bad. Rather they are descriptive categories which carry no necessary evaluative connotations of a good/bad, pleasing/frustrating kind.

In the discussion of Paisley's debilitating effect upon the character of Unionism, feelings of dependence and of loss-anxiety are quite apparent. Two 'objects' are referenced here. First, the Britain–Ulster relationship, 'the link with Britain'. This is highly valued, as is evident from the use of such terms as 'respect', 'desire' and 'longing'. There is a feeling of dependence upon the object and of anxiety that it may be lost. Secondly, Unionism itself is referenced. There is profound anxiety lest this object (which is both an internalised and a cathected object for 'James') should be sullied and destroyed. It should be noticed that in both of these instances the anxieties are not persecutory but rather relate to the loss of a valued object.

Integrated with the above affects are feelings of guilt and responsibility. (Notice that all of these affects are quite unknown to 'Elizabeth' within the ideological context.) 'James' recognises the negative aspects of Unionism and is also able to recognise that Unionism must take some responsibility for the prevailing situation in Northern Ireland. (Again, contrast 'Elizabeth'.) The hesitations etc. regarding his own Official Unionist Party are one indicator of these feelings of guilt and responsibility for the character of Unionism. Clearly he feels that insofar as the Official Unionist Party is like the Democratic Unionist Party in this regard, it is guilty of degrading Unionism and of threatening the link with Britain. Also of significance is the acceptance of the DUP as a part of Unionism; a bad part but nevertheless an acknowledged part. In 'James'' construction of the political order Unionism is a whole object which has positive and negative aspects.

Finally, we should notice that there are clear elements of splitting and projection in this example. Unionism is split more or less into good and bad and the DUP comes to contain most of the negative elements. The crucial aspects of this to notice are the following. The processes of splitting and projection are not dominant to the exclusion of the other defensive processes. Neither are the split objects dehumanised in either of the ways we have seen in the cases of the dehumanising and persecutory positions. Rather these defences and attendant affects play a partial role within the much more complex system of constructions, defences and affects which constitute the ambivalent position of ideology. Consequently they do not take the same form as in the prior positions. Rather their form is governed by the other operations of the ambivalent position.

CONCLUSION

This chapter has suggested that Unionist ideology is typically organised according to one of three psychodynamic positions and that these are best understood as positions of subjectivity which carry significant implications for the political process in Northern Ireland.[34] Political conflict in Northern Ireland is as much concerned with which of these three positions will prevail as it is with any stark conflict between Unionism on the one hand and Republicanism or Nationalism on the other. Furthermore these different aspects of the conflict are interactive and, as such, the character of the intercommunal conflict is itself affected by the outcome of the conflict within

[34]   See Frank Wright's fine study of Unionism for some broadly similar distinctions between 'extreme' and 'liberal' forms of Unionist ideology. Where Wright remains descriptive throughout (apart from a footnote which defines extreme Unionism in terms of its 'monolithic' construction of Catholics) this study has attempted to develop a theory of ideology which can capture an ideology's affective components in a systematic manner. See F. Wright, 'Protestant Ideology and Politics in Ulster', *European Journal of Sociology*, vol. 14 (1973). The footnote is on p. 216.

Unionism as to which form of subjectivity is dominant. The shift from 'O'Neillism' to 'Paisleyism', to speak in a very metaphoric manner for the moment, is surely indicative of this. O'Neillism attempted to reorganise intercommunal and intracommunal relations in Northern Ireland in line with what I have characterised as the ambivalent position. Whilst always a fragile project, the 'new deal' promised by O'Neillism did have some significant effects. For instance, it is telling that Eddie McAteer and John Cole should have commented as follows at the time of the 1965 election campaign in Northern Ireland:

The most welcome new feature of the election is that 'some of the hate seems to have been drained out' said the Nationalist leader of the Opposition, Mr. Eddie McAteer, speaking at a press conference to launch the Nationalist party manifesto. But he urged the PM (O'Neill) to show more vigour in pursuing the initiative of the talks with Mr. Lemass (PM of the Republic) in January.

Never has Ulster had an election where the Orange and Green issue has been less evident, says Belfastman John Cole writing in the *Guardian*. Under the heading 'Farewell to 1690' he says of the present campaign: 'It seems a different age from that of the first election I reported in 1949. The change is primarily a change of generations. Mr O'Neill has made a break with the simple frontier politics of his predecessor (as Prime Minister of Northern Ireland) Lord Brookeborough'. (*Belfast Telegraph*, 19 November 1965 (both statements))

Strikingly, neither of these comments reveals any premonition of the civil conflict which was to ensue in Northern Ireland. Rather, they both register a profound change in the Unionist ideological formation and they both rely on assumptions regarding the transformative effects of modernisation to explain this change. This is quite explicit in John Cole's emphasis on 'a change of generations'. Likewise both are agreed that structures of feeling have been considerably altered; that 'some of the hate' or, in Cole's euphemism, 'the simple frontier politics' has been dissipated.

Interestingly, the vast literature written on Northern Ireland since the time of this election either fails to notice this change in 1965 or feels obliged to drastically discount it. Yet, as we will see in subsequent chapters, my own research on this election campaign, which draws upon reports of election speeches etc. in the regional and local newspapers, indicates that this campaign was structured, principally, by the rules of the ambivalent position. By 1969, however, the more familiar rules of the dehumanising and persecutory positions were again calling the tune, though contested every step of the way. This intra-Unionist ideological conflict was institutionalised in the battle between the pro-O'Neill faction of the Ulster Unionist Party, on the one hand, and the various anti-O'Neill Unionist groupings, on the other hand. It was played out in the bitter election campaign of 1969 and has continued to organise the politics of Northern Ireland ever since. Any constructive analysis of the politics of Northern Ireland must engage this reality by taking ideology, including its affective components, seriously; thereby moving beyond the repression of affects which has so seriously disfigured the academic study of ideology and politics.

CHAPTER 5

Ideology and reasoning

I am convinced that normative structures do not simply follow the path of development of reproductive processes and do not simply respond to the pattern of system problems, but that they have instead an *internal history*.

(Jurgen Habermas, 'The Development of Normative Structures', emphasis in original)

In this chapter I will draw upon a second psychological theory, cognitive-developmental theory, in order to delineate a specific set of rules for the structuration of political subjectivities and social and political relations in Northern Ireland. Habermas argues that the rules, or rationality structures, which have been specified for ego identities, ego development and, in particular, moral judgements and actions, can also be observed, through a reconstructive exercise, in the structuration of the three domains of group identities, world views, and legal and moral systems. Habermas has suggested, furthermore, that cognitive-developmental theory may be utilised to analyse the specific rationality structures which organise these three cultural domains and to explore their 'internal history'.[1] It is my intention to develop this general position by specifying a cognitive-developmental method for the analysis of Unionist ideology. This method will be used to specify the rationality structures which organise this ideological field; i.e. it will be used to specify the cognitive unconscious of Unionist ideology. In order to do so, I will begin by reviewing the work of Lawrence Kohlberg and his associates on moral reasoning. To facilitate a ready distinction from the affective-cognitive *positions* which I specified in chapter 4, I have

---

[1]   J. Habermas, *Communication and the Evolution of Society*, translated by T. McCarthy (Boston: Beacon Press, 1979), passim. The discussion of the 'internal history' of normative structures is on p. 116.

chosen to term these cognitive-developmental rationality structures so many *modes* of Unionist ideology.[2]

SPECIFYING SOME RULES OF THE COGNITIVE UNCONSCIOUS

Building upon the work of Piaget, Kohlberg developed a method for the analysis of moral reasoning which delineates six major stages. These stages are not distinguished on the basis of an analysis of their thematic content *per se*. Rather they are distinguished on the basis of variation in the psychological rules according to which they construct the moral domain. One consequence is that the presence of similar thematic content in two statements does not necessarily imply that they share the same stage characteristics. This similar thematic content may be structured in quite distinct ways and thus carry quite different meanings and implications.

One of the moral dilemmas which Kohlberg used to elicit moral reasoning is the hypothetical Heinz dilemma in which a man (Heinz) has to choose between stealing a drug to save his wife's life or allowing her to die. Research has indicated that this type of moral dilemma occasions a variety of response-types at each of the stages. These have been classified as the life norm, the property norm, the affiliation norm etc. In other words these amount to classifications according to type of content. By looking in closer detail at some examples which have been classified under the same affiliation norm, we can underline the way in which structural variation may transform the meanings and implications of statements despite their similar content. Consider the following statements:

(Heinz should steal the drug)
A: If you had a wife who had cancer and you only had half of the money, and you had to break into a store for a good reason, if your wife is dying you'd do it.[3]
B: I believe he should have. It is wrong by principles, but to save his wife, I

2   See L. Kohlberg, *Essays on Moral Development, Volume Two: The Psychology of Moral Development* (San Francisco: Harper and Row, 1984), esp. ch. 3. Shawn Rosenberg is one political scientist who has explored the political reasoning of individual subjects by drawing critically upon Kohlberg's cognitive-developmental theory. See S. Rosenberg, *Reason, Ideology and Politics* (Cambridge: Polity, 1988).

3   A. Colby J. Gibbs, L. Kohlberg, B. Speicher-Dubin and D. Candee, *Standard Form Scoring Manual, Part Three, Form A* (Cambridge, MA: Centre for Moral Education, Harvard University, 1979), p. 14.

think he should have. *Someone so close to him means so much more than breaking into the store.*[4]

C: (Should he steal the drug for a friend?)

No I don't think so. In that case it's really another family, and it's their concern. *In the first example it was his wife and someone who was very dear to him.*[5]

In these instances the same conclusion is drawn on each occasion: Heinz should steal for his wife. Broadly speaking, the same type of reason is advanced in each case; it is something about the relationship between husband and wife which warrants the conclusion. Yet A (an example of stage two reasoning) is quite distinct from B and C (both examples of stage three reasoning).

In the case of A, according to the *Standard Form Scoring Manual*, 'moral approval is based on a concrete projection of what the self would do, or the self's needs and wants, into Heinz's situation. The fact that the self would do it automatically makes it right or approved.'[6] This stage constructs the moral situation according to a rule of instrumental relativism. If it would satisfy me, or my needs, then it is right. However B and C construct the moral dilemma according to a rule of interpersonal concordance: 'Stealing is justified because it conforms in this case to a norm of affiliation and concern between husband and wife or friends.'[7]

In these instances it is not needs or preference which warrant the action but the character and closeness of the relationship. This relationship is privileged, not on a basis of a duty to preserve life or whatever, but on the basis of its being special in some way. Example C highlights this. Here the duty to steal is extinguished as soon as the relationship ceases to be sufficiently close or special. (Of course not everyone will draw the boundary between special and other relationships along the wife-friend axis.) Now consider the following stage four example:

D: Yes (he should steal the drug). I mean if we were just dating, and all of a sudden I found out that she was – I don't think I would have the actual obligation, even though there might be just as much love (Why not?) I don't know, maybe just because of the laws of marriage (Why does that make it more binding?) It is just the simple contract of marriage. I don't know if I am sounding too – (What is the contract?) Just service and a devotion to each other and just obligation. There is where obligation comes in.[8]

In this example it is not the closeness of the relationship which

---

[4]   Ibid., p. 27 (emphasis in original).   [5]   Ibid., p. 14 (emphasis in original).
[6]   Ibid., p. 14.   [7]   Ibid., p. 26.   [8]   Ibid., p. 64.

warrants the theft. The distinction drawn on the basis of the differing status of girlfriend or wife makes this evident. Rather the justification is in this instance provided by the conventional social norms attached to the marriage relationship. The quality of the personal relationship is set aside and universal social or religious norms of a conventional character construct the moral dilemma. Now consider this stage five example:

E: I don't think it matters whether the person is close to you or even if you know them at all. When you are dealing with human life, that doesn't enter into it. The right to live is a universal thing, to be applied to all people whose lives can be saved, regardless of personal ties.[9]

Here neither individual preference, nor a special relationship, nor a conventional set of expectations attached to a social relationship warrants the theft. Rather this position is supported by a primary and universal valuing of life. Affiliation is here the affiliation between all members of the human species. This stage is structured as follows: 'There is a hierarchy of rights and values. Stealing is justified as serving a universal right to, or value of, life which is prior to laws. This hierarchy is not just one recognised by society or religion, but a judgement of hierarchy rational individuals would make based on logic (i.e., property values presuppose the value of life).'[10]

Crucial to this stage is its post-conventional, reflexive character. Preference, attachment and social norms are evaluated against criteria of individual rights and may be found wanting. This stage adopts an autonomous stance which may involve the advocacy of either change or the flexible interpretation of laws and social norms. The apparent flexibility of stage three is recovered, but now in the form of an assessment conducted in terms of a hierarchy of universal values, rather than in terms of a hierarchy of affective attachments. Indeed we can now see that this apparent flexibility of stage three is merely a chimera. The hierarchy of affective attachments is as binding as any conventional social morality. However it binds in different ways.

Any reliance on Kohlberg's theory of moral reasoning, even an unorthodox reliance, carries with it certain limitations.[11] Despite his

---

9   Ibid., p. 82. The manual provides no examples of the affiliation norm at stage five. This
     example is classified as a life norm.
10   Ibid., p. 80.
11   See Carol Gilligan's critical revaluation of Kohlberg's work for the most powerful
     illustration of this. C. Gilligan, *In a Different Voice* (Cambridge, MA: Harvard University
     Press, 1982).

many protestations, Kohlberg's work is clearly impregnated with liberal values. The close parallel between Kohlberg's highest stage and the Rawlsian conception of justice is one example of this. The liberal character of Kohlberg's highest stages does not necessarily mean, however, that the analytic distinction between structure and content cannot be maintained. It may merely suggest that Kohlberg and his associates failed to adequately separate these two aspects. The difficulty of so doing should not be underestimated. Clearly it is impossible to develop a detailed account of structures without specifying some contents. At the higher stages the distinction, in practice, between contents and structure is likely to become imprecise. This reflects the fact that at the higher stages the contents are themselves structured.

Although I am sympathetic to certain features of Habermas' position, a position which draws, though not uncritically, on Hegel and Marx as well as Piaget and Kohlberg, none of what follows presupposes any decision regarding the strong empirical claim regarding a universal sequence of structural forms. One possible position is to recognise that these forms will always tend to be contaminated by the particular elements of the culture from within which they are described, especially in the case of the higher stages. This leaves open any issue of universality. A second position, one which recognises what Giddens has termed the double hermeneutic, occupies an intermediate position between universalism and relativism. Irrespective of the validity of any assumptions regarding the universality of an hierarchically ordered, determinate set of rationality structures, within Western societies these rationality structures have a broad provenance; in this respect they might be described as relatively universal. Consequently, Kohlberg's method for the analysis of moral reasoning may be regarded as well suited to the particular concerns of this research, namely the delineation of the rationality structures which organise an undeniably Western ideological formation. However, my own way of handling this issue is distinct from both of the above. For my purposes I have no need to follow Kohlberg, or Habermas, in the search for the holy grail of a universal ethics, let alone for one which can be hierarchically ordered. Instead, as I argued with regard to Habermas in chapter 2, I prefer to recognise the inevitable historical embeddedness of all ideological forms and to utilise cognitive-developmental theory as one means of specifying the specific, positive characteristics of the particular forms under investigation.[12]

There are some further considerations which highlight the fact that cognitive-developmental theory, as developed by Kohlberg and his associates, requires adaptation for the purposes of this study of a particular ideological formation. First of all, the evidence used in this research was not gathered by the administration of a set of hypothetical dilemmas of little and unknown relevance to the subjects. Rather, for this study of Unionist ideology, evidence was gathered in two ways. First, a group of politically active individuals was interviewed and encouraged to reflect on their understanding of the recent and contemporary situation in Northern Ireland. The interviews were conducted so as to elicit both the reasoning process underlying the subject's construction of the political order and the feelings of the subject towards various aspects of this order. That is to say, the interviewees were asked to state and explain their position regarding a political situation about which they care and which impinges upon them in quite palpable ways.[13]

Secondly, evidence was also gathered from the record of public discourse. The political debate as recorded in newspaper reports of political speeches, in the vigorous pamphlet literature and in books and other publications was sampled in a very thorough and extensive manner. The great virtues of this latter approach are its status as an 'unobtrusive measure' of the ideological formation and its capacity to enable diachronic as well as synchronic observation. Although, from the technical point of view, such methods of gathering evidence may lack a certain reliability, the validity of evidence gathered in this manner is unquestionable as it is drawn directly from the political discourse under investigation. This is especially so in the case of material drawn from the public record. In part 2, where I focus in detail on the public, political discourse of Northern Ireland, I have attempted to provide, following the model of good historical research, sufficient primary evidence to enable the reader to make his or her own assessment of the manner in which I handle empirical evidence.

[12] See chapter 6 for more on this matter.
[13] The group consisted of fifteen members of the Democratic Unionist Party and fifteen members of the Official Unionist Party. The first eight in each group were selected from a list of local (council) government members. Randomising procedures were used to reduce any selection bias as far as possible. The subsequent seven in each group were contacted by referral from those first selected.

THE COGNITIVE UNCONSCIOUS OF UNIONIST IDEOLOGY

With the above discussion of moral reasoning as background I will now set out a characterisation of the structural rules underlying ideological reasoning in Northern Ireland. Four modes of ideological reasoning can be identified: an instrumental-corporate mode, an affiliative-corporate mode, a conventional-liberal mode and a post-conventional-liberal mode. These overlap broadly with Kohlberg's stages two, three, four and five. I leave aside any 'equivalents' to Kohlberg's stages one and six as the first of these is quite rare empirically in ideological reasoning and because of Kohlberg's later concern over whether there is any real structural difference between stages five and six.

Consider the categories Protestant and Roman Catholic. These are basic elements of the Unionist ideological formation, appearing in each of the four modes designated above. However these terms do not carry the same meaning in each of the above modes. For instance, in the conventional-liberal mode these terms simply denote an attribute of persons all of whom are constituted as citizens of a democratic state, the United Kingdom. Consequently these terms may form part of a series of descriptive attributes: e.g. Patrick is a lawyer, a fine horseman and a Roman Catholic. Within the conventional-liberal mode of Unionist ideology it will, of course, be well understood that the characteristic of being a Roman Catholic is, in fact, a significant one which is likely (though not certain) to indicate general political allegiance, patterns of social intercourse etc. However it is not a privileged, defining characteristic in principle.

In the affiliative-corporate mode the person is constituted and exhausted by the ethno-religious category. In this mode the individual human being is first of all a member of a sociopolitical grouping of an ascriptive kind and is evaluated in terms of his or her loyalty or allegiance to group norms. The other elements in the series describing Patrick remain descriptive, but the group characteristic, in this case an ethnoreligious one, now becomes constitutive and exhaustive.

For the postconventional-liberal mode it is neither citizenship nor group membership, but rather the attribute of being a human being, which is constitutive and exhaustive. The shift from the conventional to the postconventional mode involves a change in which the characteristic of being a citizen of a state becomes descriptive where before it had been constitutive. Entitlement has its basis in an immanent universal ethics which attaches to the species characteristics of all human beings. Clearly a tension may exist between the positive law of a particular state and the immanent rights of all human beings. The postconventional mode is a reflective mode which is able to confront such an issue and is thus capable of the creative innovation which may, under ideal circumstances, overcome the established antipathies of a society such as Northern Ireland.

As with the affiliative-corporate mode, for the instrumental-corporate mode the terms Protestant and Roman Catholic are both constitutive and exhaustive of the political order. However for the instrumental mode it is not allegiance to the group which determines right. Instead desire constitutes right. If something is desired then it is justified to do all that is necessary to achieve it. Consequently group membership is not a function of loyalty and allegiance but rather of shared objectives. The terms Protestant and Roman Catholic are constitutive solely in terms of an identity based on interest and desire. The connection between the wish and its assessment as appropriate is immediate and thoroughgoing. There is no need of an intervening construct such as loyalty to secure the connection.

By focusing in more detail on these modes we can fill out some central distinctions and their implications in a more elaborate manner. (In the main the two corporate modes will be discussed together.) Let us begin with the familiar. The conventional-liberal mode locates the subject within a system of subjects in which all are formally equal, which is divided into public and private domains, and in which the state is seen as the neutral arbiter between conflicting interests within the public sphere and the protector of the liberty of the private sphere. The primary, constitutive relationship is that between the individual subject and the state with its system of legal equality; i.e. each individual is first of all an equally entitled subject and is equally subject to a non-ascriptive, universalist system of law. At a second level the individual may be a member of a group, or class, etc. but this in no way modifies the centrality of the state-individual subject relationship.

In both corporate modes the primary, constitutive relationship is that between the group and the state. Hence the individual human being is first of all a group member. His or her individuality is recognised only in a secondary and derived form. Entitlement to

claims upon the state has expression only through group membership. Typically, whereas the conventional-liberal mode would regard
all individuals and the functional categories to which they belong as
equally entitled on the basis of need or other criteria of eligibility of a
universal nature (e.g. a farmer may be entitled to assistance as he
lives in a deprived rural area) the corporate modes would regard one
group and its members as especially entitled *per se*; that is, on an
ascriptive basis. A classic example in this regard is housing policy.
The first Civil Rights march in 1968 took place in protest against
housing allocation by a local authority. The Dungannon council
evicted Catholic/Nationalist families from some new housing in
which they had squatted and allocated one of these houses to an
unmarried Protestant/Unionist woman who happened to be the
secretary of the local Unionist MP. As construed from within the
pluralist modes, such 'favouritism' is quite appropriate, as was the
more general phenomenon which it highlighted; a systematic bias in
favour of Protestants/Unionists within the public housing sector.

The corporate modes evaluate the behaviour, beliefs and aspirations of other groupings in terms of their compatibility with those of
one's own grouping. Authority is granted legitimacy to the extent
that it maintains and furthers the interests of one's own group, whilst
excluding (for the instrumental mode) or controlling (for the affiliative mode) incompatible groups and their interests. Within these
parameters authority is granted undivided and uncritical loyalty.
Should it step outside these parameters it is ridiculed and despised.
Thus from within the corporate modes a good law is one which
serves group ends; and the criterion of its rightness is the extent to
which it does so effectively. The ideal law is a draconian and
discretionary one enforced by the 'right' people. An example of such
a law would be the Special Powers Act which empowered the
minister of home affairs in the Stormont government 'to take all such
steps and issue all such orders as may be necessary for preserving the
peace'.[14]

We should notice some of the advantages and disadvantages of the
corporate modes within a situation of intergroup conflict. On the
one hand, they can successfully integrate a group because they see
members as valued by the very fact of membership and ascribe
entitlement on this basis. Outgroup members are less entitled or are

---

[14] Cited in M. Farrell, *Northern Ireland: The Orange State* (London: Pluto Press, 1980), p. 93.

conditionally entitled for so long as they demonstrate their subservience – or that they know their place. On the other hand, the negative aspect or limit to the corporate modes is that the only 'solutions' they can offer to intergroup conflict are differential incorporation (formal or substantive apartheid), 'repatriation' or partition and, at the extreme, genocide.

These advantages and disadvantages of the corporate modes become apparent if we consider the following sections from a set of interviews with some Unionist councillors in Northern Ireland. At one point 'Robert' responded as follows:

F. And as far as the settlement of the troubles here. If you keep on giving in to a spoiled child eventually that spoiled child tells you what to do. So in actual fact if they stop giving in and give them a real good spanking – I mean if I have my child there and it's doing wrong, I mean if I don't give it a spanking it just goes wild and does what it likes. But when I give it a good spanking I have it under control. What's wrong here is that there's no control. Until we get the Roman Catholic community, as it were, to heel, to realise that we're not out to do them down but they must realise that they must be subject to the law.[15]

In this statement the appropriate order of things is one in which the Roman Catholic community has been brought 'to heel'. The imagery of this statement powerfully underlines this point. The Roman Catholic community is imaged as a 'spoiled child' in need of a 'good spanking' to achieve 'control' and eliminate 'wild' tendencies.

In the statement we notice the following:

First, the political order is construed in ethnoreligious terms as, principally, one in which Roman Catholics are to be kept subordinate and separate from Protestants. That is, the political order is composed of ascriptive groups with impervious boundaries and is organised in an hierarchical form. Secondly, persons are unequivocally designated as, primarily, members of an ethno-religious grouping. Thirdly, authority is construed as a relationship of coercive power through which such an hierarchical ordering of intergroup relations is to be achieved. Any failure to achieve this preferred arrangement is construed as a failing of authority *per se*, and may become the basis for criticism of the government of the day (or the executive or secretary of state). Viewed from this perspective, or in terms of this mode of rationality, we can well understand why the

[15] Drawn from an interview conducted by the author in 1981.

Northern Ireland power-sharing executive, in which Protestants and Catholics shared power as equals, should have proved such an anathema, and why it called forth the kind of civil disruption (the Ulster Workers' Council strike) which led to the toppling of the executive.

The following kind of statement was repeated, usually in strikingly similar terms, by a majority of interviewees. One example will suffice for our current purpose. When questioned about the Ulster Workers' Council strike 'Robert' replied:

G: But the main views of the mainstream of the Protestant people was strongly against this power sharing executive. And when, I know, I took part in it, they asked for this strike and all throughout the area they just voluntarily accepted. I mean it wasn't the thing that there was any opposition from the people. It was really, as it were, what would you say; the people just were with it, as it were, you know. This was the thing to do. And even looking back on it, it was unbelievable the way that people – I know farmers and they threw the milk down the drains, just because they wanted this thing to be a complete ... and because they were completely against it. They were so sickened by the way that boys like Currie and Paddy Devlin and Gerry Fitt jumped from, I mean you take these boys. Gerry Fitt was in Derry whenever there was a riot in Derry. Paddy Devlin was one of the mainstream boys in the gun running. And that was still fresh in the people's minds. Austin Currie was on about a rent and rate strike to bring down the government a short time previously and yet whenever he got into this power sharing executive he told the people this was it, the rent and rate strike was over and for them to start and pay rents. And I think that these were the things that really sickened the people. That from today they were in out and out rebellion and from the next day they were lauded as persons of great esteem and responsibility. People just, as it were, took this onus [animus?!] against them, you know. I think that was one of the main things that really sickened the people. They just couldn't take it, you know.[16]

Returning to statement F, we should not be misled by the rhetorical flourish of the concluding 'subject to the law'. Clearly in this instance the law, itself a pre-eminent form of authority, is seen as the instrument for establishing a set of corporate norms which justify the preferred political order and thus justify the exercise of control necessary to achieve or realise this. The rule of law is construed as rule by an authority which achieves the separation and hierarchical ordering which the corporate mode of ideology requires.

[16]   Drawn from an interview conducted by the author in 1981.

The Loyalist theme within Unionist ideology highlights further characteristics of the corporate modes. Many commentators are puzzled by the following phenomenon. On the one hand, many Unionists will make fierce declarations of loyalty and of profound affection towards the British Crown. The British identity and connection are greatly valued, indeed they are prized, and are regarded as the rightful patrimony of all loyal Ulstermen. On the other hand, the same individuals will display distrust and an unwillingness, which often approaches contemptuous dismissal, to accept the authority of British governments and ministers. And in many cases they will indicate a readiness to use force to oppose governmental authority.

These apparently contradictory stances are exemplified by the 1974 Ulster Workers' Council strike. Following the appointment of a power-sharing executive the Ulster Workers' Council (UWC) organised a province-wide strike. This strike lasted for several days during which the province came to a virtual standstill, and finally achieved its objective of compelling the dissolution of the Northern Ireland power-sharing executive. This executive or 'ministry' was composed of individuals from both the majority and minority communities in Northern Ireland working together as a 'government'. It was the preferred solution of the UK government and parliament to the Ulster crisis, and indeed enjoyed bi-partisan support at Westminster. It lasted for a mere five months, being brought down by the thoroughgoing refusal of a significant section of the Unionist population to accept its authority. Construed from within either the conventional or postconventional-liberal modes of ideology such a 'Loyalist rebellion' indeed appears anomalous. However there is no inconsistency at all when viewed within a corporate mode. In this mode the welfare of the group is primary and the 'rightness' of legal or institutional arrangements is judged according to their capacity to maintain group supremacy. It is the group and its interests to which loyalty is pledged, and this is symbolised by the crown. Any institution or individual that challenges this supremacy – and this includes Her Majesty's government and prime minister – is characterised as disloyal. If the monarch were so foolhardy as to express a critical opinion, no doubt she too would be seen as disloyal.

The difference between the liberal and corporate modes of Unionist ideology is not merely thematic. Indeed there may be, and quite often are, thematic similarities which disguise the radical discontinuity between the modes of ideology. This becomes apparent if we contrast the above characterisation of the corporate modes of loyalism with the following example of the conventional-liberal mode. In another of the interviews, as we have already seen in chapter 4, 'James' spoke of the need to revive 'traditional Unionism'. This extract is used again to demonstrate that both the psychodynamic and the cognitive-developmental methods of analysis can be used on the same material. However, as the full text of this extract is available on pp. 88–9, only the first segment is quoted here.

E: I would like to see restored the old ideals of what you might call decent traditional Unionism. But Paisley's brand of Unionism is this fiery politics, he appeals to the gut instincts of the, well in many cases, some of the least desirable members of the community and that's why it's so easy for him to stir up hatred and fear. He plays on the fears, but in many ways I fear that traditional Unionism, vaguely decent Unionism, is going under.[17]

This statement is of interest on several counts. Firstly 'James' quite poignantly conveys the depth of the emotional attachment which Unionists have to the maintenance of the British connection. He discusses this in terms of feelings of 'desire', 'longing' and 'respect'. The subtext of this suggests the profound role which this connection plays in the formation of both individual and group identity.

Secondly we should note certain limits to James' historical sense which are, no doubt, attributable to his desire to differentiate traditional Unionism, as he construes this, from Paisley Unionism. Ironically the crucial phrase 'a Protestant parliament for a Protestant people' is itself a core element of traditional Unionism.

'James' sketches in a version of history in which an old, traditional Unionism of a liberal character has been vulgarised and debased by 'some of the least desirable members of the community' following the lead given by Ian Paisley in the period from about 1969. In order to sustain this version of history he evades, or denies, at least in this context, the fact that this motto has its source in the declaration, 'All I boast is that we are a Protestant Parliament and a Protestant State' made by Lord Craigavon in 1934 when prime minister of Northern Ireland. This occurred in the context of a public discourse regarding the purported need and obligation of 'Protestants' or 'Loyalists' or 'Orangemen' to employ solely 'good Protestant lads and lassies'

[17] Drawn from an interview conducted by the author in 1981.

rather than 'Roman Catholics 99% of whom are disloyal'.[18] Clearly
'James' is uncomfortable with the notion that Paisley is a natural
inheritor of a major ideological element of traditional Unionism.
The fragility of his 'white-wash' of traditional Unionism has its echo
in his anxiety regarding the true character of his own, contemporary,
Official Unionist Party. This is registered in the hesitations, qualifica-
tions and doubts e.g. 'I would hope the rest of my party ...' which
mark his description of the membership.

'James'' discourse is itself an exemplar of the conventional-liberal
mode of Unionist ideology; what he would refer to as 'decent',
'traditional' Unionism. In this construction of reality persons are
categorised on the basis of individual characteristics and behaviour.
All are seen as equally entitled to the rights and privileges of the state
and equally subject to its obligations and laws, irrespective of their
own system of values and its likeness or dissimilarity to the values of
Unionism. Thus for 'James' the primary distinction is between
'ordinary decent people' and 'terrorists'. In 'James'' conceptual
universe the former are all those who accept the authority of the
state, at least insofar as they limit their opposition to constitutional
forms. Terrorists, on the other hand, are quite plainly those from
either community who through the use of weapons, explosives or
other violent and unconstitutional means challenge the authority of
the state.

'James' explicitly rejects a categorisation of the political order in
terms of Protestant and Roman Catholic, or more precisely 'Prods
and Micks'. As he puts it, 'The people who support Paisley would
talk about Prods and Micks. I would talk about ordinary decent
people and terrorists.' In effect 'James' is objecting to the use of such
terms in a constitutive and exhaustive manner. That is, he is
objecting to the construction of the political order which characterises both corporate modes.

We should also note the limit of the conventional-liberal mode, as
exemplified in this statement. By suggesting that the appropriate
distinction is between the 'decent' and the 'terrorist', 'James' is
offering and accepting the positive law of the United Kingdom as the
criterion of evaluation. This is not unlike Margaret Thatcher's oft-
repeated statement at the time of the hunger strikes in 1981 that 'a

---

[18] These quotations come from political speeches delivered by Sir Basil Brooke and Lord
Craigavon in, respectively, 1933 and 1932. They are quoted in A. C. Hepburn, *The Conflict
of Nationality in Modern Ireland* (London, Edward Arnold, 1980), pp. 164, 165.

law is a law is a law'. Whilst the legal system of the UK may and indeed does have many virtues it is unable to adequately accommodate the reality of Northern Ireland. That is, it is unable to reflect upon and to enquire into the political and social factors which lie behind and animate 'terrorism'. The transformations of this legal system in Northern Ireland, for instance the experiment with detention and the introduction of Diplock courts in which judges rule alone on matters of fact and in which requirements of evidence have been modified, are clear examples of this. The conventional-liberal mode cannot address such issues, hence while it is not the source of the Northern Ireland 'problem' neither is it capable of providing the 'solution'.

Thus, in the conventional liberal mode the political order is composed, first of all, of individuals bound together through their relationship to the authority of the state and its attendant constitutional and legal system. These individuals also may be members of particular religious groupings, ethnic groupings or whatever. However, no imputation or conclusions regarding either their character, or their entitlement to the protections and privileges of the state, may be drawn from such membership. In this mode distinctions and categorisations are made in a contingent manner, depending upon the actual characteristics and behaviour of these individuals. Thus no-one is born a terrorist, inclusion in this category is contingent upon behaviour. Persons are construed as individuals with multifaceted aspects. They are seen as individuals and are not reduced to either a microcosm or expression of a group characteristic, nor are they dehumanised in a more thoroughgoing manner.

PART 2

The analysis of an ideology in crisis

CHAPTER 6

Towards a depth hermeneutics
of Unionist ideology

'Who are the loyalists of Ulster? To many outsiders they are the
'voice of unreason, the voice of illogicality'. They are loyal to
Britain, yet ready to disobey her; they reject clerical tyranny,
yet oppose secularism; they proclaim an ideology of freedom
and equality, except for Catholics; they revere law and
authority, then break the law. And they refuse to do the
rational, obvious thing.'   (Sarah Nelson, *Ulster's Uncertain Defenders*)

What is Unionism? What are the central themes, beliefs and values
which characterise this particular ideological formation? As I will
demonstrate in this second part of my study, there is no simple answer
to such apparently innocent questions. Indeed, such questions are not
sufficient for an adequate account of Unionist ideology. Unionism is
not monolithic and is not univocal. Rather it is a vital, dynamic and
diverse field of signification, communication and subjection. Hence
no considered summary, however apparently basic, can capture its
specificity, its complexity and its variety.[1] There is no essence to be
discerned. Likewise no moment of observation is sufficiently privileged
to afford a 'freezing' of its contents. Unionism is a dynamic set of
constructions, evaluations and beliefs regarding political experience
in Northern Ireland. It is constantly being reconstituted, gaining new
inflections and losing old concerns in response to prevailing political
exigencies. In these respects Unionism is like all other ideologies.

It is my argument that, along with these dynamic and contingent
aspects of Unionist ideology it is possible to discern a limited set of
unconscious rules which are characteristically drawn upon for the
production and organisation of subjectivity and intersubjectivity.
These rules carry no necessary implications as to the specific content

---

[1]   For a magisterial historical account which is consistent with this claim, see A. T. Q.
Stewart, *The Narrow Ground: Aspects of Ulster, 1609–1969* (London: Faber & Faber, 1977).

of Unionist ideology, and there is nothing inevitable about their reproduction.[2] The extent to which any particular set of rules is re-produced through the structuration process, and the domain over which any set of rules has predominance, is always contingent upon the communicative actions of subjects and the intended and unin-tended consequences which follow from such actions. Subjects always act with an already organised subjectivity, at least for that moment, and with a set of cognitive understandings and emotional investments concerning the horizon or context within which they are acting. At the same time, in so acting subjects inevitably draw upon some set of rules of structuration which are more or less deeply embedded in social institutions and social structure.[3] Through drawing upon specific rules of structuration subjects may re-produce, modify or, very occasionally, transform these rules and/or the range and depth of their embeddedness.

Northern Ireland is a fascinating case study, in part, because it so clearly exemplifies these processes of structuration through which apparently primordial identities and patterns of relationship have been consistently re-produced. As I argued in chapter 1, the plur-alism paradigm is consonant, in the main, with the ways in which social reality presents itself in Northern Ireland. Its related limita-tions are two-fold. First, it tends to discount those ideological forms and social or political movements which are not plural or corporate in form; in so doing it misconstrues the dynamic complexity of the ideological and political field under investigation. Second, pluralism theory has no way of looking behind its observations regarding the institutionalisation of corporate difference and asking questions about the recursive processes of structuration through which this history is made and remade. Therefore, while it can observe the reproduction of difference it cannot adequately account for this. In particular it cannot analyse ideological and political conflict ade-

---

[2] I use this hyphenated form of writing 're-production' so as to emphasise a major theoretical point about the ways in which the making of history from one moment to the next is always a contingent process in which outcomes are not inevitable, even in those circumstances in which they may be predictable to a very high degree of accuracy. This is a primary claim of structuration theory, as developed by Giddens, Bourdieu and others.

[3] I follow Thompson's definition of social structure as 'the relatively stable asymmetries and differentials which characterise social institutions and fields of interaction'. Further I agree with his claim that to analyse social structure 'involves the attempt to ascertain the criteria, categories and principles which underlie these differences and account for their systematic and durable character'. See J. Thompson, *Ideology and Modern Culture* (Cambridge: Polity Press, 1990), chapter 6. The quotes are from pp. 282, 283.

quately as it reads all ideological and political processes through its plural or corporate lens. A revised structuration theory such as I have developed in this study, one which specifies a variety of unconscious rules of structuration which are themselves the 'site and stake' of political conflict, is able to open out this very issue of reproduction through understanding it as a recursive, but contingent, process in which no particular outcome is inevitable and within which the rules for organising subjectivity and intersubjectivity are constantly being fought over by political actors and movements. If, in Northern Ireland, the politics of corporate identity and corporate difference are re-produced as the dominant form for the organisation of subjectivity and intersubjectivity, this does not happen automatically. Rather, this process is always contingent and usually conflictual. This will become apparent when we look at a critical moment in the history of Northern Ireland in chapters 7 and 8.

The purpose of this current chapter is to address some preliminary matters prior to taking my attempt to write theory with an empirical intent to the study of an empirical setting: Northern Ireland. Initially I conceived this study of Unionist ideology as one which I would base on the analysis of an extensive set of interviews conducted with members of the two principal Unionist parties in Northern Ireland. However, as my research progressed I realised that such a synchronic analysis could not adequately address what I now take to be the most fascinating question regarding a society such as Northern Ireland, the question of how this society has been *re-produced* as a divided society. Hence the interview material I had gathered took on two new functions; first as a set of field notes through which I was able to acquaint myself with the thoughts and feelings of a group of committed Unionists and, second, as a set of evidence upon which I could draw to develop the characterisations of ideological modes and positions developed in chapters 4 and 5. I had come to realise that, for the study of Unionist ideology over time, I needed evidence drawn directly from the political process and evidence which could be gathered retrospectively and as a time series, so to speak, for the period with which I was concerned. This evidence, in the form of discursive material produced by the principal political actors and movements in Northern Ireland, has been gathered from the public political discourse as recorded in newspapers and in publications by the relevant actors and groupings. It is on the basis of this evidence that I attempt, in chapters 7 and 8, to develop a depth hermeneutics of Unionist ideology during a critical period of its recent history.

DEPTH HERMENEUTICS AND THE SOCIAL-HISTORICAL EMBEDDEDNESS OF IDEOLOGICAL RULES

Hermeneutics may be described, briefly, as a method of analysis which foregrounds the requirement of interpretation and understanding while recognising that all social actors (including social scientists) think and act within a pre-constituted and pre-interpreted domain of symbolic forms. Hermeneutics places this pre-constituted and pre-interpreted domain of symbolic forms in the analytic frame and it approaches this domain through privileging the self-understandings of subjects involved in communication. As John Thompson has argued, such an emphasis on what he terms 'doxa' (no doubt borrowing the term from Bourdieu), by which he means 'the opinions, beliefs and understandings which are held and shared by the individuals who comprise the social world', is an essential, if preliminary, hermeneutic aspect of a depth hermeneutics.[4] However, while such a concern with the hermeneutics of everyday life is critical, it needs to be gone beyond in an attempt to explore the embedded rules of structuration, which order everyday life. Thompson says of this:

> Symbolic forms are meaningful constructs which are interpreted and understood by the individuals who produce and receive them, but they are *also* meaningful constructs which are structured in definite ways and which are embedded in specific social and historical conditions. To take account of the ways in which symbolic forms are structured, and of the social-historical conditions in which they are embedded, we must move beyond the interpretation of doxa and engage in kinds of analysis which fall within the methodological framework of depth hermeneutics.[5]

Thompson also claims that the analysis of ideology is one specific domain of inquiry for which a depth hermeneutics is peculiarly appropriate. As he puts it: 'To interpret ideology is to explicate the connection between the meaning mobilised by symbolic forms and the relations of domination which that meaning serves to establish and sustain.'[6]

---

[4]   For a fuller discussion of these issues which is consistent with my own approach see Thompson, *Ideology and Modern Culture*, chapter 6.
[5]   Ibid., p. 280, emphasis in original.
[6]   Ibid., p. 293, emphasis in original.

My own way of approaching this connection between meaning and domination has already been outlined in the preceding chapters. There I have explained how psychoanalytic theory, as the depth hermeneutic method par excellence, can be joined with a revised structuration theory so as to provide a means of 'taking ideology seriously'.[7] As we will see in the following chapters, such a focus upon the unconscious rules of structuration for subjectivity and intersubjectivity may be used to explore the embedded ideological rules of a specific social-historical order, the contingent and conflictual processes through which the relative predominance and dispersal of any one set of rules has been achieved and maintained and, finally, the extent to which, and the spaces within which, any dominant rules of ideology have been contested and, at least potentially, modified or transformed. To describe such a complex set of processes under the term 'relations of domination', as Thompson does, while consistent with the history of the concept of ideology, may be potentially misleading as such a description has an unduly one-dimensional character to it. My own conceptualisation of ideology overcomes this limitation by emphasising that it is critical to talk of communicative rationalities in the plural, to specify the positive and particular features of these various rationalities (or rules) and to specify their characteristic forms and deformations. To take such an approach is to focus upon systematic patterns of distorted communication within and between social and political groupings by revealing the particular, positive bases of such distortions in the particular features of the various rules drawn upon in the organisation of subjectivity and intersubjectivity. Further, it is to approach the re-production of subjectivities, social institutions and social structure as a social and political process which is always contingent and frequently conflictual. Such an approach overcomes the less satisfactory critique of ideology in terms of some such counterfactual as an 'ideal speech situation' for the very reason that it draws our attention to the social-historical embeddedness of the variety of particular rules drawn upon in the structuration process.[8]

---

[7] In part following Habermas, I have also suggested and indicated that an analogous move may be made with cognitive-developmental theory.

[8] For a statement by Habermas on discourse ethics see J. Habermas, *Moral Consciousness and Communicative Action*, translated by C. Lenhardt and S. W. Nicholsen (Cambridge: Polity Press, 1990).

IMAGINED UNIONS

Unionism originated in the nineteenth century, drawing upon the then current ideological formation and reorganising this in response to the political threat of home rule for Ireland. Since then it has been modified and reconstituted in a multiplicity of ways. Indeed not even its immediate nominal denotation – constitutional and territorial union with Great Britain – has remained constant over the past one hundred years. While Unionism initially laid claim to the whole of Ireland, political exigencies necessitated the limiting of this claim to the territory of Northern Ireland. This in turn gave rise to the issue of a six-county or a nine-county Northern Ireland. Should the traditional nine-county Ulster become Northern Ireland or should a newly imagined six-county 'Ulster' be preferred? In the political debate produced by this issue themes of loyalty and betrayal and of the desire for Unionist ascendancy run throughout the discourse.[9] Two vivid examples help make the point. The decision by the Ulster Unionist Council, on 10 March 1920, to opt for a six-county Ulster seemed to involve a breach of the Solemn League and Covenant of 1912 in which 450,000 men and women, including many from the three subsequently excluded counties, pledged 'to stand by one another in defending for ourselves and our children our cherished position of equal citizenship in the United Kingdom and in using all means which may be found necessary to defeat the present conspiracy to set up a home rule parliament in Ireland'.[10] In a leaflet printed and circulated in April 1920 by Lt-Colonel F. H. Crawford the following justification for a six-county Ulster was offered:

Take another illustration. Three men are walking on a pier. None of them can swim. One falls into the sea and is being carried away. The remaining two can either jump in and drown with their friend or they can throw him a rope. Standing on the pier they can make a good effort to save their drowning friend. Jumping in all three will be drowned. For the six counties to jump into an Irish Parliament in Dublin and drown in it with the other three may look heroic, but it would be disastrous to all nine of the counties. If, however, six strong Unionist Protestant counties hold together on the firm pier of a Protestant Ulster Parliament they will be able to help their brother Unionists in the three counties when these need assistance far

[9] See P. Buckland, *Irish Unionism: 1885–1923, A Documentary History* (Belfast: HMSO, 1973), pp. 395–420.
[10] Ibid., p. 224.

better than if all nine were in a hopeless minority in an Irish Parliament, as they undoubtedly would be.[11]

Viewing this re-invented Ulster from the perspective of an excluded party, Lord Farnham found analogies with lifeboats, ropes and piers less convincing:

Our people look upon themselves as betrayed and deserted, and the people of 6 counties looked upon themselves as shamed and dishonoured. It has gone far further and far deeper than you imagine . . . . We only protest and resign from Council. How can we remain members of a body that have plainly told us they don't want us and that we are an incumbrance to them and have, 'you may say what you will, but you can't get away from the fact,' have broken a solemn Covenant, in order to get rid of us.[12]

During this moment of crisis Unionism radically reconstituted itself, opting to 'sacrifice' its least secure 'brothers' for a six-county Northern Ireland with a clear Unionist majority. It is thus clear, that in a relatively short historical period an apparently fundamental aspect of Unionism – the territorial scope to which it laid claim – was modified drastically in the face of political exigency. The desire to maintain Unionist supremacy, at least numerically, eventually led to a preference for the current six-county boundaries of Northern Ireland. The contingencies of the political process produced an ever diminishing claim regarding the geographic scope of the Union and thereby revealed that the requirement for Unionist supremacy was paramount

If the ceding of territory may be understood as political expediency fuelled by a 'siege mentality' in which Unionist supremacy was regarded as the sole guarantee of the preservation of valued ideal and material interests, interests which could only be secured by the link with Britain, in the 1970s a more curious modification occurred within Unionism when advocacy of an 'independent Ulster' and the flying of the Ulster flag (The Red Hand of Ulster) became a striking feature of so-called Loyalist opinion. In this instance, for a time, the revocation of the Union became a central tenet of one major strand of Unionist opinion!

Sarah Nelson captures this curious logic in the opening paragraph of her study of Loyalism, which appears above as the epigraph to this chapter. In this introductory statement Nelson states, both nicely and succinctly, a common observation regarding the dominant Loyalist

[11] Ibid., p. 411.
[12] Ibid., p. 419.

attitude within Ulster Unionist ideology. It is oppositional and, apparently, flagrantly illogical. It makes demands, but never makes concessions. It sees the world entirely from its own point of view and fails to see that others, be they Nationalist, British or third parties, may have other points of view which are themselves legitimate. It is zero-sum in character, believing that a gain for 'them' is inevitably a loss for 'us'. It is an exclusivist construction of the world which is drawn upon in the maintenance and reassertion of the dominant and exclusivist form of Unionist identity. Nelson's study focused upon members of various Loyalist groupings (political, paramilitary, work-place and community groups) and was concerned to describe their worldviews. She defined Loyalism as a term describing not 'those who gave unequivocal loyalty to governments at Stormont and Westminster' but rather those 'Protestants who have opposed conces-sions to the Catholic minority, condemned links between Northern Ireland and the Irish Republic, and resisted Westminster's attempts to enforce political change ... they have all seen loyalty to elected governments as conditional'. In their view, Stormont and Westmin-ster governments have been disloyal to the Protestant ideals they were founded to uphold, and must be re-called to the 'true' principles of their 'glorious past'.[13] In what follows I shall attempt to trace out the conflict within Unionism between Loyalist and more liberal forms of Unionist ideology during a period in which Unionist hegemony in Northern Ireland suffered a series of profound disrup-tions.

[13]   S. Nelson, *Ulster's Uncertain Defenders* (Belfast: Appletree Press, 1984), pp. 9, 10.

CHAPTER 7

Crisis and the structuration of Unionist ideology, *1962–1969*

It has been said over and over again, 'You want to oppress the Catholic minority, you want to get a Protestant ascendancy over there'. We have never asked to govern any Catholic. We are perfectly satisfied that all of them, Protestant and Catholic, should be governed from this Parliament, and we have always said that it was the fact that this Parliament was aloof entirely from these racial distinctions and religious distinctions, which was the strongest foundation for the Government of Ulster. Therefore, not only have we never asked to get an opportunity of dealing in a hostile way with the minority, but we have sought from the beginning to end of this controversy to be left alone and go hand in hand with Great Britain as one nation with Great Britain ... We will do our best, but it is idle for any man to pretend that our Ulster Parliament, or any other Parliament in the midst of a community of that kind, will not ... find very great difficulty in making progress as they would wish to do in the Parliament set up. No, sir, I urge even now at this hour that the proper course is that Ulster should remain as she is and that you should govern her, as you are governing her now, from here; there is very little difficulty about it, and that you should above all things have it as a place of your own with feelings towards you exactly like your own people ... I say try to look ahead, and looking ahead, I believe the policy we have urged from the beginning of retaining Ulster as she is now as part of the United Kingdom, and treating the people of Ulster exactly as you treat the people of Great Britain, is the truest and surest policy for His Majesty's Government to pursue.
(Sir Edward Carson, the Unionist leader, in May 1920 when the
Government of Ireland Act was going through its Committee
stage at Westminster)

In this and in chapter 8 I attempt to develop a novel understanding of the political process in Northern Ireland during one period of intense political conflict. I do so by taking the theory and methods of analysis I have outlined and developed in earlier chapters to the study of a critical moment in the structuration of Unionist ideology. This moment is the fourteen-year period from 1962 to 1975. But before focusing on this period it is useful to specify, in the form of some general propositions, the principal implications to be drawn from the argument to date.

TWO PROPOSITIONS

I put forward two related sets of propositions; the first structural or reconstructive in character, the second relating to causal sequences. For present purposes these may be stated as follows: First the structural or reconstructive propositions:

(1)   An ideological formation is a complex system of signification which has structural as well as thematic dimensions. The various thematic elements of an ideology are not merely articulated into a discourse. They are organised in terms of a determinate set of unconscious rules. As the previous chapters have established, these rules may usefully be separated into two groups; the (three) psychodynamic positions of ideology and the (four) cognitive modes of ideology.

(2)   Both the psychodynamic positions and the cognitive modes involve qualitative distinctions between the various forms of ideology; they each distinguish various forms of reasoning, or reasoning and feeling, by specifying the unconscious rules of structuration which are peculiar to each particular mode or position. The crucial implication of this is that any change of rules within an ideological formation will involve a qualitative alteration or 'movement' in the form of reasoning, or reasoning and feeling, involved in the structuration of the ideological field. The principal implications of this are outlined immediately below.

Second, some propositions regarding causal sequences

(1)   Crisis, whether the product of political, economic, ideological or other processes, will tend to generate defensive and/ or coping procedures within the ideological formation in crisis.

This carries two types of implication

(2)   Moments of crisis (in contrast with moments of relative calm) will tend to affect the ideological formation (and the political

order which it constructs and organises) in the following ways:[1]

(3)   Those groupings for which the crisis is challenging but not overwhelming will tend to construct the political order in relatively 'sophisticated' forms (*vis-à-vis* their habitual construction).[2]

There are two subsidiary aspects to this:

(3 i)   Those groupings which have habitually constructed the political order in 'sophisticated' forms will tend to do so more firmly and with enhanced confidence at moments of crisis. This is so to the extent and during the period that there has been a general shift of the ideology in this direction.

(3 ii) These same groupings should come into relative political prominence at moments of crisis; again to the extent and during the period that there has been a general shift of the ideology in this direction.

(4)   Those groupings, if any, for which the crisis is irrelevant will tend to construct the political order in established, habitual forms.

(5)   Those groupings for which the crisis is overwhelming (ideologically, politically, economically or whatever) will tend to construct the political order in more 'primitive' forms. There are two subsidiary aspects to this:

(5 i)   Those groupings which have habitually constructed the political order in 'primitive' forms will do so more firmly and with enhanced confidence at moments of crisis. This is the result of a general shift in the predominant form of the ideology.

(5 ii) These same groupings should come into relative political prominence at moments of crisis; again to the extent and during the period that there has been a general shift of the ideology in this direction.

(6)   Given that moments of severe crisis affect most groupings within a social formation to some extent, we would expect, on the basis of the above propositions, intragroup polarisation of ideological forms at such moments i.e. an antagonistic coex-

---

[1]   For a discussion of the concept of crisis and the depiction of four possible crisis tendencies of late-capitalist societies, see J. Habermas, *Legitimation Crisis*, translated by T. McCarthy (Boston: Beacon Books, 1975). See also, J. O'Connor, *The Meaning of Crisis* (Oxford: Basil Blackwell, 1987), especially chapters 3 and 4.

[2]   See my earlier discussion of work by Janis, Janis and Mann and Lazarus in chapter 1.

istence of relatively 'sophisticated' and relatively 'primitive' forms of ideology.

(7) Prolonged crisis, during which political and armed conflict become a persistent feature of the conduct of political life, will tend to generate an unfolding process of ideological transformation, with the relatively 'primitive' forms of ideology becoming predominant as the crisis unfolds.

(8) An interactive aspect of (7) above is that as the relatively 'primitive' forms become entrenched their very predominance may create an ideological crisis for those groupings which, previously, have rejected their assumptions. Thus there should be a perverse multiplier effect within the process of ideological transformation as it proceeds towards more 'primitive' forms.

(9) Generally, those ideological formations which have been subject to endemic crisis will contain a high concentration of relatively 'primitive' modes and positions, *vis-à-vis* any less crisis ridden ideological formation.[3]

(10) Even ideological formations such as described in (9) above will also contain more 'inclusivist'[4] forms through which a re-working of intergroup relations may be both imagined and enacted.

(11) Actual outcomes within the field of intergroup relations remain contingent upon the actions and reactions of the various parties to the process. However all such parties or actors inevitably work within the ideological formation and are subjected to its

---

[3] Only a comparative study would allow a direct examination of this last proposition. This study can only approach this particular issue indirectly, through a reflection upon and consideration of accumulated knowledge. The fact that Northern Ireland has appeared such an extraordinary exception within the set of Western polities suggests that it reveals some unusual distinguishing characteristics. Commonly these have been identified as the inappropriate persistence of ideologies more suited to the seventeenth than to the twentieth century (i.e. a pluralism thesis is implied). On the basis of this research I propose a reconceptualisation of this whole matter. The Unionist ideological formation has not simply persisted. It has been re-produced and transformed throughout the whole period. Its striking character as apparently primordial is actually one quite appropriate ideological response to the persistent crisis which has prevailed prior to and since the establishment of the state of Northern Ireland. Moreover, throughout its history Unionist ideology has taken diverse forms, both diachronically and synchronically. These have included forms which did not rely upon supposedly primordial identities and which did not denigrate others on the basis of some ascriptive criteria such as religion or language. Why some of these various forms have achieved dominance at least for a time and the ways in which the 'balance of power' between the various forms has changed over time in Northern Ireland are two central concerns of this study.

[4] See footnote 5 below for a definition of this term and its antonym.

rules; in the sense that such rules, in their variety, constitute so many forms of commonsense. Actors must engage with such rules of commonsense, either to re-make or to transform them. Even strong external actors with many resources cannot by-pass such an engagement with the rules of ideology. Any attempt to transform such rules, or to privilege 'inclusivist' over 'exclusivist'[5] forms of such rules, inevitably involves both the reading of such attempts through the already established ideological forms and, more critically, an engagement with such rules in the very attempt to displace them.

These propositions attempt to spell out some of the principal features of the structuration of ideological processes during periods of on-going political crisis. They offer a more elaborate, and, hopefully, a more precise formulation of the frequently observed phenomena of polarisation within a grouping followed by a drift towards the predominance of 'hard-line', uncompromising or exclusivist positions. They also suggest that to arrest such a drift to exclusivism, political actors, individual and group, inevitably need to engage in an ideological conflict; that the re-making of political and social relations is always a process which takes place within ideology. Northern Ireland during its most critical period is a valuable case in terms of which to explore these propositions.

In chapter 2 I raised the issue of developing a productive way of drawing into empirical research Habermas' notion of ideology as systematically distorted communication. I indicated the need to develop methods of analysis which would reveal the characteristic forms and deformations of a particular ideology. The subsequent discussion in chapters 4, 5 and 6 has attempted to do this. Although Habermas' conceptualisation of a 'pattern of systematically distorted communication' is very helpful in approaching the study of ideology, Habermas' own concern with an immanent 'ideal speech situation' which is tacitly invoked in every instance of human communication obscures the pressing need to specify the particular, 'positive' features of existing ideologies and the particular features of the systematically distorted patterns of communication which they

---

[5]   For the purposes of clarity and simplicity of exposition, I will tend to use the term 'exclusivist' and its antonym 'inclusivist' to distinguish between, on the one hand, those rules which are corporate in mode and dehumanising or, more typically, persecutory in position and, on the other, those rules which are 'liberal' in mode and ambivalent in position.

involve. In attempting to redress this limitation I have specified some principal rules involved in the recursive structuration of Unionist ideology and I have explored their particular constructions of the subject, of the proper relations between subjects, and their constructions of authority and the proper exercise of power. This approach has enabled me, in chapters 4 and 5, to specify the distortions which arise when a particular rule is drawn upon for the construction of any particular political or social practice. It has also enabled me to develop the proposition that some major aspects of intra-Unionist disagreement or conflict can be understood exactly as disagreement or conflict regarding which rules for the structuration of Unionist ideology are regarded as appropriate.

In these final chapters I want to extend this analysis in two related ways. As we have already seen, the approach developed in this study can be used to analyse an ideological process as a conflict over which rules will dominate in the construction of the public and institutional space. In this sense systematically distorted communication arises not only due to the suppression or repression of generalisable interests but also due to the qualitative differences between one set of rules and another; for instance between the rules of the persecutory position as against the rules of the ambivalent position, or between the rules of the corporate modes and those of the liberal modes. In such instances similar thematic concerns, such as the preservation of the Union with Britain, are construed quite differently in one form of rules as against another. For instance, while agreeing on the general principle of union with Great Britain, political actors drawing on one set of rules will construe the implications of the commitment to Union in quite different ways from those who draw on another set of rules. Systematic distortions in communication within a political grouping and *between* its various sections will occur whenever a disagreement arises regarding which rules are 'proper' for the construction of a particular political or social moment. In these chapters concerning a critical period in the history of Unionism it is this second type of systematically distorted communication with which I am most concerned.

BREAKING THE RULES

As Bob Purdie has noted, the civil rights movement may be regarded as a catalyst which activated the dormant and deep-seated ethnic divisions within Northern Ireland. For a brief period it placed a liberal ideology in a position of some centrality within the public discourse of Northern Ireland. As Purdie puts this, the civil rights movement was one of several 'new departures and new experiments' which were attempted in the 1960s. He describes this movement, in its beginnings, as 'a new way of conceptualising an old problem', adding that, for the Catholic community, 'until the 1960s nationalism supplied the grammar with which to discuss possible solutions'.[6] While endorsing Purdie's understanding, what I would add to this is two claims.

First, during the period from 1962 until 1975 Northern Ireland can be said to have experienced an attempt at modernisation which eventually 'failed'. That is to say, it failed in the sense that the expected consequences of a variety of attempts at economic, political and 'civil and constitutional rights' reform failed to have the expected transformative effects upon the character of social and political relations and social and political identities. Three major groupings can be identified as the carriers of this modernisation project: the Northern Ireland Labour Party (NILP), the O'Neill faction within the Ulster Unionist Party (UUP) and the civil rights movement. What each of these groupings managed to do was to raise the serious possibility of a different ordering of relations and identities in Northern Ireland. They imagined a different form of society and, usually in a halting and compromised way, initiated political actions which were intended to institute these imagined identities and relations.

Second, my purpose is to go beyond an historical reconstruction of the rise and fall of modernity in Northern Ireland during the critical fourteen-year period from 1962 and to offer an account of the various psychosocial processes at play; to offer an explanatory reconstruction which, in one sense, goes beyond an historical reconstruction. It is important to note that I am not claiming that these three groupings invented, de novo, this new, imagined society. Such liberal rules had been a part of the ideological discourse of Northern Ireland since at least the late eighteenth century. What we see, from the mid-1950s on, is a renewed attempt to institutionalise this imagined society as a new form of social and political relations entailing a new set of identities, one in which ethnic or religious

---

[6]   B. Purdie, *Politics in the Streets* (Belfast: Blackstaff Press, 1990), pp. 1, 2.

identity plays a subsidiary role. Apart from the three political or social movements which I identified above, the principal actor in this modernising impulse was the state itself. From the 1930s, but with renewed vigour after the Second World War, Westminster had introduced a vast array of social welfare legislation, offering entitlement to state support or assistance on the basis of non-ascriptive criteria. This state-sanctioned set of rules was administered and implemented within Northern Ireland by the Stormont regime and by the various local councils in ways which often, but not always, attempted to rewrite these rules in ascriptive terms. The classic example in this regard is the allocation of public housing according to sectarian criteria rather than universal needs-based criteria. This conflict between the universal, liberal rules of the welfare state legislation and the, frequently, exclusivist, sectarian rules of the local governments and agencies charged with the implementation of such legislation introduced a profound tension into the daily administration of the state, one which the three political and social movements mentioned above attempted to resolve, or at least explore or exploit, through their attempts to institutionalise non-ascriptive rules in the domains of economic, political, civil and constitutional life. No doubt the most ambivalent and, perhaps, compromised of these three groupings was the O'Neill faction of the UUP. At the same time this was clearly the most powerful of the three groupings. If successful it could, through its pivotal role as the principal governmental faction, make a profound difference. Of course, whether broader ideological and social forces would facilitate such a transformation of the dominant rules is the issue of major concern.

As stated above, a striking feature of post-war Northern Ireland was the growing intrusion of the British (UK) state into its regulation and administration. The rapid growth of the welfare state in the UK and the increasingly interventionist role of the state in the direction of the economy (both of which came together in regional economic policies, for instance) turned the Stormont regime in Northern Ireland into something akin to a ventriloquist's doll with a mind of its own. On the one hand the amount of financial support attached to state development and welfare policies was so attractive as to lead Stormont to almost automatically pass matching legislation so as to guarantee access to the British exchequer. On the other hand the conventional-liberal norms institutionalised by such practices were not often as welcome as their accompanying travellers' cheques, so to speak.

One instance highlights this. In 1956 the UK government increased family allowances for third and subsequent children by 2 shillings a week. In Northern Ireland, for many Unionists, such a redistributive policy carried with it the spectre of political and cultural annihilation. Such a policy could only encourage Roman Catholics to have even more children! Thus the Unionist government took the extraordinary step of introducing legislation which was at variance with the Westminster legislation, despite the implications this carried for the maintenance of parity with the rest of the UK. Given that Northern Ireland was hugely subsidised by the rest of the UK on the principle of parity, to stray from this principle was to raise a significant question mark regarding the continued prosperity of the regional economy. Nevertheless, 'Ivan Neill, the Stormont Minister for Labour, announced that he was departing from the British scheme and would increase the allowances for second and third but not subsequent children.'[7] Amidst howls of opposition, principally from the Nationalist Party, the Irish Congress of Trade Unions and the Presbyterian Church, this regional initiative was abandoned at the stage of the Bill's second reading.

This example is of interest on at least two counts. That it occurred at all, despite the self-evident nature of its sectarian intention and against the whole trend of maintaining parity with Britain, indicates the ideological conflict which economic dependence on Westminster carried for the Unionist government at Stormont. That it was ultimately abandoned indicates the power of both Westminster as an integral part of the state and economy in Northern Ireland and the residual power of the liberal modes of Unionist ideology. Captain Terence O'Neill was a central political actor who, first as minister of finance and subsequently, from 1963 to 1969, as prime minister, attempted to resolve this inherent tension within traditional Unionism by promoting a modernisation process in Northern Ireland which would maintain and strengthen the union with Britain by means of economic 'progress' and its anticipated modernising effects upon political identities, rather than by sectarian means.

Throughout the 1960s the old certainties upon which the sectarian basis of Ulster politics was based came under challenge. First, the IRA campaign which had been mounted throughout the late 1950s and early 1960s came to a desultory, but official, conclusion in 1962.

---

[7]   M. Farrell, *Northern Ireland: The Orange State* (London: Pluto Press, 1980), p. 213.

This cessation of paramilitary violence created a new political possibility for Northern Ireland. The very fact that the Republican paramilitary campaign had ended with a whimper highlighted the limited extent of support amongst Nationalists for such a campaign. It removed the most potent source of the Unionist 'siege mentality', the fear of being shot and bombed into a United Ireland. It also signalled a broader change, a willingness among a significant proportion of the Catholic/Nationalist community to work towards 'new solutions to old problems'. Beyond this, it indicated the possibility of new political identities, ones which were not so firmly attached to the sectarian verities. The social movement which gave public and institutional form to this new possibility was the civil rights movement with its insistence upon the equal rights of all citizens; perhaps best exemplified in its 'one man (sic), one vote' campaign slogan. This movement, which initially drew its support from both Nationalist and Unionist communities, took the novel step of insisting that British standards and norms should be fully extended to Northern Ireland. Rather than looking to Nationalist and Republican ideology for its identity and programme, the civil rights movement looked to similar movements elsewhere in the world and, in particular, to the American civil rights movement.

Within Unionism a parallel transformation was under way. The prime minister of the Unionist party, Captain Terence O'Neill, proposed to 'transform the face of Ulster'.[8] This claim has met with a very mixed reception among commentators on Northern Ireland; a reception which mirrors the manner in which O'Neill's initiatives were received within Northern Ireland at the time. One group of commentators regards O'Neill as a positive force for change. For instance, F. S. L. Lyons wrote in *Ireland Since the Famine* that 'Captain O'Neill set himself not only to divert domestic energies away from internecine quarrels and towards constructive policies but also to cultivate more amicable relations with the south.'[9] In *Northern Ireland Since 1968* Paul Arthur and Keith Jeffery describe O'Neill as 'a man with a mission, an innovator who wanted to prepare Northern Ireland for the late twentieth century and its place in the affluent sun'.[10] Barry White, a distinguished journalist with the *Belfast Telegraph*, has claimed that 'O'Neill genuinely wanted to make

---

[8]   *Belfast Telegraph*, 24 November 1965.
[9]   F. S. L. Lyons, *Ireland Since the Famine* (Oxford: Oxford University Press, 1979), p. 78.
[10] P. Arthur and K. Jeffery, *Northern Ireland Since 1968* (Oxford: Blackwell, 1988), p. 6.

Northern Ireland a model, modern province.'[11] Other commentators
have either dismissed O'Neill completely as a hypocritical meddler
and a traitor to Unionism or have treated his purported liberalism
with great scepticism.[12] Generally, this last group base their dismissal
of the significance of O'Neill's reforms on the fact that these reforms
were largely symbolic in character.[13] As I have argued above in my
introduction, to make such a claim is to miss the point.[14] O'Neill's
personal virtues or failings are hardly the issue, yet, typically, most
discussion is reduced to this. Rather, what is at issue is the political
meanings which attached to O'Neill's various initiatives, modest as
these initiatives were from some perspectives. My argument is that
we can only begin to adequately comprehend the character of such
initiatives and the responses they produced if we take seriously the
ideological process within Northern Ireland.

As we have seen in previous chapters, the Unionist ideological
formation can be analysed in terms of the various rules of structuration (both modes and positions) which organise its several ways of
construing the person or subject; the proper relations between
persons or subjects; and the proper form of authority and the proper
exercise of power. At any historical moment all of the various rules of
structuration which we have discerned have a certain provenance; at
certain moments and within certain institutional spaces these various
rules constitute the pre-understood forms for the performance of
speech-acts and social interaction. They find their way into the
cultures of particular institutions and organisations where they
establish the commonsense understandings in terms of which saying
and doing is organised. The questions which I now wish to address
relate to the relative prominence of these rules within the public
discourse regarding the proper ordering of social and political
relations in Northern Ireland. Which rules, if any, have achieved a
degree of hegemony over the institutional and public space of
Northern Ireland, and for which time periods? What forms of

---

[11] B. White, *John Hume – Statesman of the Troubles* (Belfast: Blackstaff Press, 1984), p. 37.
[12] An interesting and idiosyncratic example of the genre which dismisses O'Neill as a traitor
is D. Gordon, *The O'Neill Years: Unionist Politics 1963–1969* (Belfast: Athol Books, 1989).
[13] See Purdie for the most intelligent version of this assessment of O'Neill. Purdie summarises
his position as follows: 'The most innovative aspect of O'Neill's premiership was his
"style", which consisted of making liberal and modernist statements and gestures, while
using extreme caution in nudging his party towards changes in its traditional outlook.'
Purdie, *Politics in the Streets*, p. 14.
[14] See page 13 above.

opposition have arisen and how has this conflict been fought at the ideological level?

Throughout the fifty-year period subsequent to the creation of the state of Northern Ireland in 1920, Unionist ideology was formed and represented by the UUP. Of course there were always some independent Unionists, and the UUP was itself subject to influence and persuasion by a variety of other organisations and institutions. These included the various Protestant churches, the various Chambers of Commerce and representatives of the principal industries as well as the British government and bureaucracy (both Westminster and Whitehall) and the Loyal Orange Order. However the United Ulster Unionist Council and its political arm, the UUP, were the specific organisations charged by their community with the propagation and preservation of Unionist principles and Unionist power. The party was remarkably successful in this regard, winning election after election over the fifty-odd years of Stormont government. Indeed the party was never defeated electorally. Only the proroguing of the Northern Ireland parliament by Westminster in 1974 could succeed in halting its dominant role in the governing of Northern Ireland.

Reflecting on this history of Unionist supremacy, one commentator has noted what he terms some 'curious' features of democracy in Northern Ireland.[15] For approximately fifty years the UUP formed the government of Northern Ireland, and its leader, as though automatically, held the position of prime minister. At election after election the Unionist party achieved sweeping victories and in many cases its candidates stood unopposed. One telling example of this 'curious parliamentary history' is provided by the career of Captain Terence O'Neill. O'Neill was first elected to his seat of Antrim Bannside at a by-election in 1946. He subsequently successfully defended his seat at elections in 1949, 1953, 1958, 1962, 1965 and 1969. In 1969 he was opposed by Ian Paisley, a rising figure within the Unionist community and the leader of a political organisation which eventually formed itself as the Democratic Unionist Party (DUP). O'Neill was also opposed by Michael Farrell, a leader of People's Democracy and a central figure in the Civil Rights movement. In this bitter three-cornered contest O'Neill was returned with a small but comfortable majority. However, the curious part of all this is that all *three* candidates were facing electoral opposition for the

[15] See A. M. Gallagher, untitled paper which was presented to the First International Conference of the Ethnic Studies Network in Portrush in June 1992, p. 1.

very first time. In other words, in all the previous elections at which Terence O'Neill had been successful over a twenty-year period he had always been returned unopposed. As Gallagher notes, 'this parliamentary career was not atypical'.[16] In the nine general elections between 1929 and 1965 there were, on each occasion, at least 20 of the 52 Stormont seats which went unopposed; that is 39 per cent. In some cases these percentages were much higher. For instance, in 1933 64 per cent of seats (or 33 seats) were returned unopposed and as late as 1958 more than half (52 per cent or 27 seats) of the seats were decided without a ballot. The same pattern existed at by-elections where, in the period between 1929 and 1965, 32 of the total of 58 by-elections (or 55 per cent) went unopposed.[17] This is hardly what one would expect from a modern democracy in which politics is a vital preoccupation.

This curious situation underlines the unusual character of politics in Northern Ireland. The question of the Union with Great Britain was a recurrent obsession at every election up until 1958. For so long as the party could convince those voters who identified themselves as Unionists that only the UUP could protect the union, then it could be certain of electoral victory. This certainty followed, at least in the early years, directly from the contrived Unionist dominance within the Northern Ireland community. When Northern Ireland was first established as a distinct governmental entity its boundaries were drawn so as to maximise the Protestant-Unionist proportion of the population. Hence, as I discussed in chapter 6, the old nine-county Ulster, in which the population balance was approximately half Protestant-Unionist and half Catholic-Nationalist was not preserved as the new state of Northern Ireland. Rather a six-county 'Ulster' was created in which the population balance was approximately two-thirds Protestant-Unionist and one-third Catholic-Nationalist. This formula guaranteed Unionist dominance in the short term, especially following upon the recent civil war in Ireland and the intense conflict between Unionists and Nationalists over the issues of home rule and partition into 'North and South'. However it was an open question as to the duration of such identity politics in the new state. If the more typical Western model of class-based politics, in which various parties 'represented' the interests of labour and capital, were to become dominant in Northern Ireland, then the old identity politics

---

[16] Ibid., p. 1.   [17] These figures are drawn from Gallagher, ibid.

upon which the continued dominance of the Unionist community and the UUP was based might start to disintegrate. Hence the very political structure of Northern Ireland presented the ruling party with the need to maintain the prevalence of a form of Unionist political subjectivity which was exclusivist in character and which gave priority to issues of identity over issues of a material or class nature. In the terms which I have previously developed, the predominant rules of Unionist ideology throughout the first forty years of UUP government were corporate in mode and dehumanising or, more typically, persecutory in position; in a single term of convenience these rules were exclusivist in form.[18] I base this judgement on a detailed reading of several hundred documents and speeches from this period. However it is not my purpose to establish such a claim in this study; in any case it is more or less commonly accepted by most scholars, although, of course, they do not use my terminology. All I wish to do is to indicate the presence of such rules while acknowledging the occasional co-presence of 'liberal' modes and the ambivalent position, or, more simply, inclusivist rules.

Perhaps the classic example of the predominance of such exclusivist rules is provided by Sir Basil Brooke, later Lord Brookeborough, speaking in 1933 at a Twelfth of July meeting:

Continuing, Sir Basil said there was a great number of Protestants and Orangemen who employed Roman Catholics. He felt he could speak freely on this subject as he had not a Roman Catholic about his own place. (Cheers) He appreciated the great difficulty experienced by some of them in procuring suitable Protestant labour, but he would point out that the Roman Catholics were endeavouring to get in everywhere and were out with all their force and might to destroy the power and constitution of Ulster. There was a definite plot to overpower the vote of Unionists in the North. He would appeal to loyalists therefore, wherever possible to employ good Protestant lads and lassies (Cheers). ... Mr. Cahir Healy [Nationalist MP] complained that no appointments were given to Roman Catholics, but in that he was quite wrong as in his (Sir Basil's) opinion they had got too many appointments for *men who were really out to cut their throats* if opportunity arose (Hear, hear). It would be sheer madness to keep on giving such men appointments under existing conditions. ... (emphasis mine) (*Fermanagh Times*, 13 July 1933)[19]

This speech was delivered during the depression, when, for

---

[18]   See footnote 5, above.
[19]   Taken from A. C. Hepburn, *The Conflict of Nationality in Modern Ireland* (London, Edward Arnold, 1980), p. 164.

Unionism, the spectre of working-class solidarity across the sectarian divide had arisen. Quite clearly, the speech draws upon the rules of the persecutory position and the rules of the affiliative-corporate mode to construct its preferred pattern of social relations in Northern Ireland. This speech created considerable controversy, but Brooke himself did not resile from it. Instead he reiterated it on several occasions and added that if Protestants 'were put in the power of the Free State ... not only would they be condemned to death, but they might be ... drawn and quartered'. Later that year, speaking in Enniskillen, again he affirmed that his comments were 'not a political stunt as some say ... he believed from the bottom of his heart all he said'.[20] The prime minister of the time, Lord Craigavon, defended Brooke's statement without reservation, stating that Brooke 'spoke as a member of his majesty's government. He spoke entirely on his own when he made the speech ... but there is not one of my colleagues who does not entirely agree with him, and I would not ask him to withdraw one word ... I do not think that a single word said ... [by Brooke] ... could cause any offence to those who are loyal to the constitution of Northern Ireland.'[21] The *Fermanagh Times* commented: 'The whole country will rejoice at the strong and frank attitude taken up by the prime minister ... and not one of his colleagues did not agree.'[22] Amongst other things this episode highlights the wisdom of Sir Edward Carson's advice to parliament, which I have quoted above as the epigraph to this chapter. The very existence of a Northern Ireland parliament, born out of conflict and compromise, created a situation in which the issues of loyalty and the preservation of the Union were pervasive throughout the political and social life of the province.

However, from around 1958, the hegemony of such exclusivist rules began to enter a period of crisis. It appeared as if a new wind of change was beginning to blow. This crisis for exclusivism was promoted by several factors including, principally, the imminent economic decline in the traditional Ulster industries following upon the end of the Korean war; the growing complexity of the Northern Ireland economy and the increasing supervision of Northern Ireland expenditure by Whitehall, the on-going but successful resistance to the IRA offensive and the rise of the ecumenical movement. For

---

[20]   B. Barton, *Brookeborough: The Making of a Prime Minister* (Belfast: Institute of Irish Studies, the Queen's University of Belfast, 1988), pp. 78–9.
[21]   Ibid., p. 80.   [22]   Ibid., p. 80.

these and other reasons the major political conflict faced by the UUP
at the 1958 elections was not with the traditional Nationalist 'enemy'
but rather with the pro-union (with Britain) NILP, and it was played
out in the industrial centre of Belfast around issues of economic
prosperity and growth and welfare state provision for the working
class. Unlike in the 1930s, the Unionist party could not rely, so
readily, upon the traditional exclusivist ideology to compete with the
NILP, a party attempting, from a Unionist position, to establish a
constituency based on issues of class.

This same conflict over issues of class and prosperity figured
prominently in the 1962 Stormont election. In this election the
premier, Lord Brookeborough, relied on exclusivist rules to promote
the interests of the UUP, just as he had done in the 1930s as a back-
bencher. During the election campaign Brookeborough made the
following sorts of statement. At an open air meeting in Portadown on
26 May 1962 he reminded the audience of what 'our boys' on the
border had come through in the past number of years and not to let
them down on this occasion. In reference to social services he said
Northern Ireland had Éire beaten into a 'cocked hat'.[23] Speaking in
Cromac on 31 May 1962, Brookeborough said that '[v]oting Socialist
is as much an attack on the constitution as voting Nationalist'.[24] In
these instances we see Brookeborough approaching the issue of
economic development in an idiom borrowed from the traditional
Unionist concerns with the dangers of Nationalism. He is not as
provocative as he was in 1932, but the same rules are in play.
However Terence O'Neill, the minister for finance, who was to
replace Brookeborough as prime minister in 1963 after Brookeborough's retirement, spoke as follows:

There are two roads along which Ulster can travel in the future. Both will
be hard but only one can reach the destination entitled 'prosperity'. Along
one road there will be trouble between management and labour tending to
give Ulster a bad name for industrial relations. Can we possibly afford to
take this turning? Along the other road we can build together the finest
industrial atmosphere in Western Europe which will be more valuable in
attracting industry than any financial incentive. It isn't then so much a
question of can the government afford to attract new industry to Ulster –
but rather can we afford to let our name for industrial relations become
tarnished in any way. (*Belfast Telegraph*, 31 May 1962)

As we will see in detail when I examine the 1965 Stormont election

[23]   *Belfast Telegraph*, 26 May 1962.   [24]   *Belfast Telegraph*, 31 May 1962.

campaign, this concern with economic development, and the convic-
tion that it could deliver a new political and social order which had
been purged of the traditional sectarian enmities which had so
disfigured social and commercial life in Northern Ireland, became
the new faith of liberal Unionism under O'Neill's direction. At the
same time this faith in the social virtues of economic development
was seen to have certain pragmatic advantages. So, in reflecting
upon the 1962 election immediately after the results had been
announced, the prime minister, Lord Brookeborough, said:

This was probably the most powerful challenge we have had to face in over
40 years. To retain all our seats with two exceptions in the face of this
massive onslaught was truly a magnificent achievement, especially when we
take into account that it was fought on a purely bread and butter policy.

The Government's industrial and economic record was the main issue
and the policies have been endorsed by the electorate. They have emerged
from this contest strengthened and invigorated and the people have shown
this confidence in a Unionist government despite the so-called winds of
change. *Belfast Telegraph*, 1 June 1962

In this statement Brookeborough is recording that the threat to
UUP dominance, a threat which the UUP failed to repel under his
leadership, was coming from the NILP; with the uncharacteristic
effect of placing 'bread and butter' issues at the heart of the political
conflict!

THE 1965 ELECTION: PLAYING BY THE NEW RULES

In the conclusion to chapter 4 I quoted Eddie McAteer, leader of the
Nationalist opposition, claiming that the 1965 Stormont election was
quite different from previous elections in that 'some of the hate
seems to have been drained out'. I also quoted John Cole's suggestion that '[n]ever has Ulster had an election where the Orange and
Green issue has been less evident'.[25] In both cases this sense of a
liberal tolerance of difference was understood to have its basis in the
'modernisation' of the Northern Irish economy. No longer were the
old atavistic attitudes of much relevance, or so it seemed. Under the
direction of Captain Terence O'Neill the Unionist party was seen to
be charting new territory, to be more concerned with a future of
material progress than a past of sectarian difference and discrimination. For McAteer, O'Neill's most promising step prior to the 1965

[25] Purdie provides further examples of a like kind. See Purdie, *Politics in The Streets*, p. 15.

election had been his invitation to the taoiseach of the Republic of Ireland to visit Stormont for talks about economic cooperation between the two parts of Ireland.

The 1965 election was O'Neill's first as prime minister and was seen by him as a critical opportunity to defeat the new challenger to Unionist supremacy in Ulster, namely the NILP. The *Belfast Telegraph*, in its post-election commentary, analysed the Unionist victory as follows:

O'Neill has done what he said he would do – push back the rising tide of Labour in Belfast ... Labour was hard put to pick a quarrel on the main economic issues that the Government put to the country. The planks on which they consolidated their 1958 position in the last election – the dry dock, rising unemployment – had been quietly removed from under their feet ...

This blurring of policy distinctions between Labour and Unionists was probably a major factor (in the election result). (*Belfast Telegraph*, 26 November 1965)

As this comment indicates, the NILP, itself a predominantly Unionist party with strong connections to the trade union movement and with a commitment to policy initiatives in line with those of the British Labour Party, was regarded by the UUP as the principal opposition party, the one which could encroach most dangerously on its 'natural' constituency. Such encroachment had begun in the 1958 Stormont election when the NILP had won four seats. This success was consolidated in the 1962 Stormont election when the NILP again won four seats, but with vastly increased support. As the historian, Patrick Buckland, has commented about the effects within Unionism of the 1962 election results: the 'revival' of the NILP, 'sustained through two elections, created considerable outrage and even panic among Unionists in Belfast who feared that the NILP had not reached the limit of the Protestant vote'.[26] This 'revival' of the NILP can be attributed to a number of overlapping factors. The old Ulster industries such as ship-building and linen manufacture had a last lease of life during the Korean war, but thereafter had fallen into decline. The predominantly Unionist 'labour aristocracy' which worked in these industries was far more interested in economic growth than it was in the old Unionist bogey of sectarian difference. In the 1962 Stormont election Sir Basil Brooke had failed to recognise the need to modify his exclusivist position with the result

---

[26]   P. Buckland, *A History of Northern Ireland* (Dublin: Gill & Macmillan, 1981), p. 109.

that, in Belfast, the Unionist party held seven seats with a total vote of 67,450 as against the NILP holding four seats with a total vote of 60,170. For the NILP this 1962 election saw an increase in its total vote of 40,000 and an increase in its total majority in the seats it won of more than 2,000.[27]

When O'Neill took over as prime minister in 1963 he was moving from a long and influential period as minister for finance. With such a background he was the ideal leader to restore the UUP's dominance over the NILP as he was both a committed Unionist, although one who typically construed the political order in inclusivist terms, and also a technocrat who was committed to the achievement of economic growth and prosperity for all in a new Ulster. Over the next few years, in a series of mainly symbolic initiatives, he began to demonstrate that he was keen to improve the quality of community relations between Protestant and Catholic and that he wished to go beyond the old exclusivist traditions of Unionism. During this period in the middle of the 1960s O'Neill was one major political actor who began to re-work the dominant rules of Unionist ideology by beginning to construe the potential future of Northern Ireland according to inclusivist rules and by taking some tentative steps towards the institutionalisation of such rules.

The *Belfast Telegraph* reported O'Neill's Twelfth of July address of 1964 as follows:

'All around you, the signs of modernisation and progress – new schools and hospitals, farm buildings and factories, roads and bridges – are to be seen.'

They would be less than true to the memory of those who signed the Covenant if they let the development of Ulster fall below the very highest standards.

'*I think it was very revealing when a prominent Nationalist said, not very long ago, that he would rather see his constituents prosperous under the Union Jack than emigrating under the Tricolour,*' the Prime Minister went on.

[. . .] 'As British citizens they had to bear responsibilities but they also enjoyed many privileges. *Without the economic and financial strength of the British nation behind us we could not face with confidence the tasks which still lay before us.*'

'There was much work still to be done for Ulster. There were vast and expensive programmes of development under way or still being planned.'

'There will be ever greater opportunities for our people, in education, in training, in useful and fulfilling employment. Without our British connections many of these things would be totally beyond our reach,' the Prime Minister concluded. (*Belfast Telegraph*, 13 July 1964; emphases mine)

[27] Purdie, *Politics in The Streets*, p. 65.

In this statement O'Neill promotes the virtues of the Union in
economic and social terms and makes reference to a prominent
Nationalist politician who is described as putting similar economic
concerns ahead of the identity politics of the past.

These halting steps towards the re-ordering of the rules of Unionist
ideology quickly produced a storm of protest and internal division
within Unionism. At the same Twelfth of July demonstrations in
1964 at which O'Neill made the above statement, other Unionists
and Orangemen were sounding a more familiar note. So Mr Rafton
Pounder, MP for South Belfast at Westminster, speaking at Brookeborough, addressed the crowds as follows: 'Appeasement has never
solved anything. Unity by surrender would be contemptible. If a
principle is worth holding, it is worth fighting for. The forces of the
counter-Reformation are again at work, again they must be defeated.' (*Belfast Telegraph*, 13 July 1964)

And Mr Norman Porter made an even stronger case. The *Belfast
Telegraph* reported his speech as follows:

Danger in being too friendly
At Annalong, Mr. Norman Porter, hit out at Protestant clergy who want
closer unity with the Roman Catholic Church.

'There is a great and imminent danger in this ever increasing age of good
neighbourliness and friendship,' he said. 'It can be overdone, leading not
only to compromise but to betrayal.' He warned, 'When you become too
friendly with those of different religious persuasion, you find it increasingly
hard and difficult to oppose their beliefs – this leads to compromise.'

[...] 'It is alright to feed the lion in its cage, but to get too close to it and
start patting its head is inviting serious trouble.' (*Belfast Telegraph*, 13 July
1964)

These two statements register a concern with both the ecumenical
movement within the Protestant churches and the liberal movement
within Unionism. Norman Porter's speech highlights some of the
intricacies of an exclusivist position. Porter, president of the Evangelical Protestant Society, had been a long-time associate of Ian
Paisley, until he and Paisley broke with each other in 1963 over
Paisley's 'increasingly strong attacks on the Presbyterian Church'.[28]
In this speech Porter warns of the dangers of 'good neighbourliness
and friendship' which can lead to the slippery slope of 'compromise'

28 S. Bruce, *God Save Ulster! The Religion and Politics of Paisleyism* (Oxford: Oxford University
Press, 1989), p. 39.

and 'betrayal'. The speech is so clearly marked by the rules of the corporate modes and the dehumanising position that this hardly needs to be established. What does warrant comment are the anxieties provoked by the ecumenical and liberal movements. It is as if 'fraternisation', or 'good neighbourliness and friendship' have an inevitable outcome in 'betrayal'. The paranoid component of this is surely evident. In this particular construction Protestants and Unionists who fraternise are regarded as though they are children who need to be told the harsh facts of life. In this way their liberal intentions and actions are recast as an innocent ignorance which, however, is fatally open to perverse corruption at the hands of 'those of different religious persuasion'. In this manner such liberal norms are denied a legitimate place within Protestantism and Unionism, they are cast out beyond the pale of what can count as 'true' Protestantism and Unionism. The paranoid-schizoid mechanisms at play here become quite apparent in the dehumanising image of Catholics as 'the lion in its cage'. This image contains the persecutory anxieties to which the rise of modernity in Northern Ireland had lent a renewed urgency. It condenses into one signification both these persecutory anxieties and their preferred 'solution'; a public policy of discrimination which tolerates Catholics and Nationalists only for so long as they are kept in their place; 'but to get too close to it and start patting its head is inviting serious trouble'. As we have seen previously, the 'exclusivist' forms of Unionist ideology produce a particular construction or reading of the on-going social and political process in Northern Ireland. The social and political process, with all its inevitable complexities, is read as a story of on-going threat and imminent betrayal. Indeed two distinguished historians use the term 'siege mentality' to describe this form of Unionist ideology.[29] The predominance within Unionism of such 'exclusivist' rules creates a set of presumptions in which attempts to change the rules in a liberal direction are themselves read as further examples of threat and betrayal, performed either through ignorance or with malevolence. If such initiatives fail to 're-groove' Unionist ideology as inclusivist then the agents of change within Unionism themselves become the focus of

---

[29] See A. T. Q. Stewart, *The Narrow Ground: Aspects of Ulster, 1609–1969* (London: Faber & Faber, 1977), pp. 47–8. See, also, F. S. L. Lyons, *Ireland Since The Famine* (London: Fontana Books, 1973), pp. 715–28 and F. S. L. Lyons, *Culture and Anarchy in Ireland* (Oxford: Oxford University Press, 1979), pp. 113–45 and, especially, p. 117.

anxieties about threat and betrayal. We can see this in some of the actions of Ian Paisley.

Paisley launched a series of attacks on liberal Unionism in the mid-1960s, long before the Civil Rights marches were to provoke hostile reaction from Loyalists. For instance, he protested vigorously about the visit to Stormont by the taoiseach of the Republic of Ireland, Sean Lemass, in February of 1965. O'Neill invited Lemass to visit him at Stormont to discuss economic cooperation between Northern Ireland and the Republic, but Paisley regarded this visit as grounds for a defence of traditional Unionist beliefs. Farrell comments that 'The Lemass–O'Neill meeting gave Paisley new ammunition, and in February 1965 a massive Paisley rally outside the building forced O'Neill to abandon a function in the Unionist Party headquarters. For the rest of the year Paisley stomped the country denouncing "O'Neillism".'[30] Paisley made similar capital of the O'Neill government's uneasy toleration of Nationalist celebrations of the 50th anniversary of the 1916 Easter Rising in 1966. In the *Protestant Telegraph* he wrote:

Capt. Terence O'Neill will soon have to make up his mind whether he intends to appease the Republican minority or serve the vast so-called extremist majority. Surely he does not seriously think that appeasement will stop the IRA attacks or the cries of discrimination. Or is he secretly selling us to the South? (*Protestant Telegraph*, 18 June 1966)

Earlier, on 6 June 1966, Paisley led a group of Free Presbyterian Church demonstrators on a protest march on the Assembly Hall, to picket the General Assembly of the Irish Presbyterians. Along its approved route this march encountered a group of Nationalist/ Catholic youths who were 'armed with a good supply of bricks and metal objects to hurl at the marchers'.[31] With police protection, the marchers eventually arrived at the Assembly Hall where, amidst much confusion, they managed to surround its entrance and heckle the Presbyterian dignitaries and the governor and his wife as they left the building. For his part in this demonstration Paisley was charged, and eventually convicted, with offences against the maintenance of public order. Although his fine was paid for him anonymously, Paisley was not prepared to sign a bond, binding him over to keep the peace. He claimed that such an undertaking would ban him from

[30] Farrell, *Northern Ireland*, p. 234.   [31] Bruce, *God Save Ulster!*, p. 81.

making any public protests. So on 20 July, along with three others, he was imprisoned at Crumlin Road jail.

Ten days later the following appeared in his paper, *The Protestant Telegraph:*

The reasons why I chose jail – Ian R.K. Paisley
I have chosen jail:
1 To focus attention on the fact that there seem to be two laws in Ulster. One for Papists and O'Neillites and another for the loyalist Protestants. [...]
2 To focus attention on the actions of the Prime Minister.
The term of the present Prime Minister, Capt. Terence O'Neill, has been one sad story of appeasement with the enemies of Northern Ireland. His secret meetings with Lemass were acts of treachery. By his words and actions he has shown himself to be more interested in his political dictatorship than in keeping Northern Ireland truly Protestant. In the conspiracy with Capt. O'Neill, the Moderator of the Irish Presbyterian Church and the Clerk of the Presbytery, was Mr. Brian McConnell. A study should be made of Mr. McConnell's pedigree, and then you will know why he is leaning over backwards to placate the Papists. *See the blood in his veins* and you will get a surprise. Look at the blood of 'Seamus' O'Neill – the blood of O'Neill was linked with Roman Catholic conspiracy. And *the old rebel strain* is coming out in this prodigy we now have in Stormont. We want to show that this is not a democratic country, but that it has been run by a group of dictators from Glengall Street. [UUP headquarters] For years these men have tried to tell the Protestants of Ulster that they are loyal and true blues, but they are being found out now. The hidden things of darkness are being exposed. O'Neill thinks elections are far away, but the memory of the Ulster people is long. All the political activity of the police, all the manipulations of the law, all the perjury, will never stop the Protestant people of Ulster from attempting to rid us of that Lundy, O'Neill. With the grace of God and the help of the Protestants of Ulster, the day will come when I will be in Stormont – the only way true Protestant people can deal with the *ruling junta of Lundies* is to have someone there to root out the nest of traitors. (*Protestant Telegraph*, 30 July 1966; emphases mine)

This statement is structured by the rules of the persecutory position and the affiliative-corporate mode. In this instance the nominal category of 'Unionist' is split into an all-good and an all-bad group. The recent history of Northern Ireland is construed as a process of 'appeasement' and 'conspiracy'. Clearly the Nationalist community, or 'the Papists', are referenced as the group which O'Neill is 'leaning over backwards to placate' and appease. However the animus of the statement is directed to O'Neill and other liberal

Unionists. It is they who are engaged in a 'conspiracy' and the purported contamination which 'explains' this betrayal is 'the blood in [their] veins.' 'The old rebel strain is coming out in this prodigy we now have in Stormont.' They are, then, construed as constitutionally (or genetically) different and inferior to 'loyal and true blue' Unionists. This construction involves a denigration of these political actors through its attribution that they carry an hereditary taint. By implication those who support Paisley's vision for Northern Ireland are 'pure bred' Loyalists.

The principal affects which animate this statement are persecutory anxiety, rage and contempt, all features of the persecutory position. The main affect attributed to O'Neill and the other 'conspirators' and 'appeasers' is greed for power. The sole admitted affect is a confident, though not omnipotent, pride by Paisley in his own manifest destiny; 'the day will come when I will be in Stormont ... to root out the nest of traitors'.

As we have seen with previous examples, this persecutory position construes a split world of good and bad in which the 'other' is denied any complexity and any capacity to interact in a productive and creative manner with oneself and one's own grouping. The affective characteristics of this position also render constructive interaction unmanageable as the affects which are deployed operate to maintain the boundaries of the split world; they are characteristic of the paranoid-schizoid position discussed in chapter 4. As I have previously noted, for instance in my discussion of Elizabeth in chapter 4, the overall effect of such a construction is to maintain a set of exclusivist subjectivities which, for their integrity, rely upon the maintenance of difference. Such subjectivities, and Loyalism is one of them, involve an emotional investment, or cathexis, of exactly those constructions of 'self' and 'other' which preserve such exclusivist differences. This generates an inability to deal constructively with the 'other' for two related reasons. First, to recognise the complexity of the 'other' would be to question the bases of one's own self-identity and group-identity. Such questioning threatens the integrity of the exclusivist subject position and, as a consequence, it is experienced as a betrayal or 'appeasement'. Second, the construction of the 'other' according to the rules of the persecutory position generates an object which is seen as so hostile and treacherous that any interaction, on the basis of equal entitlement, is to be avoided and the actors and conditions which might require such interaction are to be vigorously opposed.

Paisley also draws upon the rules of the affiliative-corporate mode in his statement. The principal feature of this mode is that 'the individual human being is first of all a member of a sociopolitical grouping of an ascriptive kind and is evaluated in terms of his or her loyalty or allegiance to group norms'. In his account of why he has 'chosen jail' Paisley constructs a social and political order which is patently ascriptive; consanguinity being the explicit criterion of determining loyalty to the group. Those Unionists such as O'Neill who have constructed this social and political order according to different rules and whose actions have been organised by different forms of Unionist ideology are read as disloyal, as having betrayed group norms. They thereby have become an enemy within who must be exposed for what they are; 'the hidden things of darkness are being exposed'.

Paisley brands both O'Neill and the 'ruling junta' of the UUP as 'Lundies', thereby delivering the harshest of possible denigrations available within the Unionist lexicon. Interestingly, the distinguished historian, A. T. Q. Stewart, when discussing his concept of a 'siege mentality' (which he regards as a recurrent cultural inclination of Unionism, a concrete rule of structuration for Unionism, so to speak) says of the original Lundy:

The unfortunate Governor of Derry whose notoriety is so preserved in Protestant mythology was in no sense a traitor, but simply a prudent soldier acting in the interests of the preservation of the people under his care. He has become the archetype of those who truck with the enemy; therefore each crisis inevitably produces a new Lundy. It is not an archaic survival but a recurrent nightmare. *If Lundy had not existed, it would have been necessary to invent him.*[32]

As if to confirm Stewart's proposition, Ian Paisley reinvented Lundy from a prison cell in 1966. It is important to note that this construction pre-dated the civil rights marches and was a direct response to the crisis within traditional Unionism promoted by O'Neill's attempt to re-work Unionism as an inclusivist ideology. Those critics of O'Neill who dismiss the extent of his reforms typically overlook the significance of this ideological conflict within Unionism and thereby fail to develop an adequate account of the political process in Northern Ireland during this moment of crisis.

[32] Stewart, *The Narrow Ground*, p. 48; emphasis mine.

If O'Neill's inclusivist vision for Northern Ireland had a profoundly disturbing effect on those Unionists who regarded themselves
as Loyalists, in the 1965 election campaign the concerns of such
Loyalists were hardly on the agenda. The tenor of this campaign is
well represented by a party political broadcast which was reported in
the *Belfast Telegraph*:

'The Unionist Party is doing all it can to foster the new community spirit
that is emerging in Ulster,' said Mr. Roy Bradford, Unionist candidate for
Victoria, in a party political broadcast last night.

'Its aim was to act with malice towards none, and with charity to all, but
it would be foolish to say that this great endeavour would succeed this year
or next,' he said. *People wanted more than cries of indignation and protest, they
wanted leadership, and this did not lie along the top of a fence green on one side and
orange on the other.* (*Belfast Telegraph*, 20 November 1965; emphasis mine)

O'Neill himself took up this theme consistently. For instance, on
20 November he attacked the NILP for making the campaign an
'election of false scares and political stunts' and went on to claim:
'They are afraid to fight us on our record of achievement because in
their hearts they know that the last few years have been years of
concrete progress. Jobs, houses, hospitals, roads, agriculture; these
are the real issues of this campaign' (*Belfast Telegraph*, 20 November
1965).

Certainly, the NILP regarded itself as the unfair recipient of UUP
attentions. So much so that David Bleakley, NILP member for
Victoria, turned such attentions into a campaign issue. On 23
November he complained as follows:

'Capt. O'Neill in his latest call to drive the Labour members out of public
life had let the cat out of the bag,' said Mr. David Bleakley, Labour
candidate for Victoria.

He had made it quite clear that this had been the central aim of the
general election all along.

Even the Nationalists had been let off nearly scot-free by the Unionist machine.
Only two Nationalist seats had been fought and the P.M. rarely bothered to
mention them.

He had been prepared to leave his colleagues in these areas in the lurch
and concentrate his attention elsewhere. The real mote in his eye is the
small Labour group. (*Belfast Telegraph*, 23 November 1965; emphasis mine)

It seems that O'Neill would be damned whichever way he turned.
The irony in all this is two-fold. First, the NILP deserves considerable
credit for the steps it took towards breaking up the old patterns of
identity politics which had dominated so much of political life in

Northern Ireland and in placing a moderate, reformist Labour programme on the political agenda. But as the above indicates, the party itself was relying on the old identity politics to provide it with its rationale as the alternative. When the UUP successfully defeated its growing influence in Belfast at the 1965 election, the NILP, and the careful cross-denominational alliances upon which its support had been based, began to disintegrate. Second, it is a bitter irony of politics in Northern Ireland that the NILP eventually broke up over the issue of the opening of public facilities on a Sunday. This sabbatarian issue was one of the most traditional of all within Orange and Unionist ideology and a constant thorn in the side of better relations between Catholics and Protestants.[33] Once the NILP began to lose momentum, such traditional concerns of Unionist ideology began to re-surface; they were again drawn on in the construction of what was judged as proper.

THE 1969 CAMPAIGN: ULSTER AT THE CROSSROADS

In a sermon on 3 February 1969, the dean of Belfast, in a service at St Anne's Cathedral which was attended by the prime minister and Mrs O'Neill, spoke of the election campaign as follows:

Within the family of the Church there are people who, legitimately, have different political affiliations and who view things from different angles, but there come times when issues are of wider concern than mere party politics or sectional interests.

The enlightened and forward-looking policies which are associated with Captain O'Neill and his Government brought a breath of fresh air into the tensions which have bedevilled our community for so long. We felt we were entering a new era.

Let there be no doubt that the overthrow of the present government would endanger the pursuit of the enlightened policies – and be a return to

[33] During the 1965 election campaign the issue of the future of a major employer (of Protestants) in Belfast, the shipyard of Harland and Wolff, came under scrutiny, due to the leaking of a consultants' report into the firm which questioned its ability to diversify in order to maintain employment. As this report had been commissioned by the British Labour government, the leak carried negative implications for the NILP's claim of a special relationship with British Labour. Forced to defend his party over this matter Mr David Bleakley, Labour candidate in Victoria, replied: 'To suggest that the industry is on the rocks is *sheer disloyalty to our economy* and a very cheap way to win votes' (*Belfast Telegraph*, 22 November 1965, 1; emphasis mine). What is so striking about this rhetoric is the manner in which it turns traditional issues of loyalty and disloyalty regarding the constitutional position of Northern Ireland into a reproach regarding the economy. This highlights the manner in which NILP ideology was locked into the more traditional themes of Unionism.

the view of those who have been most vociferous against them and who would be able to claim that they could dictate, by violence and the threat of violence, the policies they want.

I do not believe the mass of people want to go back. I believe they want to see justice, tolerance and peace; they want contentment and fair play for all in our province; they want loyalty and integrity in high places, they want community responsibility as well as community rights.

I believe the policies of the present government can produce such a community and those of us who believe so must show our loyalty to them in whatever way we can and that we abhor any attempt to overthrow them. (*Belfast Telegraph*, 3 February 1969)

This endorsement of the O'Neill government highlights the fact that the 1969 election was viewed, at the time, as a watershed election. This statement is a good example of the conventional-liberal mode of Unionism and of the ambivalent position. It draws a sharp distinction between those who seek 'justice, tolerance and peace ... contentment and fair play for all in our province' and those 'who would ... dictate, by violence and the threat of violence, the policies they want'. The criterion of distinction is related to actual behaviour and not to some ascribed feature such as religion or 'blood'. Moreover the boundary between those regarded as seekers of 'justice' and those regarded as promoters of 'violence' is permeable; the category is proposed in inclusivist terms as one towards which all should aspire. The affects involved are those of hope and trust.

O'Neill himself, perhaps caught up in his own rhetoric which placed a huge emphasis on the development of roads and other infrastructure, dubbed this the 'Crossroads' election. The UUP election manifesto proclaimed as follows:

The Ulster Unionist Party believes in an Ulster in which the obligations and rights of all citizens will be fully recognised. It expects of all citizens that loyalty toward the State which is due when the institutions of that State have the expressed support of a clear majority. It seeks from every individual a proper sense of responsibility and whole hearted participation in the life of the State.

The Party acknowledges and proclaims the right of all citizens to equal treatment under the law, to full equality in the enjoyment of health, education and other social benefits and to the protection of authority against every kind of injustice.

We believe in the creation of new opportunities in which all will share; new jobs, new houses, and new economic development for all parts of the country.

The Party will work to heal those divisions in our community which have so far prevented Northern Ireland from fulfilling its best hopes ...

In all our policies we will combine firmness with fairness. We believe in the rule of the law and that no person is above the law. [Those who] seek to disrupt society and benefit from divisions they create and attempt to take the law into their own hands must be answerable to the law.

We shall resist every attempt to usurp the authority of Parliament, as to substitute the rule of force for the rule of law. Our aim will be to create the fullest confidence in our democratic system. Parliament is the centre of that system and it is in Parliament, by the process of debate and discussion, that the answers to our problems must be found. *(Belfast Telegraph*, 14 February 1969)

And in his televised election speech O'Neill stated:

You are being asked to give us a mandate for all we have been doing to make Ulster a better place to live in. You are being asked to say whether you approve of the motorways, the hospitals, the schools and universities, the houses and factories which make up the New Ulster.

But you are also being asked to take a much bigger decision. It is one which has never been put to you before at any General Election. I am asking you all to trust one another, to accept one another, to respect one another. I am asking you to put our old religious divisions aside to work together for the good of the country.

I think religion ought to be a private matter, a matter of conscience. It has bedevilled Ulster politics for far too long. Let every man worship God in his own way. And let us assume that our fellow-citizens have, for the most part, the same concerns as we do ourselves. They want a steady job. They want a decent home. They want the best for their children. They want, above all, to be allowed to live in peace.

[...] I do not believe that the man or woman who is assured of a fair deal in Northern Ireland will want to sacrifice all the benefits he or she enjoys in the United Kingdom.

I now say this clearly to you all. It is the declared and unmistakable policy of the Unionist Party that everyone shall have a fair deal in Ulster. Let there be no more hesitation about supporting the British connection. Its benefits are for all. We recognize no class of citizenship other than the first class. *(Belfast Telegraph*, 21 February 1969)

This 1969 campaign marked the breakdown of party discipline within the UUP. A party which had dominated Ulster politics from the time of partition in 1921 and which had managed to contain a broad and various spectrum of political belief, ranging from openly sectarian to cautiously liberal, now began to fall apart. The UUP was so split that all the traditional Unionist seats were contested by both a pro-O'Neill and an anti-O'Neill Unionist candidate. In many instances the prime minister and leader of the UUP endorsed an unofficial pro-O'Neill candidate against the official party candidate. In such a situation as this only the electoral process itself could, potentially, sort out a range of internal conflicts within Unionism which the Unionist party itself could no longer manage. However the electoral process failed to solve the political impasse. While O'Neill and his supporters were returned in sufficient numbers to retain the leadership of the party and the government, they received a reduced level of electoral support which began to sap away at the authority of their leadership. Within a few months O'Neill accepted the inevitable and resigned as party leader, to be replaced by his cousin, James Chichester-Clark.

A PARTY 'SPLIT IN MANY BITS'[34]

In 1968 O'Neill found himself caught between his need to respond to the civil rights claims which had been forced onto the political agenda by a series of civil rights marches and his need to retain support within the Unionist party and the electorate. He proceeded cautiously, initiating modest reforms such as a new and equitable points system for the allocation of public housing, the appointment of an ombudsman, the dissolution of the infamously gerrymandered Derry Council, a review and restriction of the Special Powers Act and a general review of the franchise.[35] At the same time he chastised the civil rights marchers, characterising the Belfast to Derry march in October of 1968 as 'a foolhardy and irresponsible undertaking' and admonishing those involved in the following terms: 'Enough is enough. We have heard sufficient for now about civil rights; let us hear a little about civic responsibility.'[36] For Loyalists, who construed the civil rights campaign and the government's reactions according to the rules of the corporate modes and the persecutory or dehumanising positions, such modest reforms were regarded as 'appeasement' and as positive proof of O'Neill's betrayal of Unionism. For the civil rights marchers, the reforms were too little and too late, and O'Neill's admonishments were regarded as stalling tactics.

Faced with an accelerating breakdown of social and political

---

[34] *News Letter*, 14 February 1969. See below for the context.
[35] J. Darby, *Conflict in Northern Ireland: The Development of a Polarised Community* (Dublin: Gill & Macmillan, 1976), p. xiii.
[36] Cited in Farrell, *Northern Ireland*, p. 251.

order, O'Neill called a snap election in 1969 in an attempt to restore his authority. It is telling that he looked to both the Unionist and Nationalist communities for support. This very fact highlights the extent to which O'Neill was experimenting with the creation of novel rules for the conduct of politics in Northern Ireland. As we have seen, the exclusivist forms of Unionist ideology had become so dominant in Northern Irish politics that in election after election from 1922 onwards most candidates were returned unopposed. However in 1969 the commodious vehicle of Unionist supremacy since the inception of the state of Northern Ireland, the UUP, itself split into pro-O'Neill and anti-O'Neill factions.

An opinion poll taken just before the election suggested that O'Neill was right in his belief that he could draw support from both communities. Published in the *Belfast Telegraph* on 13 February 1969, the Marplan survey of a random sample of 660 electors found that pro-O'Neill candidates had 'the backing of 61% of the electorate. In religious terms they are supported by 69% of Protestants and 45% of Roman Catholics'. The issue of 'paramount importance' was the maintenance of law and order. It was 'held to be "very important" by 92% of all voters'. On the issue of the pace of reform, 'more than half the electorate thinks Capt. O'Neill's pace on policies to improve civil rights has been "about right". This view is endorsed by 57% of Roman Catholics, but one Catholic in three believes the Premier to have moved "too slowly".' Amongst Unionists, only 10 per cent of the pro-O'Neill but 49 per cent of the anti-O'Neill Unionists believed that 'the speed at which Capt. O'Neill has been implementing his policies to improve civil rights' was 'too quickly'.[37]

The intensity of this election campaign can be seen from the following instance of a conflict in Coleraine between a pro-O'Neill constituency association executive and an anti-O'Neill sitting member and his local supporters:

Mr. Joseph Burns, M.P., for North Derry, was unrepentant after being rapped by his constituency association's executive ... This followed his resignation last week as assistant Government Whip and his signing of a letter calling for a change in leadership. After the no confidence resolution he told 150 of his supporters at a meeting in Coleraine Orange Hall: 'Over the past number of years our party has been getting torn apart. So I became convinced that there was only one answer: one answer for Unionism, and one answer for Northern Ireland. And that was that the

[37] *Belfast Telegraph*, 13 February 1969.

Prime Minister must go and someone else must take his place. I did not arrive at this decision overnight. I thought about this for quite a long time because my first thought was for the party.'

When Mr. Burns ended his address by saying: 'By your presence here you have shown me you are supporting me and I can assure you that in the days to come I will need your support', the crowd shouted repeatedly, 'You will get it.'

Then the meeting gave him a unanimous vote of confidence and also passed a unanimous vote of no confidence in the Prime Minister. The executive committee had met earlier in the downstairs Committee room. After their decision was announced there were rowdy scenes in the foyer outside. Supporters of Mr. Burns banged the door of the committee room and shouted 'Lundies' and 'O'Neill out'. (*Belfast Telegraph*, 3 February 1969)

Commenting after the election, Lord Brookeborough, now in retirement, was loyal to his successor but firm in his critique:

The Prime Minister did what he thought was right, but the election, to my mind, was one of the most damaging things that ever happened to the Ulster Unionist Party. I do not want to exacerbate the position. God knows, it will be nearly impossible to get things back to normal. *The party is not only split in half, but split in many bits.* I am not bitter, but I am merely stating facts as I see them. (*News Letter*, 14 February 1969; emphasis mine)

Despite the overwhelming support which O'Neill had received going into this election campaign, by the time it was over his own support within his constituency and the support for pro-O'Neill candidates throughout the province was greatly reduced. In Bannside O'Neill received only 29 per cent of first preferences. Paisley, his principal opponent, received 24 per cent of first preferences. Throughout the province, in the twenty-three constituencies contested by both pro-O'Neill and anti-O'Neill candidates, the pro-O'Neill candidates won eleven seats and the anti-O'Neill candidates won twelve.[38] It is in the aftermath of this election campaign that we can most clearly see the sharp conflict over which rules were to be dominant in the structuration of political life in Northern Ireland.

[38]   Farrell, *Northern Ireland*, pp. 253–54.

CHAPTER 8

Crisis and the structuration of Unionist ideology, 1969–1975

I walked through the Falls to school every day and I know these people. They're very generous, on both sides. The man on the Shankill resents being called a bigot, even though he may sometimes act like one. But if you give him an opportunity where you don't hassle him, don't frighten him and don't fill him full of fear, you make him a generous and magnanimous man ... If you frighten a people, and knock their confidence, it doesn't make them reasonable. It makes them absolutely unreasonable.

(Robert McCartney interviewed by Barry White, *Belfast Telegraph*, 11 December 1981)

In this chapter I will explore the structuration of Unionist ideology in the period from 1969 to 1975. First, I will trace the unfolding political and civil crisis in Northern Ireland in the period from the introduction of British troops in August 1969 until the events of Bloody Sunday in January 1972. My intention in this discussion is to explore the structuration of Unionist ideology, and the changing internal differentiation within Unionist ideology, during a period in which, broadly speaking, Unionism can be seen to have consolidated around exclusivist forms. This consolidation prepared the ground for Unionism's most startling political achievement since the commencement of the 'troubles'; the successful Ulster Workers' Council (UWC) strike in May 1974, a general strike which, even with the presence of the British army on the streets of Northern Ireland, succeeded in defeating British policy by causing the collapse of the cross-community power-sharing executive and the restoration of direct rule from Westminster.[1] In this discussion I will also attend to the structuration of Nationalist ideology over this period up until 1972. The events of

---

[1]   The power-sharing executive consisted of six Unionist, four SDLP (i.e. nationalist) and one Alliance member.

Bloody Sunday will be treated as the fulcrum around which this discussion will swing.

Secondly, I will focus on two new Unionist groupings which formed in the early 1970s: Vanguard, which formed just after Bloody Sunday in February 1972, and the Democratic Unionist Party (DUP), which formed in October 1971. I do not intend to develop a detailed descriptive history of these two groupings, although I will need to briefly cover certain aspects of the same. Rather, I intend to explore the characteristic forms through which each of these groupings constructed the social and political process in Northern Ireland in the period from 1972 until 1975. In doing this I will pay particular attention to the Vanguard movement, for reasons which will become apparent as I proceed. Thirdly, I will consider a case of what I term 'breaking the rules from the inside'. In 1975 William Craig, the Vanguard leader and a Unionist with impeccable loyalist credentials, attempted to institute a voluntary power-sharing agreement with the nationalist SDLP and immediately found himself beyond the pale within the United Ulster Unionist Coalition (UUUC), of which he was the nominated leader.

The dimensions of the unfolding crisis in Northern Ireland can be indicated in a variety of ways. Table 1 of official statistics gives one such indication.

The various changes to the organisation of policing, politics and government in Northern Ireland over this time period also indicate

Table 1 *Statistics regarding violence in Northern Ireland, 1970–1974*

	1970	1971	1972	1973	1974
Shootings	213	1,756	10,628	5,018	3,206
Explosions	153	1,022	1,382	978	3,206
Deaths: Army & Police	2	59	146	79	50
Deaths: Civilian	23	115	322	171	166
Injuries: Army & Police	811	707	1,044	839	718
Injuries: Civilian	(no figures)	1,800	3,813	1,812	1,680
Houses Searched	3,107	17,262	36,617	74,556	71,914

Source: J. Darby, *Conflict in Northern Ireland*, p. xix.

the scope of the crisis. *Policing:* On 15 August, 1969, British army troops were introduced into Belfast in an attempt to restore public order and to protect the citizenry, especially Catholic citizens living in the Falls district of Belfast. Later the same year the disarming of the Royal Ulster Constabulary (RUC) and the disbanding of the B-Specials (the Ulster Special Constabulary, a police reserve composed almost entirely of Unionists) was announced. In 1971 internment without trial was introduced and was retained until 1975. *Political Parties:* In 1970 the liberal-Unionist Alliance party and the liberal-nationalist Social Democratic and Labour Party were formed. In 1971 the Democratic Unionist Party was formed and in 1972 the Ulster Vanguard movement was formed. In 1973 the Vanguard Unionist Party grew out of the Vanguard movement. In 1974 Brian Faulkner, previously leader of the UUP, established the Unionist Party of Northern Ireland. *Government:* On 24 March 1972, following Brian Faulkner's refusal to accept, as premier of Northern Ireland, 'that the responsibility of law and order in Northern Ireland should be transferred to Westminster', the United Kingdom prime minister, Edward Heath, prorogued the Stormont parliament 'until a political solution of the problems of the province can be worked out in consultation with all those concerned'.[2] In 1973, under the direction of Westminster, and its secretary of state for Northern Ireland, William Whitelaw, a Northern Ireland Assembly was elected and a power-sharing executive was formed, in which representatives of the UUP, the SDLP and Alliance shared power. A tripartite conference between the UK, Ireland and representatives of the Northern Ireland Assembly was held at Sunningdale and recommended closer and formal ties (a Council of Ireland) between the Republic and Northern Ireland. In 1974 the Ulster Workers' Council general strike succeeded in destroying the power-sharing executive, which collapsed on 28 May with the effect of restoring direct rule from Westminster. In May 1975 the government conducted further elections, this time to a Northern Ireland Constitutional Assembly.

These facts and figures establish the profound character of the changes which occurred in Northern Ireland over this five to six year period, and, of course, these have been noted in numerous studies.

[2]   House of Commons Debates, 5th series, vol. 833, cols. 1859–1861 (24 March 1972). Cited in A. C. Hepburn, *The Conflict of Nationality in Modern Ireland* (London: Edward Arnold, 1980), p. 208.

My intention is to look closely at the rules of structuration which were drawn upon by a variety of Unionist political actors in an attempt to better understand the character of this crisis within Unionism.

A PERVERSE MULTIPLIER EFFECT AND THE 'DRIFT' TO EXCLUSIVISM

From late in 1968 the divided society of Northern Ireland became, as well, an increasingly violent one. Fierce repression of the civil rights marches by the RUC; the disintegration and destruction of 'mixed' areas of housing (i.e. areas in which Unionists and Nationalists lived contiguously) in Belfast and elsewhere; the continual presence (from August 1969) of armed British troops on the streets; the intensification of various 'policing' activities such as house searching and internment; the murderous activities of the various paramilitary groupings; the everyday spectacle of rowdy demonstrations, with petrol-bombs and rubber bullets as symbol and substance of violent confrontation; all these signs marked a society in crisis. Both the Nationalist/Catholic and the Unionist/Protestant communities were confronted with a complex and confusing situation which they had to make sense of as best they could. So long as both communities held to exclusivist rules for the construction of these complex and disturbing phenomena they could be certain of both their own identity and the source of the mayhem surrounding them. They were a corporate group confronted by an implacable enemy. For Unionists this enemy was trying to destroy their very identity and way of life; for Nationalists the enemy was trying to continue with its regime of oppression and discrimination while denying to them their national identity. At the same time, for so long as both communities continued to rely on exclusivist rules they remained locked into a perverse spiral. In drawing upon such exclusivist rules for the structuration of both subjectivity and intersubjectivity both communities assured the re-production of these rules. Actions and interpretations which were exclusivist in form returned, in the next moment, as the rules for the organisation of both subjectivity and intersubjectivity.

Given the deep-rootedness of such exclusivist rules it should come as no surprise that plural or divided society interpretations of the political and social process in Northern Ireland tend to predominate in the interpretative literature.[3] Although the political and social process in Northern Ireland is open, and contingent upon action, such action tends to be organised by the exclusivist rules of structuration; and this is especially so at moments of crisis. Consequently, for Northern Ireland and like societies, pluralism theory is a good predictor of outcomes, although it lacks the capacity to observe and analyse processes. Indeed, as we have seen already, there were groupings associated with both communities which were attempting to make a difference by institutionalising inclusivist rules; thereby beginning to change the forms of subjectivity and intersubjectivity routinely available in Northern Ireland. These liberal groupings, principally the O'Neillites and the civil rights movement, were in no sense pure cultures; in part they continued to carry within them the very exclusivist forms they hoped to eradicate. Furthermore, apart from responding to their actual features, it was always open to one community, or sections of it, to read the other community solely through exclusivist forms. For one, given the mixed, rather than pure, culture of the liberalising movements, these movements always contained features which could be construed as 'evidence' of their implacable and hostile difference. Second, even in the absence of actual evidence, the exclusivist forms of both Unionism and Nationalism could successfully read events and the actions of others so that they conformed to the already established pre-understandings. Further, within the nominal groupings of Nationalism or Unionism it was always open to read the actions of the liberal sections of one's own nominal grouping by drawing on exclusivist rules; thereby seeing them as traitorous, deceitful or naive. In a society in which, for fifty years and more, the dominant rules of subjectivity and intersubjectivity in both communities were exclusivist and in which threats to the identity of both communities were apparently perennial (itself a product of the dominance of exclusivist rules), the breaking of the traditional rules was inevitably fraught with conflict and the possibility of systematically distorted readings. In this section of my discussion I will focus on one significant event, the killings in Derry on Bloody Sunday in January 1972, and on the various readings of this event and the ways in which these readings fed into the structuration of political relations in Northern Ireland. I will do so in an attempt to explore the dynamics of a shift within Unionism

---

[3] Again, as explained in chapter 1, this pluralism or divided society paradigm is quite distinct from the pluralist democratic theory developed by such writers as Robert Dahl.

to the reassertion of the 'proper' dominance of exclusivist identities and patterns of relationship. We will see how this shift occurred both within the Unionist community, broadly conceived, and within the UUP as it tried to hold onto its mantle as the traditional Unionist party, while negotiating the dynamics of a political system in crisis. I begin by filling in some essential background.

The arrival of British troops in Northern Ireland in August 1969 created a new situation for all groupings, including the UK government. These new arrangements were rife with ambiguity, as they involved both the maintenance of the Stormont regime and the transfer of principal, though not total, responsibility for security to the UK government. Within the Nationalist/Catholic community we can trace two major effects of the heightened UK involvement: the formation of both the SDLP and the Provisional IRA.[4] While both were committed to the achievement of a United Ireland, these two organisations drew on quite distinct rules in constructing their own identity, their role within Northern Ireland, their relationship to Unionism and Unionists, their relationship to Britain and their judgement regarding the appropriate means by which the cause of a united Ireland should be pursued. The Provisionals drew on exclusivist rules to construe all of the above and hence their opposition to both Unionism and the union with Britain was organised in terms of corporate criteria. The SDLP, a party which formed in August 1970, while not inoculated against the occasional reliance on corporate rules, attempted to develop and institutionalise within the Nationalist community a conception of the above roles, relationships and appropriate means which was organised by inclusivist rules (i.e. liberal and ambivalent). As a party of reform with a Nationalist constituency, the SDLP was committed to both the institutionalisation of inclusivist rules within Northern Ireland and the promotion of a united Ireland through political means which themselves were organised in an inclusivist form. The effect of this was to accord the

---

[4]   Of course I am not claiming that the involvement of British troops was the sole determinant of the formation of these two groupings, only that it was a principal and precipitating one. Another proximate effect of significance was the splitting of the civil rights movement in 1970. See B. Purdie, *Politics in the Streets* (Belfast: Blackstaff Press, 1990), for more on this. For more on the formation of the SDLP see I. McAllister, *The Northern Ireland Social Democratic and Labour Party: political opposition in a divided society* (London: Macmillan Press, 1977), passim. In preparing this discussion of the structuration of Nationalist ideology I have drawn upon research notes prepared for me, under supervision, by Peter Collins, formerly an undergraduate student of mine. I wish to thank Mr Collins for his careful research assistance.

Unionist community a legitimate role in any negotiations regarding a united Ireland and to respect their status as a majority within Northern Ireland. As we will see, unfolding events made this inclusivist vision a difficult one to sustain.

For Unionists also, British intervention was problematic and led to an accentuation of internal differences. The disbandment of the B-Specials, which accompanied the arrival of British troops, was taken by many Unionists, drawing on exclusivist rules, as a sure sign that they had been betrayed and left defenceless. They read the disbanding of the B Specials as a punishment and betrayal for past loyalty; i.e. as an unwarranted taking from them of their, assumed, 'proper' right to differential protection by representatives of their own group. They had been stripped of their last bulwark against 'terror' and left subject to an ineffective (i.e. more impartial) form of policing. Westminster was no longer trustworthy and, with the re-emergence of the IRA in its Provisional form, the civil rights movement was, purportedly, exposed for what it had always been; a front for Republicanism. Unionism was split and found itself engaged in an internal conflict regarding the proper rules for ordering subjectivity and intersubjectivity. For both communities in Northern Ireland, Bloody Sunday became a critical moment in this political conflict.

The march in Derry on 30 January 1972 followed approximately six months after the shooting, also in Derry and also by the British army, of two young men on 7 July 1971. Concerned that these shootings were a direct consequence of Prime Minister Faulkner's advocacy of 'shooting with effect', the SDLP demanded an official inquiry.[5] After British refusal to grant such an inquiry, the SDLP withdrew from the Stormont parliament and announced a new campaign of civil disobedience. Within Stormont, this withdrawal was met with clear hostility. So, the minister with special responsibility for overseeing law and order, John Taylor, stated on 20 July that it may prove 'necessary for more people to be shot on the streets'.[6] On the basis of this experience the SDLP demanded the abolition of Stormont as a prerequisite to its further involvement in formal political institutions.

A few weeks later, on 9 August 1971, Brian Faulkner and his government requested the British army to implement an internment

[5] *Irish Times*, 9 July 1971, p. 1.
[6] *Irish Times*, 21 July 1971.

policy in which, in the first instance, approximately 300 suspects were 'lifted'; the vast majority of them from the Nationalist/Catholic community. During this exercise the army often acted on highly questionable 'intelligence'. The fact that they tried to intern several people who were long dead and one man who had been involved in the IRA campaign of 1920–1, and was currently in his nineties, threw great doubt over the accuracy of the information upon which they acted in all cases.[7]

As was to be expected, this policy of internment drew hostile responses from both the SDLP and the Provisionals. However the rules which organised these two responses were quite different. For the SDLP the policy of internment indicated the final bankruptcy of the Stormont regime. It also demonstrated British commitment to the maintenance of an overtly oppressive institution. Drawing on the liberal modes the SDLP read internment as political repression, the arbitrary and particularist employment of oppressive laws. They constructed their campaign of dissent in liberal forms. Continuing to advocate non-violence, they extended the civil disobedience campaign which they had renewed after their withdrawal from Stormont in July. In the following terms they called on civil servants to resign and announced a 'rent and rates' strike against local government institutions:

We call on all who hold public positions in Northern Ireland, whether elected or appointed, to express their opposition by immediately withdrawing from those positions and to announce their withdrawal publicly and without delay ... We call on the general public to participate in this protest by immediately withholding all rent and rates. We expect one hundred percent support from all opponents of internment ...[8]

This call to Nationalists by the SDLP is a good example of the 'mixed' culture which the SDLP drew upon at such moments. While I have already noted the liberal character of its response to intern-

---

7   McAllister, in his excellent history of the SDLP, writes regarding internment: 'To many Catholics internment appeared not as a carefully planned and executed military operation against the IRA, but a punitive expedition against their community. As the stories of ill-treatment began to filter back, Catholics closed ranks around the single issue of internment. The raw statistics of violence before and after internment have been frequently quoted, but they attest directly to its failure. In the six months preceding August there were 288 explosions; in the succeeding six months, this increased three-fold. In the same two periods, shooting incidents multiplied six-fold, security forces deaths four-fold and civilian deaths over eight-fold, respectively.' McAllister, *The Northern Ireland Social Democratic and Labour Party*, p. 99.
8   Quoted in ibid., p. 100.

ment, the above statement revives, at the same time, a traditional Nationalist policy of abstention and non-cooperation with the state; a policy which, to a varying extent, remained the hallmark of the Nationalist movement and the Nationalist party from the inception of the Northern Ireland state until the O'Neill period. There is also a hint of intimidation in the final sentence quoted above. However, the SDLP did, in the main, construe this abstentionist policy differently. As we will see below, one major instance of this replaying of traditional Nationalist tactics within a new liberal form was the SDLP's establishment of an alternative assembly for 'non-Unionists'.

Republican News, a publication of the Provisionals, drew on exclusivist forms to construct its reading of internment. Internment was characterised as 'genocidal' and as a 'rape' of the North. Both Stormont and Britain had acted 'with a cold blooded ruthlessness that could do justice to Adolf Hitler or Mussolini'. Their agents, the British army, purportedly committed numerous 'atrocities' and were 'pillaging, murdering, [and] wantonly destroying all that lay in their path'.[9] The Provisionals demanded an all-Ireland Republic and claimed that 'things have now gone beyond the stage of civil rights. National rights is now the demand.'[10]

In contra-distinction, even after internment the SDLP continued to construe Northern Ireland in inclusivist forms. The party and its followers developed the civil disobedience campaign and criticised the Provisionals' exclusivist constructions, especially their claim that violence was a justified means for the self-defence of the Nationalist grouping. In these criticisms of the Provisionals (and the less central Official IRA) the SDLP was joined by liberal leaders within the Catholic Church. At this time the Unionist prime minister, Brian Faulkner called for an end to 'equivocation about the IRA ... and the profound evil it represents'.[11] This call was answered by a pastoral letter from the Bishops of Ireland (i.e. Northern Ireland and the Republic) in which they stated that 'we condemn the violence and the vicious evil of intimidation from whatever source and on whatever side'.[12]

As well as condemning violence, those Nationalists drawing on inclusivist rules to construe the complexities of Northern Ireland

[9] *Republican News*, August 1971, pp. 1, 12.
[10] *An Phoblacht*, September 1971, p. 9.
[11] *Irish Times*, 4 September 1971, p. 5.
[12] *Irish Times*, 13 September 1971, p. 1.

were able to face the reality of the 1 million Unionists in their society
who would not go away. Hence, while maintaining their long-term
commitment to a United Ireland, they insisted upon the necessity of
gaining the consent of Unionists to any changed political arrangements. They also turned to consociational models as a way of
breaking the old exclusivist impasse. So the SDLP declared that
'mathematical "majority rule" (either Unionist or Nationalist) simply
does not work in a community of this kind'.[13] By so doing they
committed themselves to an interim solution which addressed in an
inclusivist form the so-called 'double minority' dilemma confronting
the establishment of 'normal' politics in Northern Ireland. If Nationalists were excluded from power because they formed an exclusivist
community which was in a numerical minority, Unionists feared a
similar minority status within a united Ireland. By extending their
critique of 'mathematical majority rule' beyond the Northern
Ireland boundaries the SDLP committed itself to a consociational
model for the whole of Ireland which, in their understanding, would
facilitate the breakdown of exclusivist identities and politics.

As noted above, on 26 October 1971 the SDLP convened an
alternative Assembly for the 'non-Unionist' community in Northern
Ireland. As McAllister notes, a 'major condition of membership' was
a preparedness to give written assent to the first three articles of the
Assembly's Constitution. These articles were as follows:

Article One: the Assembly of the Northern Irish People is the principal
representative body of the non-Unionist community in Northern Ireland.
Article Two: pending the peaceful reunification of the country, the Assembly
shall work towards the objective of obtaining equality of treatment for
everyone in Northern Ireland, irrespective of political views or religion.
Article Three: the Assembly shall pursue this objective by non-violent
means.[14]

As will be apparent, Articles Two and Three underline the distinction I have made between the SDLP and the IRA.

Of further interest in this regard are the discussions within both
the SDLP and the Assembly regarding Article Two. At the SDLP's
annual conference, held in Dungiven on 24 October 1971, a
motion was put by the Derry City and Foyle branch to change the
article in the party's constitution which read that the promotion of
the cause of Irish unity should be 'based on the consent of the

13   *Irish Times*, 13 September 1971, p. 7.
14   McAllister, *The Northern Ireland Social Democratic and Labour Party*, p. 105.

majority of people in Northern Ireland'. It was proposed that this article (clause 2, section 4) should be changed to read that the promotion of the cause of Irish unity should be 'based on the consent of people in Northern Ireland and the Republic of Ireland'. After discussion, this motion was withdrawn.[15] To have supported such a motion would have involved the effective denial of any legitimate role for Unionists in any discussions or referenda regarding the future of Northern Ireland. For the SDLP it would have involved a move back to a more traditional, exclusivist Nationalist tradition. Instead inclusivist Nationalism moved in the opposite direction. Only a few days after the defeat of the above motion, the first Assembly of the Northern Irish People met in Dungiven Castle. At this meeting on 24 October Article Two above was discussed. It was eventually agreed to change the wording from 'pending the peaceful reunification of the country' to 'without prejudice to our ultimate objective of the reunification of Ireland'.[16] This modest change signalled a preparedness to work within inclusivist institutions in Northern Ireland and to bracket the objective of a united Ireland indefinitely.

This principled pursuit of a liberal direction produced very positive results for the SDLP. They were rewarded by both Harold Wilson, the leader of the Labour opposition at Westminster, and Edward Heath, the Conservative prime minister, in the following terms. Wilson called for an end to internment and sanctioned a united Ireland as a possible long-term 'solution' to the Troubles. Heath agreed, adding: 'It is legitimate that they (the SDLP) should seek to further that aim by democratic and constitutional means. If at some future date the majority of the north want unification and express that desire in the appropriate constitutional manner I do not believe the British government would stand in their way.'[17] This was the first occasion on which a British prime minister had given substantial support to the possibility of a united Ireland under 'appropriate' circumstances.

In the climate created by the above and like statements by the British government, inclusivist forms began to set the agenda for political debate within the Nationalist/Catholic community. The SDLP reasserted its total rejection of violence as a legitimate means

[15] *Irish Times*, 25 October 1971, p. 5.
[16] *Irish Times*, 27 October 1971, pp. 1, 11.
[17] *Irish Times*, 19 November 1971, p. 1.

for pursuing the object of a united Ireland.[18] The Catholic Church condemned the IRA's December bombing campaign in unambiguous terms by stating: 'do not call evil by any other name ... the man who takes an innocent life is committing a crime ... whatever side he is on'.[19] However, the New Year was to witness, within the Nationalist/Catholic community, a rapid erosion of this new-found opening for inclusivist forms of Nationalism. The event that precipitated this erosion was to become known, within the Nationalist community, as Bloody Sunday.

On 30 January 1972, thirteen people were killed, and another thirteen wounded, by the British army's 1st Battalion of the Parachute Regiment during a protest march through the streets of Derry.[20] Opinions vary as to whether the troops acted with or without provocation, and it is not my intention to make any particular judgement here.[21] Rather, as I indicated above, I intend to explore the various constructions of this event and the ways in which these constructions fed back into the structuration of political relations in Northern Ireland.

For the Northern Ireland Civil Rights Association (NICRA) there was a 'qualitative difference' between Bloody Sunday and anything that had 'occurred to date in the struggle for civil rights and democracy in Northern Ireland. The 1969 attempted pogrom was not ordered or directed by the British government. This massacre was.'[22] The NICRA publication, *Civil Rights*, declared that, 'Those marching in Derry ... were marching to open the gates of concentra-

---

[18]   *Irish Times*, 16 December 1971, p. 1.

[19]   *Irish Times*, 28 November 1971, p. 13.

[20]   All such marches had been prohibited in August 1971, after the introduction of internment.

[21]   Two such judgements made close to the event are worth recording. The British government ordered a public inquiry into the events to be conducted by Lord Chief Justice Widgery. In one of its conclusions this inquiry found as follows: '(10) None of the deceased or wounded is proved to have been shot whilst handling a firearm or bomb. Some are wholly acquitted of complicity in such action; but there is a strong suspicion that some others had been firing weapons or handling bombs in the course of the afternoon and that yet others had been closely supporting them.' The Londonderry City Coroner, Major Hubert O'Neill, said at the end of the Inquest on the thirteen deaths, on 21 August 1973: 'It strikes me that the Army ran amok that day and they shot without thinking of what they were doing. They were shooting innocent people. These people may have been taking part in a parade that was banned – but I don't think that justifies the firing of live rounds indiscriminately. I say it without reservation – it was sheer unadulterated murder.' Both quotations are taken from T. Downing, ed., *The Troubles* (London: Maxwell and Co., 1980), p. 163.

[22]   *Massacre At Derry*, Northern Ireland Civil Rights Association, 1972, p. 1.

tion camps, smash torture chambers, end repression and military terror.'[23] McAllister comments that, 'Many of the Catholics remaining in public service withdrew, particularly in the legal profession.'[24] He quotes one barrister who commented 'many of us stayed on, even after internment, but for nearly all of us Sunday in Derry is the end'.[25] Finally, Maurice Hayes, a very prominent liberal Nationalist/Catholic who held the position of chairman of the Community Relations Commission resigned on 9 February, citing the prevailing security policies as his reason.[26]

Speaking in the House of Commons on Monday, 31 January, the SDLP founding leader, Gerry Fitt, raised the most traditional of questions in its new version: 'What is the difference between a backlash from the Protestants and a backlash from the paratroopers?' The proceedings witnessed a physical attack in the parliamentary chamber upon the British home secretary, Maudling, by Bernadette Devlin, the member for Mid-Ulster, involving the slapping of Maudling's face and the pulling of his hair. The *Irish Times* reported these proceedings as follows:

While the Home Secretary was being questioned on his statement on the Derry Massacre Miss Devlin rose on a point of order to say she was the only person in the House who had been present in Derry. 'I have a right', she said, 'to ask a question of that murdering hypocrite.' As the Speaker of the House ... was saying that she had no such right, she left her place on an opposition back bench and ran down the gangway shouting: 'If I am not allowed to inform the House of what I know, I'll inform Mr. Maudling of what I feel.' She then launched herself, a tiny furious figure, upon the rotund mass of the Home Secretary on the Government front bench.

[Later, in debate] Miss Devlin said there were at least 15,000 'unarmed, peaceful civilians' at the demonstration. They had been perfectly well aware that there was a ban on parades but were quite prepared to be singled out by the authorities and if need be face the six months mandatory jail sentence.

'*None of them had been informed that overnight the death penalty had been imposed for breaking the ban on marches in Northern Ireland.*'[27]

If Bernadette Devlin was outraged by Bloody Sunday, Gerry Fitt was profoundly shocked. Speaking after Devlin in the House of Commons he began by agreeing 'with all vehemence at my

[23] *Civil Rights*, no. 1, 10 March 1972, p. 1.
[24] McAllister, *The Northern Ireland Social Democratic and Labour Party*, p. 110.
[25] Ibid., p. 110.
[26] Ibid., p. 110.
[27] *Irish Times*, 1 February 1972, pp. 1, 6. Emphasis mine.

command with every single sentence uttered by Miss Devlin'. He continued:

'*What happened last Sunday has dramatically changed the whole political outlook. Until Sunday, I regarded myself as a man of moderation in Northern Ireland* as I have consistently condemned violence. I condemn the violence of the British Army meted out to the people of Londonderry last Sunday.'

When several Conservative back-benchers protested Mr. Fitt shouted: 'I realise more and more as the debate progresses that I am an Irishman, and you are Englishmen. You have no understanding, no sympathy, and no conscience for the people who live in Londonderry.'

Mr. Fitt claimed that a political solution which may have applied last Saturday would no longer be acceptable. 'May I tell the Home Secretary in all seriousness what is happening in Ireland at this moment. There is an upsurge of national fervour and national awareness throughout the 32 counties that has not existed since our country was so unnaturally partitioned.'

Mr. Fitt said that some time ago he had said in the Commons that it would be 'a disaster' if the British Army were taken out of Northern Ireland. There would be a Protestant backlash, and the Catholic community would be threatened.

But today the people of Belfast and Derry are saying, 'what is the difference between a backlash from the Protestants and a backlash from the paratroopers?'

'The British Army is no longer welcome or acceptable in Northern Ireland. They are seen as acting in support of a discredited and corrupt Unionist Government.'[28]

In these examples we see the way in which a dramatic and tragic event involving the British army in the streets of Derry could undermine the inclusivist forms of Nationalism as the more traditional exclusivist forms were relied upon in the moment of crisis. Both Devlin and Fitt had been active in the civil rights movement and Fitt, in particular, had attempted to promote and institutionalise inclusivist Nationalism in Northern Ireland in a manner which fully recognised the requirement of accommodating, in so far as was consistent with his ultimate preference for a united Ireland achieved by peaceful and democratic means, the aspirations and interests of Unionism. However, in the heady atmosphere following Bloody Sunday the requirements of one's own emotional investments in a particular identity and history tended to promote exclusivist readings of unfolding events.

For exclusivist nationalism Bloody Sunday held no such surprises,

[28]   *Irish Times*, 1 February 1972, p. 6. Emphasis mine.

disappointments nor causes for a change of heart. Rather, for the Provisional IRA Bloody Sunday was 'the truth in pictures'.[29] 'British rule in north-east Ulster rests on the bayonet and has continually since the partition of Ireland 50 years ago', declared *An Phoblacht*, repeating an Irish Republican Publicity Bureau pamphlet produced after Bloody Sunday.[30] For these Nationalist groupings, which routinely drew upon exclusivist forms for the construction of subjectivity and intersubjectivity in 'north-east Ulster', the killings in Derry were neither a shock nor a disappointment; they were merely another event in a relentless, on-going colonisation and repression of the Irish by the 'Brits' and their Unionist surrogates.

For Unionists, Bloody Sunday highlighted the profound crisis in which they found themselves; Northern Ireland was beginning to appear ungovernable and the proroguing of the Stormont parliament seemed imminent. The crisis produced a variety of readings of the recent events. Ivan Cooper, the Alliance Party chairman, was reported as follows:

'Last Sunday, which saw the death of 13 people in Derry, must spell the end of the line for the hard-line security policy ... for three years these people have been preaching the necessity for getting tough, shooting on sight, teaching the Catholics a lesson and sorting out the "no go" areas. The Catholics have certainly been taught a lesson, and the Derry deaths in January 1972 now rank with internment in August 1971 and the Lower Falls curfew of 1970 as milestones in the creation and expansion of the I.R.A. All these milestones were examples of the British lapping up hardline Unionist propaganda.'

Mr. Cooper said that those responsible for British Government policy had, by these three events, recruited more members for the IRA than the whole efforts of all the IRA leaders. He went on: 'the hardline Unionists wanted to see an end to "no go" areas. No state can tolerate such areas. But a "no go" area is not simply one where the security forces do not operate. It is also an area which is alienated from the community. 'Thanks to the hardline Unionist policy of playing into the hands of the IRA, much of Northern Ireland now consists of "no go" areas, and they will remain 'no go' areas even if they are saturated with troops and police.'

He added: 'The only way in which the "no go" mentality can be broken down is by a security policy which does not alienate the entire Catholic population, and political initiatives designed to bring about reconciliation.' *(Irish Times*, 4 February 1972)

This is a very clear example of what I have termed the post-

---

[29] *Republican News*, 6 February 1972, p. 1.
[30] *An Phoblacht*, February 1972, p. 12.

conventional-liberal mode of ideology.[31] In his statement Ivan Neill steps back from the immediate situation and any simple prescriptions about the maintenance of law and order. Instead he reflects in a critical manner on the conditions which have produced segregation and alienation in Northern Ireland. Rather than seeing the IRA as some trans-historical force of malevolence yet again wreaking havoc in Northern Ireland, he draws attention to the 'hard-line' governmental policies which, he argues, have created conditions within the Nationalist/Catholic community which account for the growing support for the IRA. Further, throughout he maintains a categorical distinction between the Nationalist/Catholic community, on the one hand, and the IRA on the other. Both individuals and groups are assessed in terms of the particular, contingent circumstances in which they find themselves and the particular actions they perform. The sliding of the signifier 'Nationalist or 'Roman Catholic' into the signifier 'rebel' or 'terrorist', or some more dehumanising signifier such as 'vermin' and the like, does not occur. Indeed distinctions are made in such a way as to thoroughly displace even the possibility of such sliding or confusion, a characteristic which is not always so evident with the conventional-liberal mode of Unionism.

These post-conventional-liberal features stand out quite clearly if we consider other Unionist responses to Bloody Sunday. Ian Paisley responded in his characteristic manner when he declared that the march was further proof that there was a 'conspiracy against Northern Ireland behind which the Roman Catholic Church was taking the stand it had always taken: favouring an all Ireland Republic'.[32] William Craig, just prior to the formation of the Vanguard movement, stated that those who had organised the march had wanted violence.[33] As I will elaborate below, both these statements, brief as they are, are consistent with the characteristic forms through which Paisley and Craig constructed subjectivity and intersubjectivity in Northern Ireland. In Paisley's case Bloody Sunday reduces to yet another conspiracy. The Nationalist/Catholic community is eclipsed as the signifiers 'conspiracy' and 'Roman Catholic Church' fill out the full dimensions of what is to be thought and felt about the shootings in all their complexity. For Craig the actions of the troops are ignored as are the grief and outrage of the

---

[31] See chapter 5.
[32] *Irish Times*, 4 February 1972, p. 9.
[33] *Irish Times*, 2 February 1972, p. 8.

Nationalist/Catholic community. In his case the extent of what is pertinent is exhausted by the presumption that the organisers wanted violence and the knowledge that they received violence.

The *Loyalist News*, also discussed below, drew on dehumanising and instrumental-corporate rules to celebrate the killings quite explicitly:

Protestant View

No sympathy ... with the families of the rebels who were killed in Londonderry last Sunday. Now is the time for the Protestants of Ulster to realise who is against the state of Northern Ireland ... in these past few days new heads are to be counted. We have the woeful cries of the Roman priests; 'I was there' said one ... in an unlawful parade ... fine example for his calling. 'I stood beside a paratrooper ... I was three yards from him' said another, imploring him to stop the shooting.

What really did happen was – the usual I.R.A. tactics were employed ... youths and children to lure the soldiers into ambush ... only this time the paras were too quick for them. The C.R. (Civil Rights) and all the supporting cast of rebels shout about indiscriminate firing into a crowd of peace loving rebels of all ages, shapes and sizes in an illegal march, WHY was there no women and children shot dead?

There were two great surprises in Londonderry last Sunday, the first one was to Protestants that the army actually did fire 'live' bullets instead of the usual 'rubber ones and to the 'rebels' *who did not expect the army to shoot to kill.* We have information that one of the 'rebels' alleged to have been shot on Sunday, had met his Waterloo two days earlier ... no bread vans were available to take his carcase away, so now he gets 'national honours.'

NOW WE ASK ... WHAT IF IT HAD BEEN 13 PARAS DEAD. Would the priests, C.R.A., G.A.A., Alliance Party and the Law Society been so quick to condemn the 'rebel scum'. What about all the murders that has been committed in the name of 'so called freedom for Ireland'?

As we have said in these columns before, we are not hypercritic's [sic] and we only reiterate what thousands of Protestants ... all say ... in every part of the Province, to quote a few:

'Not enough of them dead'
'About time the army shot a few'
'That will teach them'
'13 unlucky for some'
'A taste of their own medicine'
'When the "Prods" get at them again there will be far more'
'It couldn't have happened to nicer people'
'Were the army short of ammo?'
(*Loyalist News*, 5 February 1972; emphasis mine)

This statement is clearly both dehumanising and corporate in form.

It relies on mechanisms of splitting and projection, it patently construes nationalists as part-objects and it identifies the various groupings involved in the events of Bloody Sunday and their aftermath as belonging to one or another corporate group; us or them.

Interviewed on Radio Eireann on 5 March 1972, two weeks prior to his 'liquidate the enemy' speech discussed above and one month after Bloody Sunday, William Craig was asked: 'Would this mean killing all Catholics in Ulster?' In a reply which harked back to to the situation in the 1920s, and Basil Brooke's statements in the 1930s, Craig replied:

It might not go as far as that but it could go as far as killing. It would be similar to the situation in the 1920s where Roman Catholics identified in Republican rebellion could find themselves unwelcome in their place of work and under pressure to leave their homes.[34]

It is evident that, as within Nationalism, within Unionism the events of Bloody Sunday gave rise to a polarisation and hardening of dominant Loyalist exclusivism, paralleled by a sharpness of critical vision within those marginal Unionist groupings, of which Alliance is the principal example, which continued to construe events in inclusivist forms. Within both communities the unfolding political process was tending towards the re-production of exclusivist forms of subjectivity and intersubjectivity.

VANGUARD: REASSERTING THE ORDER OF THINGS

Faced with serious civil disturbance promoted by both the Civil Rights marches and the reactions amongst Loyalists which these marches provoked, in December 1968 O'Neill went on television to appeal to the people of Northern Ireland for support of his modest, reformist programme. In his famous 'Ulster Stands at the Crossroads' speech he emphasised the financial and economic reliance of Northern Ireland upon Westminster and insisted that the Government of Ireland Act of 1920 gave supreme authority to the Westminster parliament.[35] The Stormont parliament was a devolved parliament and not, as some loyalists found it convenient to believe, part of a federal structure.

The next day William Craig, minister for home affairs in the

[34] Quoted in Farrell, *Northern Ireland*, p. 93.
[35] T. O'Neill, *The Autobiography of Terence O'Neill: Prime Minister of Northern Ireland 1963–1969* (London: Hart-Davis, 1972), p. 148.

Stormont government, addressed the Bloomfield Young Unionist Association and took the opportunity to contradict his prime minister on the crucial issue of the constitutional relationship between Westminster and Stormont. Craig stated the following:

I would resist any effort by any government in Great Britain, whatever its complexion might be, to exercise that power in any way to interfere with the proper jurisdiction of the Government of Northern Ireland.

It is merely a reserve of power to deal with an emergency situation. *It is difficult to envisage any situation in which it could be exercised without the consent of the Government of Northern Ireland.*

I would regret very much if we were to sit back passively and see an effort being made to depart from this very fundamental principle touching on our Parliament and Government. It is the duty of every Unionist to stand solidly and defend the Constitution on this basis. To accept any other argument is to make a laughing stock of the whole concept of democracy. (*News Letter*, 11 December 1968; emphasis mine)

This curious exclusivist reading of the Government of Ireland Act of 1920 is one of the very first instances of a new direction within Unionism towards what was to become a mainstay of the Ulster Vanguard movement; the advocacy of an independent Ulster, should relations with Westminster become unsatisfactory. In 1968, O'Neill could not overlook this breach of cabinet solidarity and he immediately demanded Craig's resignation. Craig took his place on the back-bench at Stormont and did not re-emerge as a major actor on the public political scene until 1972 when, on 9 February he was reincarnated as the leader of the Vanguard movement, a new association of Loyalist organisations.[36] Initially Vanguard did not form itself as a conventional political party but rather as 'an umbrella for traditional unionist groups'.[37] Craig announced the basic position of Vanguard by presenting a petition in which 334,095 people pledged 'unremittingly to use whatever means to defend the loyal cause'. He also announced that Vanguard would sponsor a series of rallies in defence of traditional Unionism.[38] In his recent study of the

[36] In 1971 Craig had toured Northern Ireland raising support for the Vanguard movement. Steve Bruce describes Craig as 'an intriguing character. A Lurgan solicitor who could speak menacing words in a slow quiet voice, he had come close to the leadership of the Unionist Party, had held cabinet office and retained good links with the paramilitaries and the workers' leaders who [were to plan and organize] the 1974 strike'. S. Bruce, *God Save Ulster! The Religion and Politics of Paisleyism* (Oxford: Oxford University Press, 1989), p. 111.

[37] *Irish Times*, 10 February 1972, p. 9.

[38] Perhaps it should be pointed out that 334,095 people amounts to well over half the adult Unionist population of Northern Ireland. For instance in 1971 the total 'non-Catholic' population of Northern Ireland was 971,000, constituting 63.2 per cent of the total

Protestant paramilitary groups Steve Bruce notes that the striking novelty of the Vanguard rallies was not just the fact that they involved 'the coming together of all three strands of loyalism: dissident politicians, Protestant trade unionists, and the vigilantes in the UDA. The important novelty was that the second and third groups were not just on the field listening and applauding; they were on the platforms with their "social betters", making the speeches.'[39] This feature of Vanguard greatly facilitated the recolonisation of the Unionist ideological field by exclusivist forms and prepared the ground for the successful Ulster Workers' council strike of 1974.

The Vanguard movement favoured the restoration of the old exclusivist rules which had dominated Northern Ireland since the 1920s and which O'Neill's movement within the UUP, the UK government and opposition, the NILP and the Civil Rights movement had all acted to displace. In particular, it saw itself as the necessary response to the dreaded Civil Rights movement, one which would use similar techniques for Loyalist purposes. Vanguard regarded those Unionists who constructed Northern Ireland in liberal forms as the despicable enemy in their own camp. Each concession regarding civil rights was construed as a betrayal by such liberal Unionists; they were latter-day Lundies just like the original Lundy who had treated with the enemy in 1689.

We can see this most clearly in the various critiques of liberal Unionism which Vanguard developed. Liberal Unionism was attacked both for its past record of concession and for its perceived inability to properly understand the character and extent of the prevailing Nationalist threat to Unionism. For Vanguard the current 'troubles' in Northern Ireland were the responsibility of the O'Neill and Chichester-Clark governments and their concessions on the various civil rights issues. First, they had failed to see the civil rights movement for what it was – a Republican front determined to destroy Ulster under the rubric of reform. Secondly, they refused to take the obvious steps necessary to restore the status quo ante. They remained 'soft' on law and order when what was called for was the restoration of the B Specials. As the Loyalist Association of Workers, one of the associations which joined together to form the Vanguard

---

population. I have derived these figures from Bob Rowthorn and Naomi Wayne, *Northern Ireland: The Political Economy of Conflict* (Cambridge: Polity Press, 1988), appendix 7.

[39] S. Bruce, *The Red Hand: Protestant Paramilitaries in Northern Ireland* (Oxford: Oxford University Press, 1992), p. 82.

movement, put it immediately after Bloody Sunday: 'bring back the B-specials to shoot straight at 150 yards'. In the same issue the *LAW Newsletter* also asserted that '[y]ou can only be on one side or the other'.[40] The *Loyalist News*, a pro-Vanguard publication associated with Loyalist paramilitaries, proclaimed, 'Let's kill as many as we can.'[41] In these instances we have a reading of the 'realities' of Northern Ireland organised by the affiliative-corporate mode and, in the shoot to kill instruction, a clear instance of the instrumental-corporate mode of ideology, an injunction to keep the Nationalist minority in 'their place' by the use or threat of violence. Such an injunction is also apparent in the following from the Ulster Defence Association: 'Unless you are prepared to fight, and fight now, you are condemning your children to a faith that is evil, insidiously evil. The choice is yours and you have little time to make it.'[42] Shortly after, in its 26 February issue, the *Loyalist News* again advocated the use of violence as the necessary preliminary and inevitable corollary to the 'proper' re-ordering of social and political relations in Northern Ireland: 'let the IRA and its supporters be beaten first, then can follow the talks at which the democratically elected government of Northern Ireland will tell the rebels what is required for participation in this state. NO SURRENDER'.[43]

Vanguard quickly moved to a position of real significance through its extra-parliamentary activities and the support that they managed to achieve. Craig characterised all parliamentary activity as so much 'mumbo jumbo' which distracted from the twin dangers to Ulster's survival, Nationalist aggression and British treachery.[44] Viewed from within the logic of the corporate modes and the persecutory position the very fact of the changes which Westminster and the Civil Rights movement had promoted and which the Unionist party had accepted indicated such treachery and aggression.

In the early months of 1972 Vanguard promoted its particular, mainly secular, version of exclusivist Unionism at a series of rallies which it organised around Northern Ireland. At these rallies Craig

---

40 See *L.A.W. Newsletter*, 4 February 1972, pp. 2, 5. The Loyalist Association of Workers was one of the main organisations which joined the Vanguard movement and, later, it was a principal actor in the organisation of the Ulster Workers' Council Strike which successfully brought down the power-sharing executive and returned Northern Ireland to direct rule from Westminster.

41 *Loyalist News*, 19 February 1972, p. 3   42 *U.D.A.*, no. 18, 1972.

43 The phrase 'No Surrender' was coined by the defenders of Derry in 1689 and has remained a catchphrase of Loyalists ever since.

44 *Irish Times*, 23 February 1972, p. 9.

spoke of the intense Loyalist commitment to the prevention of a sell-out of Ulster into a united Ireland and reiterated his personal pledge to 'defeat an evil conspiracy which threatened the very existence of Ulster ... and to preserve our British way of life'. He concluded these promises with the threat that, 'If Catholics declared war on their [Northern Irish] constitution, loyalists would ensure victory ... God help those who get in our way.'[45] The rules organising such constructions by Vanguard are quite evident in a Vanguard publication from the same period, *Government Without Right*, in which it is argued that to show 'neutrality to the enemies of the state is to appease [and] is incompatible with the government's own duty of allegiance'. In all these instances allegiance to the group and its particularist interests is the primary criterion of 'government *with* right'.

I now want to examine three speeches at considerable length to establish the rules of structuration which Craig drew upon in his construction of subjectivity and social and political relations in Northern Ireland. The first speech was delivered to a Loyal Orange Lodge in Glenarm on 20 June 1972, on the occasion of the unfurling of a new banner for the Lodge. This new banner would be used for various celebratory marches, such as on the Twelfth of July. The speech was reported as follows:

One side of the new banner depicts William of Orange with drawn sword and Br. (Brother) Craig said, 'I say that the Ulster loyalists have now drawn their sword and for good reason (Applause). *It is our earnest hope that we will not have to use that sword, but we have drawn it and if it is necessary to preserve our Constitution we will use it and we will use it efficiently.*

... 'I have seen men taking upon themselves the responsibility of seeing to the safety of our Province,' he said. 'I had the pleasure of taking the Salute in front of the City Hall as four battalions of Orange Volunteers marched past. I have had on many occasions the privilege of seeing a battalion of the Ulster Defence Association march past and I know of other organisations that have done themselves ready to take part in the battle for the survival of their cause.' These events were not an occasion to make one happy, but it gave one cause to feel confident.

'*We regret that all this has been necessary,*' he continued, '*but we have been grossly betrayed and let down by those who were charged with the maintenance of law and order and with our internal security. We have shown enormous patience and forbearance as even terrorists struck at our community. Our reward has been betrayal and the arrival of Whitelaw as a dictator.*

'*Whitelaw is no law ... He represents initiatives which show no design or intent to*

[45]   *Belfast Telegraph*, 15 February 1972, p. 1.

strengthen the Union but rather to appease the opponents of the Union in Ulster, and since he has taken over he has, with great recklessness, exposed the loyal people, the soldiers and the police to ever increasing risk.

... Br. Craig then declared: 'We have got to take the matter into our own hands to restore majority rule in this country. The British Government has behaved unconstitutionally and undemocratically. We have every justification for exerting ourselves to destroy this administration and for taking on our enemies who have inflicted so much misery and damage in our community, but we must see to it that there is the maximum of unity amongst all loyalists and that Party differences are pushed to one side. We must see to it that we are united to secure for Ulster a Constitution which will have the power, and the means, to safeguard Ulster's British and Protestant heritage.

'Our present Constitution has been torpedoed, but let us ask for a new one, stronger than we have ever had before. People will say: You cannot have it, London won't let you have it. We have heard that sort of talk before. It prevailed in 1912 when our grandfathers and our fathers were faced with a similar situation. They raised a loyalist army – and what they were capable of in their time we are capable of in our time.'

Br. Craig said that the message that evening was a clear and simple one to Whitelaw: 'Forget about your conferences and gimmicks and restore to the majority in Ulster their rights. Restore democracy to Ulster. Give to Ulster what you are trying to push down the throats of the people in Rhodesia – and the quicker you do it the better because we are not prepared to wait much longer. *We are not only saying "No surrender," we are declaring that we will like the men of Enniskillen, go out and meet our enemies rather than await our fate.'*

Br. Craig, whose speech got a rousing reception, said he was sure that victory would be theirs so long as they had that spirit of determination which was symbolized by the brethren of Glenarm Lodge. (*Ballymena Guardian*, 20 June 1972 (emphases mine))

This speech offers us the opportunity to explore Craig's construction of the Loyalist subject and the prevailing political situation. I will argue that the speech draws on the rules of the persecutory position.[46] In this regard it is typical of Vanguard's construction of the 'realities' of Northern Ireland. After the preliminaries, Craig uses the new Orange banner as the reference point for his characterisation of the Loyalist community as a community which will strike 'efficiently' in its defence, should this become necessary. We should note that the group who must be prepared to act are the Loyalists themselves, operating as a group or band defending its corporate

---

[46] It also draws on the rules of the affiliative-corporate mode; but see later examples for more on this.

interests. The state and its legal monopoly on the use of force is by-passed; indeed it is seen as illegitimate. The grounds for this withdrawal of consent to be governed are the perceived failure of the state to protect Loyalist interests under the Constitution. Craig then turns to the themes of self-reliance and confidence regarding the future before going on to the theme of gross betrayal as the only reward for the forbearance of Loyalists. 'Dictatorship' and 'appeasement' are the terms used to describe William Whitelaw, the serving UK Secretary of State for Northern Ireland. Even an outsider would quickly recognise the connotations of this choice of words; together they summon images of the Second World War, the very war in which loyal Unionists had fought so bravely for Britain while the 'South' had adopted a policy of unfriendly neutrality. Now, the reward for past loyalty is the imposition of a 'dictator' and the 'appeasement' of Ulster's enemies.

As with the selection from the interview with Elizabeth discussed in chapter 4, in this construction the world is split into all-good and all-bad. The very fact that Whitelaw is following a policy with which Craig does not agree places him 'beyond the pale', as it were. The Nationalist community is referenced only in terms of 'terrorists' and, not quoted, the IRA. This iconic referencing is consistent with the rules of the persecutory position, although in this speech the complete absence of any explicit reference to Catholics and Nationalists, apart from the IRA and 'terrorists', requires us to reserve any judgement in this respect. The animating affects of this speech are persecutory anxiety and omnipotent confidence, although this latter is provisional upon the willingness of Loyalist 'men' to take upon themselves 'the responsibility of seeing to the safety of our Province' and other Loyalists being prepared to follow their lead.

Speaking at Twelfth of July demonstrations several days after the above speech Craig was reported as follows:

'Certainly in living memory we have not assembled as an Institution in more difficult and trying times. Ulster is at war and it is near time that those in charge with the onerous duty of defending and maintaining Ulster's peace realised that they had a war on their hands. *It is a war which has to be won and there can be no victory by way of compromise or appeasement,*' said Bro. Craig.

... 'When the British Government brought about the first act of appeasement they set this country on an inevitable road to war. If the British Government continues in its rash policy of appeasement then we will take the law into our own hands and win for ourselves a victory. It is not enough to proclaim intent – we must now mobilise the disciplined strength of the Orange Order. There is no body of men in this land in a better position than the Orange Institution and it is our duty to lead the rest of the Province in a real stand to ensure that a democratically elected government be restored. There is *no compromise or negotiation on this position*, we must by our efforts see we have a parliament,' said Bro. Craig. (*Ballymena Guardian* 20 July 1972, emphases mine)

And at the Tobermore rally the same day Craig spoke of the need for Loyalists to be prepared, as 'in the tradition of their forefathers' to 'take up arms'. This 'warning' was delivered to a crowd of 'several thousand, including about 500 masked and hooded U.D.A. members and about 800 Orange Volunteers'. Craig continued:

the majority in Northern Ireland were *not going to stand for compromise let alone betrayal*. The loyalists had come through an extremely difficult period as those responsible for the safety and well-being of the country had failed to discharge their duties to Her Majesty's subjects in Ulster.

... '*If we are not to be allowed these rights then we will protect and maintain our heritage and way of life under a constitution outside the United Kingdom,*' he declared. 'There are some people who are not prepared to go that far. Those are people who do not value sufficiently their heritage. *We on our part, put our faith and way of life first and we will rally round to do what is necessary to maintain it.*'

Whatever the cost or sacrifices the Loyalists of Ulster would continue the fight until victory was theirs. They prayed that it might be achieved by peaceful means but if they were to be denied the right to do it in that way then they would, in the tradition of their forefathers, take up arms for their democratic rights. The Loyalists of Ulster were now prepared to come out and be involved. (*Ballymena Guardian*, 13 July 1972, emphases mine)

Again, both these speeches draw on the rules of the persecutory position, as with the speech to the Glenarm Loyal Orange Lodge discussed above. They also draw on the rules of the affiliative-corporate mode, as I will now illustrate. It will be recalled that in my description of the corporate modes of ideology in chapter 5 I pointed out that they evaluate the behaviour, beliefs and aspirations of other groupings in terms of their compatibility with those of one's own grouping. Authority is granted legitimacy to the extent that it maintains and furthers the interests of one's own group, whilst excluding (for the instrumental mode) or controlling (for the affiliative mode) incompatible groups and their interests. Within these parameters authority is granted undivided and uncritical loyalty. Should it step outside these parameters it is ridiculed and despised. Thus from within the corporate modes a good law is one which serves group ends; and the criterion of its rightness is the extent to which it does so effectively. The ideal law, then, is a draconian and discretionary one enforced by the 'right' people.

In the two Twelfth speeches quoted above these features are clearly evident. In the first of them Craig attributes responsibility for the conflict in Northern Ireland to the British government and its policy of 'appeasement'. Having stepped outside the set of rules for the organisation of social and political relations in Northern Ireland which Loyalists regard as sacrosanct, the government itself becomes the object of derision and contempt. The drift to 'war' with the IRA is seen as an 'inevitable' outcome of so-called appeasement. This mode carries no capacity for self-reflection; Loyalists are totally absolved from any responsibility for the consequences of their actions because, for so long as they are 'loyal', their motives and actions are beyond reproach. The outcome of this mode of ideology is the unhesitating endorsement of a policy which involves taking 'the law into our own hands and win(ning) for ourselves a victory'.

At the second, Tobermore, rally Craig provides a secular version of Norman Porter's advice about the dangers of 'good neighbourliness and friendship' discussed above. Hence Craig warns against tolerating 'compromise let alone betrayal'.[47] As with Porter, Craig voices concerns about betrayal, which he equates with compromise. He is also concerned with the perceived need to 'protect and maintain our heritage'. In this instance the suggestion that Loyalists might need to protect this heritage 'outside the United Kingdom' is explicitly stated. It is clear that in drawing on the affiliative-corporate mode Craig is making 'loyalty' to the constitution and government of the UK contingent upon Britain's acceptance of the dominance of exclusivist forms in the ordering of identities and relations in Northern Ireland. Unless this can be maintained, all bets are off!

Finally, the very same rules and themes are evident in a speech delivered by Tom Creighton, the Vanguard press officer. Creighton claimed that:

People were at last beginning to realise that they must make a stand. They wanted to see action and he promised that they would all 'live to see that action'. They would not put up with the 'undemocratic dictatorship' of William Whitelaw and his Ministers for very much longer.

... The speaker went on: 'Certainly we want peace, but in Vanguard we are not prepared to have peace at any price regardless of principles. Your

[47] See chapter 7 for my discussion of Norman Porter's Twelfth address.

cause and mine is a righteous cause, and it is that which the loyalist people of Ulster are going to fight to maintain. (*Ballymena Guardian*, 24 August 1972)

THE LOYALIST NEWS: ULTRA-LOYALISM SPEAKS

In this section I will explore what Sarah Nelson has termed 'ultra-loyalism' by looking closely at the rules drawn on in one publication which supported the Vanguard movement and which was close to the two principal paramilitary groups, especially the Ulster Volunteer Force (UVF).[48] This publication, *The Loyalist News*, was edited by John McKeague. McKeague, a staunch Loyalist and a 'committed Free Presbyterian and supporter of Ian Paisley', had been associated with the Ulster Protestant Volunteers' bombing campaign in 1969 and subsequently became the first chairman of the Shankill Defence Association.[49] The *Loyalist News*' political position is evident in the following, as early as October 1970:

Writing on the wall
Thanks to a weak and spineless Government and their predecessor O'Neill, we are now nearer the brink than at any time in our history. Now is the time for strong men to step forward and guide Ulster into the seventies with firmness and determination, men in whom all law abiding citizens can place their trust and evil-doers will fear. Men who are not afraid to proclaim to the world that Ulster is master in her own house, by the will of the majority of the people and will not be coerced or intimidated by republican thugs and street orators or their friends and allies in the English House of Commons. We believe that Ulster has men of proven ability to pursue such a line, namely Craig, West, and Boal etc; it is no coincidence that the present Government took a hard line with these men and deprived them of the party whip, while showering honours and position on less worthy 'YES' men. (*Loyalist News*, 24 October 1970)

This Loyalist proclamation draws its sharp line of distinction between, on the one hand, those who are 'law abiding citizens' and, on the other hand, the 'evil-doers'. It states what is to become the primary claim of Vanguard, that 'Ulster is master in her own house, by the will of the majority of the people.' Throughout this book we have frequently encountered such interpellations, although they have not always been so graphically expressed. Phrases like 'law abiding

---

[48] Sarah Nelson, *Ulster's Uncertain Defenders* (Belfast: Appletree Press, 1984), p. 61. In her book Nelson provides a detailed account of the histories and internal divisions within the two principal Loyalist paramilitary organizations, the Ulster Volunteer Force and the Ulster Defence Association.

[49] Bruce, *The Red Hand*, pp. 32–9. See also Nelson, *Uncertain Defenders*, p. 61.

citizens' or the 'loyal people of Ulster' or just 'people of Ulster' are littered throughout the Unionist discourse. Moreover, we have noticed that O'Neill had to go to elaborate lengths, when addressing his constituency, to make it plain that he was addressing all the people of Northern Ireland, irrespective of creed. The interpellation of 'citizen', 'voter' or 'subject', while lexically referencing persons according to universalist criteria, has typically carried an exclusivist connotation within Unionist ideology. In the *Loyalist News* we may observe the extent to which such exclusivist interpellations can be carried within Unionism:

Just a thought

Many people of reasonably moderate views are asking themselves, after all these years of toleration and living and working with Roman Catholics, what has gone wrong? Many people are puzzled by the lack of co-operation between the R.C. clergy and our own. Many are puzzled by the thinking and the logic of the average R.C. Perhaps the man you've worked beside for many years, suddenly trots out all the old shibboleths, what do you think or what can you say? The old lady with the pioneer badge, shuffling around the city centre store, could she be planting incendiary devices? or maybe she's scouting the lay out of the building. The priest walking unconcernedly through the city, is he really a priest, or some terrorist in disguise? Darkness falls and the streets become deserted, only those with any necessity are out and about, old people sit in their homes and long for the cold light of morning, yet dreading what the news media may bring.

In many streets and roads working men cluster around the barricaded entrances and discuss the situation. Remedies and solutions are worked out, talk, talk, talk.

Impotency swells in each man's breast, anger fills each head as the night wind brings the crunch of the bombs and the whine of the bullet. Every man remembers the proud record of Ulster and silently rededicates himself to those high ideals for which fathers and grandfathers were willing and in many cases did, lay down their lives. The morning brings work for most, unemployment for some, but depression for almost all. Grim morning headlines herald yet another night of unmolested I.R.A. activity. Somehow one must struggle on. The R.C.s one meets in the course of a day's work, in the course of a day's employment make no comment on the night before, who knows what they are thinking, perhaps they are gloating, counting the dead. Feeling sad and martyred for their own, bitter and satisfied towards their enemies.

Perhaps a look at the local Nationalist newspaper puts everything in perspective for the average Protestant. Here he learns that there are two kinds of truth, the pure unsullied Roman Catholic truth and ordinary dubious Protestant truth. Here the Loyalist realises that what is happening in Ulster is a reawakening of the ancient enmity and hatred felt by the adherents of the 'one true church' towards those who happened to say and prove logically, 'you are in error'. One has to be blind to be unable to see that there will never be peace with Rome, until Rome makes peace with God. Even the priests of the Romish Church are invariably bound up with the terrorists and the whole fabric of the church is extended towards them. People are misled by the Communist threat, but the Vatican will ally itself with anything or anyone to gain its own ends.

No matter what the year brings Rome never changes and the sooner these moderate clergy and laymen get this into their heads the nearer the solution will be. The average Protestant can also learn that mentally and theologically he has nothing in common with the alien controlled Roman Catholic.
(Signed) Defender (*Loyalist News*, December 1971)

Here, in apparently moderate tones, we find a profoundly insidious example of an imagined Ulster construed by drawing on the rules of the persecutory and dehumanising positions and the affiliative-corporate mode. This modest proposal, as it were, is offered as 'just a thought'; as if reason (or 'ordinary dubious Protestant truth'), which has suffered so much through the onslaught of a hostile world, can only voice itself in a whisper. Yet insist this reason does! It begins with an assumed, apparently benign, world-weariness. A puzzle exists; despite all its good-will and tolerance, Unionism is failing to achieve its liberal ambitions. How could this be so? The answer is provided by what some traditional Unionists have always known; there is something rotten in the state of Ulster and it can be characterised as the 'thinking and the logic of the average R.C.' But who are these people and where are they encountered? They are not, as some Unionists may care to believe, a remote and alien caste formally committed to a paramilitary group such as the IRA. Rather they are all about; the alien is in our midst, so the thought continues. They include 'the man you have worked beside for many years', 'the old lady [at] the ... store' and the priest 'walking unconcernedly' about. They are, indeed, the 'average R.C'.

The third paragraph informs us that '[e]very man remembers the proud record of Ulster'. The interpellation of 'every man' is extended only to Unionists; as if those others cannot be included in the universal term of address.[50] After all they are silent and fail to disown the events of the night, 'the crunch of the bombs and the whine of the bullet'.

---

[50] No doubt, 'every person' or 'everyone' is the non-sexist form of this interpellation, but clearly this example relies in part on the gendering of the self as male to support its attribution of treachery and inferior logic to 'Roman Catholics'.

Clearly no Unionist or Loyalist could be accused of initiating such terrors; they must have their origin in the alien netherworld. But what of those silent ones: 'the R.C.s one meets in the course of a day's work'? Could their silence be just a disguise, could they be 'gloating, counting the dead'? After all, they have failed to see the errors of their way, even after such errors have been 'prove[d] logically'. Instead they adhere to what they claim as 'the one true church'. And here is the answer to the puzzle with which the world-weary observer began. 'The Loyalist realises that what is happening in Ulster is a reawakening of the ancient enmity and hatred' felt by Roman Catholics towards Unionists and Protestants. Behind all this lies a vast network in which the Pope pulls all the strings; the priest and the terrorist are as if one. And now the 'solution' to all Ulster's ills is clear; 'moderate clergy and laymen' must see the Vatican for what it is. And the 'average Protestant', the subject to whom this message is addressed; he must learn that, 'mentally and theologically he has nothing in common with the alien controlled Roman Catholic'.

Here there is no doubt as to where the boundary is drawn between 'good' and 'bad', 'self' and 'other'. All Catholics and Nationalists are untrustworthy and to compromise with them is to treat with the dupes and agents of an 'alien' power. The persecutory constructions and affects stand out and do not require further comment. The denial of equal entitlement to Nationalists/Catholics is also self-evident.

Speaking at Ballynahinch on 30 November 1971, the prime minister of Northern Ireland, Brian Faulkner, had spoken against equating the Roman Catholic community with the IRA. Writing in the *Loyalist News*, 'Defender' took up the theme addressed above:

Help

The blind head in the sand attitude of the Prime Minister of Northern Ireland continues ... Unionists he states; must never fall in the trap of equating the Roman Catholic community with the I.R.A. It was the average Roman Catholic family which had borne the brunt of the horror and the unpleasant living conditions created by the I.R.A.'s campaign of intimidation and the constant tension which existed in areas where the gunmen operated and were combatted by the security forces. It is important that such people know that by seeking to smash the I.R.A. the Government was not in any way identifying members of the Roman Catholic community with the terrorists.

This kind of talk from a Prime Minister of a country in which the religious minority from the very birth of the state have constantly opposed and dissented, will not do. The ordinary people of this Province who desire to go about their legitimate and peaceful pursuits will not be taken by such woolly minded waffle. We have had our fill of the constant tirade of lying propaganda and high powered politics. Capt. Terence O'Neill (O Lord Forgive Me) whose name now equals that of Ulster's arch traitor Lundy, tried these moves, they did not work, nor will Faulkner's.

It is quite obvious that a cheap political stunt is being played out in this Loyal State, how else could it be, or are our leaders really stupid? Has Faulkner got the whole Unionist Party brainwashed or are the cabinet members as spineless as we suppose. Is there no one at Stormont capable of saying look, enough is enough, let the truth be known? What has happened to the men who should know better? Many of the members of the Unionist party grew up in the early days of this state, they saw the results of past I.R.A. actions, they have witnessed down through the years the constant stream of violent anti-Ulster propaganda, which has been distributed around the world. Do they imagine that the minority in Ulster have suddenly changed their attitude? . . . Do they not yet realise that a full scale terrorist war is being waged in this country? A war that could not be fought without the help and material assistance of the minority. Do our leaders think that the I.R.A. could hold the whole R.C. community to ransom? This would be impossible, we are constantly told that the Roman Catholic church is the bulwark of freedom so it follows that where this church is strong, there will be found freedom.

The truth of the matter is, that almost 100% of the R.C. minority is, if not actively, then passively behind the I.R.A.

(Signed) Defender (*Loyalist News*, 11 December 1971; emphasis mine)

This statement provides a good example of how exclusivist forms of Unionist ideology can distort communication between 'Loyalists' and those Unionists who attempt to construe the 'reality' of Northern Ireland according to inclusivist forms. Faulkner becomes the object of the persecutory position and affiliative-corporate mode because he attempts to make a distinction between the IRA and the 'Roman Catholic community' on the criterion of actual behaviour and experience rather than according to an ascriptive criterion. In stepping, at least in this instance, beyond the bounds of exclusivism he becomes part of a 'Lundy' tradition (with O'Neill at its head) which is viewed as 'stupid', 'spineless' and 'brainwashed'. Only a year later, under the pressure of events and the growing dominance within Unionism of the exclusivist 'forms', Faulkner took on an exclusivist political subjectivity in a last ditch attempt to retain his, and the UUP's, authority within the Unionist community.

Of course it might be argued that 'Defender's' understanding of the support for the IRA within the Nationalist/Catholic community is, in fact, a shrewd and pragmatic reading of the horrific situation confronting Unionists in 1970. In responding to such a claim three points should be made. First, it must be recognised that, for many Loyalists living in working-class areas contiguous with Nationalist/ Catholic areas, or living near the border, or maybe just having relations or friends in such circumstances, the everyday experience of the 'Troubles' would tend to confirm such a shrewd and pragmatic reading. Indeed, and this is the second point, such everyday experience is itself a product of ideological processes, as the structuration model I am working with helps us to understand. Social and political moments are themselves experienced through the ideological rules in terms of which the political subject and his or her field of communication are organised. As a consequence, everyday experience lived within institutions which have exclusivist rules encoded into them is 'obviously' correct in its suspicion and hostility towards the Nationalist/Catholic community. This is the 'reality effect' which such forms of Unionism produce, as Lacan and Althusser might put it. Third, although from certain perspectives such distinctions as that made by Faulkner between the IRA and the Nationalist/Catholic community could be regarded as naive, the consequence of failing to make such distinctions is disastrous, as it has the character of a self-fulfilling omission. Unless such challenges to the habitual and institutionalised rules of exclusivist Unionism are attempted, then the ideological certainties expressed by 'Defender' *produce* the very reality they have purportedly observed.[51]

A further aspect of Loyalism, as construed by the *Loyalist News*, is evident in the following article which discusses an IRA funeral:

The funerals

Last week we promised to give you the story about the funerals of the two I.R.A. sisters. Once again we saw the 'peace loving minority' out supporting the local cause. Thousands of them.

The funeral from the Falls, with the Silver Car Reg. 6917 – UZ. with *five brave yellow scum in front, six animal girls accompanied the 'dead rebels' wearing black*

---

[51] This discussion helps to highlight the significance, for my argument, of the fact that, as discussed in chapter 7, the Loyalist hostility to 'O'Neillism' long pre-dated any 'pressure' from the Nationalist/Catholic community. Regarding the IRA, the situation is even more marked. As has been noted on many occasions, in Nationalist/Catholic areas of Belfast in 1969 the term IRA appeared as graffiti which continued with the equation 'I Ran Away'. This denigration of the IRA underlines the fact that the IRA entered the scene very late in the piece, long after Unionism's exclusivist reaction was underway. Indeed there is an important sense in which it is appropriate to suggest that exclusivist Unionism reinvented the IRA in its attempt to defeat liberal Unionism.

gaberdine and dark glasses, only one was in step with black shoes. The two funerals joined at Whiterock Road the second 'dead rebel' was accompanied by six animal girls in green gaberdines, black boots not all the same, some shiny some dull, and some with dark glasses; these were fair haired animals, the first funeral they were all dark haired. . . .

Both rebel rags were tied to the boxes, containing the two animals . . . we wonder for why? Some people were asking where so and so was, and the answer was silent, with eyes cast towards the sewers! The water shortage was very evident, tears [?] for the two animals, left their tracks on the faces of the mourners.

In all it was an enjoyable affair, we only wish we could be reporting every day on two or more such like . . . deliverances.
(Signed) Roving Reporter (*Loyalist News*, 6 November 1971, emphasis mine)

This article, like the examples from the *Loyalist News* which I discussed in chapter 4, is clearly organised by the rules of the dehumanising position. I shall not belabour this point. What I would stress is the connection between this dehumanisation of members of the IRA and the construction of the Nationalist/Catholic community as a whole. Already in 'Just a thought' and 'Help' we have seen ample evidence of the equation between the IRA and the Nationalist/Catholic community. This equation is reasserted in this dehumanising context, although it is handled a little more gingerly. As with the examples discussed in chapter 4, understandable Loyalist animosity towards, and indeed understandable hatred of the IRA, is organised by unconscious rules which have sadistic and dehumanising processes at their core. Such a construction is spread along a chain of signifiers which begins with the dead person, extends to the IRA and the grieving family and friends, and ends with the Catholic community as a whole. In this manner they are all gathered under the one dehumanising construction and viewed as both alien and 'preferred-dead'.

As already noted, in 1972, immediately after its formation, Vanguard held a series of rallies throughout Northern Ireland which culminated in a rally at Stormont attended by more than 60,000 people. After marching in military style through the streets to Stormont, William Craig addressed the crowd and advised that 'We must build up a dossier of the men and women who are a menace to this country because, if and when the politicians fail us, it may be our job to liquidate the enemy.'[52] Some months later Craig visited London where he addressed the Monday Club (a Conservative Party

[52] *Irish Times*, 19 March 1972, p. 1.

club) and repeated his 'liquidation' speech. The negative response
which the speech attracted led the *Loyalist News* to join the discourse
as follows:

Craig – shoot & kill

[...] The moderates ask who will Craig and his followers shoot and kill?
Let's answer those people, like Caldwell and Bradford who in recent times
have parleyed with the I.R.A., and spell out the full meaning. Let's go back
to the signing of the Covenant and the words 'WITH OUT LET OR HINDER-
ANCE.',(sic) then take it a stage forward, SHOOT AND KILL ... ANYONE
STANDING IN THE WAY OF THE MAJORITY OF ULSTER, HAVING THEIR DEMO-
CRATIC RIGHTS. What could be clearer. The IRA have made no bones
about whom they will shoot and kill. Yet Caldwell and Bradford and quite
a number of others pretending to speak for the majority, have the gall to
ask who will Craig shoot and kill. The next few months will tell the tale if
the British Government do not give the majority what they want. (*Loyalist
News*, 28 October 1972)

And in the same issue:

Ulster will fight

When Mr. William Craig spoke to the Monday Club members in London
on Thursday night, he gave vent to the feelings of many thousands of Ulster
Protestants.

The outcry that followed was to be expected and those who shouted the
loudest were predictably enough those whose policies have led us to the
brink of disaster.

The one aspect which the moderates and appeasers were not prepared for
was the massive flood of support which flooded in for Mr. Craig's policies.

When Mr. Craig spoke on Television interviews on Friday night, he made
one point very clear, this was the disgust he felt for the hypocrisy and the
double talk which has done more to heighten the tension here and increase
frustration than anything else. ... It is not enough for the leaders of the
Unionist Party to call for tolerance, patience, and restraint while daily,
people lose their lives. No country in the world would tolerate the situation
which we find ourselves in. Why should we? We are now entitled to ask all
those who prefer to lead us and who are concerned with Ulster's future, in
the event of any sell out by Westminster or the over riding of the will of the
majority, are you prepared to fight in defence of the people who placed their
trust in you? In Northern Ireland today, under armed and physical attacks
from within and without, being undermined by weak, cowardly moderates
who would tolerate a United Ireland tomorrow, just to get their social life
going again, and grappling with a rebellious greedy minority, someone must
call a halt. Someone must speak for the Loyalist population, just as Carson
and Craigavon did over 50 years ago. The man that destiny has chosen is
William Craig. What he told the Monday Club was not a figment of his

imagination. The words that stunned his audience came from thousands of throats, he being merely the messenger chosen to deliver a warning, to a section of people who for too long have played politics with people's lives. The ordinary man in the street who has sat in front of his T.V. screen mentally urging his representatives to tell the truth, only to be frustrated time and time again by weak, polite and decent arguments, has won a victory. His point of view which has been suppressed for so long that it causes astonishment when heard, has finally been heard. To all the so called leaders, disregard it at your peril.

Let there be no mistake. Ulster is not for sale.

Now is the time to stand up and be counted, you are for us or against us, there is no middle path.

Ulster WILL fight and Ulster WILL be right. (*Loyalist News*, 28 October 1972; emphasis mine)

With great cogency, these two articles elaborate the implications of the exclusivist forms of Unionist ideology in a situation of conflict and peril. They brand the inclusivist forms of Unionism as 'hypocrisy and ... double talk' and declare that there can be 'no middle path'. They characterise the 'minority' as 'greedy' and they do not hesitate to advocate the killing of 'ANYONE STANDING IN THE WAY OF THE MAJORITY OF ULSTER HAVING THEIR DEMOCRATIC RIGHTS.'[53]

The *Loyalist News* did not speak for most Unionists; clearly it was an extremist publication whose explicit dehumanisation of Nationalists/Catholics most Unionists would repudiate. Its particular audience was members and supporters of the Loyalist paramilitary groups, in particular the UVF. This is quite evident in the cartoon series, 'Bill and Ben the IRA Men', which was a regular feature of the *Loyalist News*. In these cartoons Bill, a scrawny little man, and Ben, his large, doltish companion, are members of the IRA who consistently demonstrate their stupidity and/or their cowardice. In perhaps the most chilling of these cartoons Bill walks up to a bus stop and, approaching a larger man from the side, puts the question; 'Hey, fellah, what's my quickest way to Milltown Cemetery.' In the second 'frame' the larger man turns sideways, revealing a UVF badge on his military-like jacket and a hand-gun in his right hand, with which he shoots Bill. In the third 'frame' the UVF man has nonchalantly turned his back on Bill's body as it lies in a pool

---

[53] While I am not proposing any immediate relationship, Table 1 above (p. 152), concerning violence in Northern Ireland from 1970 to 1974, makes it evident that 1972 was an unusually violent year in Ulster, involving the highest number of incidents in all but two categories. Along with the British army, the paramilitary groups of both 'sides' were killing people in large numbers.

of blood near the bus stop. He waits for his bus, as though he has merely swatted a fly. This cartoon is a striking example of the 'telling' phenomenon which I discussed in chapter 2.[54] It relies for its chilling effect upon two features; first, the local knowledge that Milltown Cemetery is reserved for Catholic burials, and second, that the UVF man acts instantly and without speaking; his reply is the shooting itself. Significantly, the question identifies Bill as Catholic, not as a member of the IRA. The response is instantaneous and indiscriminate; Bill is shot because he has identified himself as Catholic to the wrong person; hence he is also conceived as stupid. In my judgement it is quite clear that, both then and now, most Unionists would repudiate such dehumanising constructions of Roman Catholics as we have just observed in the pages of the *Loyalist News*. However I would argue that my analysis has already indicated that exclusivist Unionism, as propounded by Vanguard and others, relied on unconscious mechanisms which bore a formal similarity to the mechanisms at play in the pages of the *Loyalist News*. Analysed in terms of their cognitive structure these ideological forms are corporate in character. By placing the interests and ideals of the corporate group above all other considerations they regard all 'necessary' means as justified. In speaking of the possible need to liquidate Catholics, and in advocating the untrammelled rights of the majority Unionist population, William Craig was not exulting in the dehumanisation of the Nationalist/Catholic population. But he was drawing upon a set of corporate rules which construct the 'minority' as differentially entitled, and only for so long as they accept their designated place as such. Moreover, if we consider the psychodynamic unconscious rules at play in these constructions we note that both the dehumanising and the persecutory positions rely upon paranoid-schizoid mechanisms; they share a 'family resemblance', so to speak.[55] In one, highly significant, sense there is a world of difference between the gross dehumanisation characteristic of the *Loyalist News* and the iconic representation of the 'other' characteristic of the persecutory position, and as drawn upon by Vanguard. This 'world of difference' needs to be

---

[54] Although this cartoon would have provided a 'classic' illustration for Burton's study of telling and riding the buses, unfortunately he seems to have been unaware of it.

[55] The concept of family resemblances is, of course, Wittgenstein's. See L. Wittgenstein, *Philosophical Investigations* (Oxford: Blackwell, 1967); L. Wittgenstein, *Culture and Value* (Oxford: Blackwell, 1980).

recognised as such. The very point of my earlier distinction between an iconic and a dehumanising construction of the other is that it offers a way of noting and elaborating the implications of such a distinction. However, it also provides us with a means of observing the 'family resemblance' noted above, and the implications which follow. In Northern Ireland, in the period from 1972 to 1975, Vanguard functioned as the umbrella organisation under which the various exclusivist forms of Unionism could shelter. It provided a public space within which the various strands of exclusivist Unionism could coalesce and re-group, prior to launching a concerted and successful attack upon those institutions and groups attempting to change the order of things towards inclusivism. It is a major part of my argument that this coming together of exclusivist Unionisms was achieved, in part, due to the family resemblance between them; despite some very significant differences, they shared a reliance on the same family of rules when it came to making sense of the crisis confronting them. We have already seen in earlier chapters that not all Unionists shared this reliance on exclusivist rules. It is worth observing that those Unionists committed to inclusivist rules not only construed the world differently, but resented those Unionists who held to and reasserted the exclusivist rules as normative. This division over the proper ordering of subjectivity and intersubjectivity lay at the root of the ideological and political conflict in Northern Ireland, and continues to do so to this day.

PAISLEY AND THE DUP: EXCLUSIVISM IN AN EVANGELICAL IDIOM

As we have seen in chapter 7, Ian Paisley became a significant political actor during Terence O'Neill's premiership. Prior to establishing the DUP in 1971 Paisley had been associated with the establishment of the Free Presbyterian Church in the 1950s and the Protestant Unionist Party in the 1960s. Through these organisations he laid claim to an independent and evangelical, Protestant and Unionist, tradition which can be readily traced back to such nineteenth-century figures as William Johnston of Ballykilbeg, the leader of a revived Belfast Orangeism in the late 1860s and Henry Cooke, Thomas Drew and the Reverend Hugh 'Roaring' Hanna, the last of these an influential street preacher of the same 'enthusiastic' period around the 1860s.[56] Wright claims that Paisley's ideology is one which, being both fundamentalist and evangelical, sees its 'major political task as being to ensure that maximum opportunity for the socialisation of Bible Protestantism is maintained: it being held that where this is not done, some implicit favour is being done to Roman Catholicism by weakening Protestantism'.[57] O'Malley claims that in the land wars of the seventeenth century the massacres of colonising Protestants by the native, Catholic, Irish, such as the 1641 massacre, reinforced the already established myth of siege with a myth of massacre. He continues:

The massacres, of course, were exaggerated in the telling, but their extraordinary symbolic significance transcended exaggeration. They became a vindication for fearfulness, vigilance, and distrust; *they made paranoia necessary for survival.* ... Northern Protestants continue to fear what they perceive as the power of the Roman Catholic Church to control individual judgment, and the political power of the Catholic Church to manipulate events, peoples, and nations. *Paisleyism is the extreme manifestation of these fears:* the Roman Catholic Church is pervasive, indivisible, clandestine, sinister, ruthless, perverse, and insidious. No intrigue is beyond her cunning, no duplicity beyond her design, no mendacity beyond her machinations, no corruption beyond her capacity.[58]

In his major study of Paisleyism, Bruce concludes as follows:

That Paisley's brand of Unionism has proved popular with such a large section of the Ulster Protestant population defies any explanation other than the obvious one: evangelicalism provides the core beliefs, values, and symbols of what it means to be a Protestant. Unionism is about avoiding becoming a subordinate minority in a Catholic state. Avoiding becoming a Catholic means remaining a Protestant. In times of stability and prosperity, the religious basis of the Protestant identity can be forgotten. Any serious challenge to the Protestant identity presents only two genuinely viable alternatives: abandonment of, or recommitment to, traditional Protestantism. I have already suggested the limits on the appeal of the first response. Those who choose the other road, even if their recommitment does not extend to religious conversion, will be attracted to a form of unionism which makes clear its evangelical foundations.[59]

Whereas both Wright and O'Malley subscribe to a pluralism thesis

---

[56] See Frank Wright's excellent study 'Protestant Ideology and Politics in Ulster', *European Journal of Sociology*, 14:2 (1972), pp. 223ff., and Peter Gibbon's *The Origins of Ulster Unionism* (Manchester: Manchester University Press, 1975) for further discussion of these four figures.

[57] Wright, 'Protestant Ideology', p. 229.

[58] P. O'Malley, *The Uncivil Wars* (Belfast: Blackstaff Press, 1983), pp. 172, 174. My emphases.

[59] Bruce, *God Save Ulster!* pp. 264–5.

regarding the perpetuation of sectarian difference in Northern Ireland, one which places at the centre of its explanation differential incorporation within the state and the perpetuation of a culture of difference through the maintenance of exclusivist institutions of socialisation, Bruce develops a more subtle, if eventually inadequate, position. Working in a Weberian tradition, Bruce argues that Unionists taking exclusivist positions should be regarded as rational actors attempting to preserve their ideal and material interests. As he puts it in a summary statement in *The Red Hand*:

[M]ost Protestants and Catholics, even those who got involved in the UDA and UVF, got on well with the other side. One needs to understand that the conflict was not a result of bad manners or social awkwardness writ large. It was the result of rational competition over resources and goals, and there is no reason why that sort of conflict should be incompatible with previously friendly everyday interaction.[60]

In making such an argument, Bruce, quite correctly, rejects any notion that Paisley's success is based upon a 'basic irrationality of Irish politics'. As he puts it, 'The notion of "tribalism" is sometimes invoked to suggest a political culture which has failed to develop out of an age of clan warfare and blood feuds.'[61] However, in rejecting such primordialist arguments in the manner in which he does, Bruce places himself in the somewhat odd position of claiming that the rational position for *all* Unionists, especially in extreme moments, is to subscribe to an identity which is evangelical and fundamentalist at its core; in effect Bruce equates a very particular set of beliefs with what is rational for all Unionists, thereby running together a pluralism theory and a rational actor theory. He does so in a manner which fails to adequately integrate these two theories. In one significant sense, despite other differences, Bruce finds himself in a position not unlike certain neo-Marxists such as John Saul writing on South Africa or Bew, Gibbon and Patterson writing on Northern Ireland. Like these writers Bruce relies upon a notion of rationality which is drawn, ultimately, from utilitarianism. Thus for Bruce, as for Saul and Bew, Gibbon and Patterson, the logic of interests can proceed outside of ideology. As I stated in chapter 1, in such cases what we are really offered is a formal analytic model of calculation (usually not explicitly developed) for decision making within an interest structure which has already determined (prior to the calcula-

---

[60] Bruce, *The Red Hand*, p. 45.
[61] Bruce, p. 250.

tion) the scope of choice and the values attached to any particular option.[62] In Bruce's hands this approach sits distinctly at odds with his detailed, variegated and highly informative, interpretative study of Paisleyism. In my opinion this problem arises from Bruce's unstated reliance upon a theory of action which places the individual actor at the centre of its concerns and an impoverished theory of rationality which relies on a crude dichotomy between the rational and the irrational. My own approach attempts to overcome such limitations by placing neither actor nor structure at the centre of its concerns. Instead, as previously explained, I opt for a revised theory of structuration. The revision I have developed is intended to redress the second type of limitation which Bruce's study, amongst others, exemplifies. Through concentrating upon the unconscious rules of structuration of Unionist ideology I have attempted to get beyond any crude distinction between rationality and irrationality by addressing different forms of rationality (or distinct rationalities) in a manner which can analyse their internal structure, or the set of rules they rely upon for the construction of subjectivity and intersubjectivity. In this way it becomes possible to analyse the systematic distortions in communication within a nominal grouping such as Unionists in a manner which is, first of all, alert to intragroup differences regarding the rules by which the proper ordering of subjectivity and intersubjectivity are organised, while, secondly, not needing either to discount certain rules as irrational or assert that all forms of an ideology rely upon the same form of reasoning. Instead, by taking such an approach I am able to recognise that various forms of an ideology are, exactly, various and distinct forms of reasoning and feeling about political identities and political relations. The relevant empirical issue becomes one of establishing the discrete rules of reasoning and feeling which are drawn upon by the particular political grouping or movement under scrutiny and the similarities or differences between any one such grouping or movement and any others.

In the remainder of this section I will examine one address by Ian Paisley, from a critical moment in 1975, with the intention of establishing the rules he drew upon to construct his preferred forms of subjectivity and intersubjectivity in Northern Ireland. Through so doing I will also provide a basis upon which to argue that Bruce's

---

[62]   See above, p. 23

explanation of Paisley's popularity, in terms of the claim that 'evangelicalism provides the core beliefs, values, and symbols of what it means to be a Protestant', is misleading. Rather, it is the shared characteristics of the exclusivist forms of Unionism, whether thematised and enacted in a secular idiom (as with Vanguard) or evangelical idiom (as with Paisley) which provide the ideological ground upon which a distinctly Loyalist-Unionist identity, spanning the secular and the religious division, may be based. In the 1970s such common ground was discovered by Unionists in their shared reliance upon exclusivist rules. It was embraced by them as it enabled a newly resurgent Loyalism (or exclusivist Unionism) to unite and, thereby, defeat the policies and policing of the state.

In one sense this argument is an extension rather than a complete rejection of Bruce's position, as it displaces Bruce's unduly restrictive concentration on the explicit and conscious content of evangelical Protestantism with a broader concern; namely, a concern with the implicit, unconscious rules of exclusivist Unionism in its various idioms. Such a broadening of focus and method of analysis is crucial if we are to make adequate sense of the internal differentiation and subsequent alliances within Unionism in the period since 1962. As my account has already established, there is more to these differentiations and alliances than can be comprehended by a theory which assesses the political and ideological processes within Unionism in terms of conformity with, or deviation from, an essential, evangelical Protestant identity.

In chapter 7 we saw instances of Paisley, in the 1960s, drawing upon the rules of the persecutory position and the affiliative-corporate mode to construct his imagined Ulster. By the 1970s he had become a major political actor but he remained constant to his earlier vision. Although the content of his political vision changed over the period, its unconscious structure remained the same.[63] O'Malley, as quoted above, notes certain features of Paisleyism which are consistent with this account when he places his explanatory emphasis upon extreme fear and paranoia. Paisley's 'call to the Protestants of Ulster' is an exemplary and characteristic statement in which we can observe the rules of structuration he drew upon in the 1970s:

[63] The principal change in content is Paisley's adoption, in May 1972, of a policy of full integration with Westminster. Later he reverted to a policy supporting the restoration of the Stormont parliament. He also changed his position on the issue of internment. See Bruce, *God Save Ulster*, for more on this.

A call to the Protestants of Ulster[64]

Fellow Protestants,

I am so deeply concerned with the present grave situation which is developing in our Province that I am urged to address to you this call.

My Protestant principles are well known and I have through good report and ill report held to them uncompromisingly thereby causing deep enmity to be generated against me by Ulster's enemies and much criticism by those who claim to be Ulster's friends. I have not hesitated to pursue unpopular paths in line with my convictions even although imprisonment and seemingly universal condemnation inevitably followed. I feel I would be failing my God, my Province and myself if I did not in this hour of crisis thus address you.

Our case is desperate. For the past five years through the treachery and weakness of those in authority, our land has become a prey to our traditional enemies. The hundreds of new made graves, the scars of thousands of mutilated bodies and the tragedies of innumerable sorrows all bear silent but eloquent testimony to Ulster's dark agony.

Let us also remember that as our case is desperate so is the case of our enemies. They must succeed or perish; they must conquer us or be destroyed themselves. They know that they are most certainly doomed if they are defeated. Hence their madness. They are devotees of that godless monster which has drenched Ireland with blood for many generations – the godless monster of a United Ireland.

In their frenzied devotion they spare neither man, woman nor child, Roman Catholic or Protestant. They are prepared to wade to victory, nay even swim to victory, in the blood of their fellow countrymen. Decency, honour, truth or morality are totally irrelevant as far as they are concerned. They trample them under their feet as of no account as they stampede forward in their base lust for power. Rev. William Arlow stands indicted of the basest of falsehoods, when he comes to their defence with the testimony that they are SINCERE MEN SEEKING PEACE.

Well might we ask what sort of sincerity is this? Yes and what sort of peace is this? Mr. Arlow has drunk the heady wine of ecumenism so deeply that his mind is in a stupor and his eyes are blind to the plain unadulterated facts. In the delusion which follows such inebriation the victim BELIEVES THE LIE.

If our enemies win then we and our children will have our future fortunes determined by a tyranny which has no parallel in Ireland's history.

Make no mistake about it we are struggling for CONSTITUTIONAL FREEDOM.

... We must not suffer the infamy of betraying the sublimest of trusts. This beautiful land cannot be allowed to be subjected to our enemies. Our fields, our homes, our firesides and the graves of our fathers, our cities and our churches, our wives and our families we must protect and defend from

---

[64] Published by the author in January 1975. Emphases mine.

every hazard. The glorious heritage which our fathers left us we must never betray. The hopes with which they died and which buoyed their spirits in the last conflict we can never permit to be extinguished.

We must grasp the torch which they so nobly bore aloft and transmit it with increasing brightness to generations yet to come.

The words 'defeat' or 'surrender' must not be named amongst us. They are not to be dreamed of. We must settle it now that we MUST SUCCEED. We cannot parley with an enemy who sees such parley as but another path in its strategy to destroy us. Peace with such a foe can only come when he has surrendered. Any other peace would have within it the seed of our destruction.

We must not, we cannot, we dare not sit down and discuss chances. There is too much at stake to think of discussing probabilities. We must make success a certainty and that by the help of Almighty God we can do. If we are prepared to do our duty, our whole duty we have nothing to fear.

What is our duty as Protestants at the present time? This is the question with which we must gravely concern ourselves. OUR FIRST DUTY IS TO BE FULLY ALERTED AS ULSTER PROTESTANTS TO THE REAL NATURE OF THE ATTACK AGAINST US.

... Ulster is the last bastion of Bible Protestantism in Europe and as such she stands the sole obstacle to this Roman Catholic Europe.

... The Roman Catholic Church is deeply involved in the IRA's terrorist campaign and officially backs the view that Northern Ireland heretofore was an unjust society. Roman Catholic priests have been deep in active service with the IRA both with bullets and bombs. Some of them are at present hiding in sanctuary in the Irish Republic ....

TWO: WE MUST ACKNOWLEDGE OUR TOTAL DEPENDENCE ON GOD AND GUARD AGAINST ANY CONFIDENCE IN THE FLESH

...

THREE: WE MUST RE-AFFIRM TO OUR ROMAN CATHOLIC FELLOW COUNTRYMEN AND WOMEN WHAT OUR PRINCIPLES ARE.

We must not for a moment longer permit the propaganda war to go unchanged. Principles and aims contrary to the very nature of Protestantism have been attributed to us.

The Ulster Protestant has been mirrored around the world as a veritable monster who would deny the right to breathe to his Roman Catholic neighbours. (As a matter of fact it is the IRA who will not let Ulstermen and women, both Protestant and Roman Catholic, breathe and have declared that they will do the same in the rest of the United Kingdom.)

Protestantism stands for civil and religious liberty. What we ask for ourselves we would not deny to any of our fellow countrymen. No man should be persecuted for his religious views. That is the heritage of Protestantism. ...

FOUR: A BANDING OF OURSELVES TOGETHER FOR THE DEFENCE AND PRESERVATION OF OUR COUNTRY.

As Ulster Protestants we must face the stern facts that the bulwarks of our society have been dismantled by successive British Governments. Bowing to the attacks of our enemies, our own defence forces, a well trained and armed RUC and Ulster Special Constabulary, were swept away. British politicians told us that if these contentious forces were disarmed, and in the case of the 'B' Specials disbanded, all would be well. ...

Our Parliament was next swept away. We were then told all would be well. What happened? The killings increased more and more.

Then Republicans with 22 per cent. of the vote must have 40 per cent. of the seats in the new Executive. Did this bring violence to an end? No, the violence escalated.

Then our future was to be placed partly in the hands of Dublin and the RUC was to be partly Dublin-controlled through the iniquitous Sunning-dale Agreement – Ulster's Munich.

Only when long-suffering Protestants rose up in wrath were the Faulknerite traitors swept from office and our Province delivered from institutions designed according to one SDLP spokesman to 'trundle Ulster into a United Ireland.'

... The time has come when all those willing to defend our Province must be called together and an overall plan devised for the protection of our homes, the defence of our Province and the preservation of our heritage. The British Government, the Republic, the IRA and the nest of traitors in our midst must see that we are determined men and will not stand idly by and see our heritage slowly but surely destroyed.

The Army Council of the IRA murderers knows what is happening. Mr. Rees knows what is happening but the Protestant people of Ulster are being kept in the dark although they are the people most deeply affected. The negotiations between representatives of Mr. Rees and the representatives of the IRA bode ill for Ulster and the attempt by the ecumenical clergy to cloak these over in the name of Christian peace is vile treachery. The Bible puts purity before peace but there is nothing pure about negotiations with those who at this very moment are killing and bombing and destroying. Those who in the name of peace want to make an arrangement with such an enemy and advocate agreement to that enemy's proposals I here and now brand as traitors. Their counsels must be rejected and their conspiracy overthrown.

Fellow Protestants, we are not struggling for fleeting or temporary interests but for our very being. Our enemies have begun to sing the songs of victory in advance and are confidently anticipating their triumph as the result of a perfidious British Government.

That triumph they must not have. The example of our forefathers forbids us their sons to surrender to such a foe. We must be prepared to expel our enemy by any and every means in our power. We fight for our lives and our national identity.

The eyes of the world are upon us. We have become a spectacle to God, to angels and to men. Can our hearts grow faint or our hands feeble in such a cause as this. The spirit of our fathers calls to us from their graves. Their heroic deeds urge us to prayer, courage and determination.

The opportunity is ours and by God's help we can redeem this Province from bondage and from ruin. May we not be found wanting.

This statement was published by Paisley and widely distributed in January 1975. It appeared, also, as a one page advertisement in the popular provincial newspaper, the *News Letter*. Such was its effect that some of Paisley's followers in the Ballymena area believed it was the prelude to Paisley's taking up arms against the British government.[65] The immediate context in which the statement was made was the introduction of a temporary cease-fire, which followed a meeting between members of the Provisional IRA and some leading Protestant clergy from the four main Protestant denominations. As a follow-up to the calling of this cease-fire, UK civil servants, under the direction of the secretary of state for Northern Ireland, Merlyn Rees, began talks with Provisional Sinn Fein (generally regarded as the political wing of PIRA). These talks led to an agreement to allow Sinn Fein to establish and run incident centres whose task was to monitor the cease-fire and take appropriate action to preserve the cease-fire if any incidents threatened its continuation. Involving, as they did, discussions with the dread Republican enemy by both Protestant clergy and representatives of the British government, these events surrounding the calling of the cease-fire were ripe for appropriation by Paisley, as they could so readily be construed in terms of the persecutory position and the affiliative-corporate mode of Unionist ideology. Further, both the meeting between the Protestant clergy and PIRA and the discussions with Sinn Fein leading to the establishment of incident centres had been facilitated by the Reverend William Arlow, associate secretary of the Irish Council of Churches. As go-between he seemed to warrant particular hostility.

Paisley's 'call' names Unionists explicitly as 'Protestants of Ulster' and it identifies Ulster as 'the last bastion of Bible Protestantism in Europe'. Enemies confront this Ulster Protestant subject from all sides. Having dominated Europe and penetrated Britain via the ecumenical movement, only Ulster and her traditions of liberty stand

---

[65]   Clifford Smyth, *Ian Paisley: Voice of Protestant Ulster*, p. 95. Clifford Smyth was a member of the DUP from 1972 to 1976 and a public representative in both the Northern Ireland Assembly and the Constitutional Convention, where he served as honorary secretary to the United Ulster Unionist Council. His knowledge of this reaction to Paisley's address is authoritive.

in the way of total domination from Rome. Hence, the IRA terrorist campaign is supported by Rome; the IRA is construed as Rome's agent. In speaking of 'our enemies' Paisley, near the beginning of his 'call', makes implicit reference to the Provisional IRA and its supporters: 'devotees of that godless monster which has drenched Ireland with blood for many generations – the godless monster of a United Ireland'. Such enemies are diabolical in character; they spare no-one, 'neither man, woman nor child, Roman Catholic or Protestant'; they are ruthless, 'prepared to wade to victory, nay even swim to victory, in the blood of their fellow countrymen' and they are without decency, honour or morality in their 'base lust for power'.

Two aspects of this construction of the 'enemy' warrant comment. First there can be no doubt but that the Unionist community felt itself besieged by 'terrorists'; most Unionists reading Paisley's 'call' could readily bring to mind a relation, friend or acquaintance who had been killed or, more usually, injured through a PIRA action. Second, it is the particular form which Paisley's repudiation of 'terrorism' takes to which I want to draw attention. The Republican enemy is construed as barbaric and as lacking the basic human dignities. Indeed their 'lust for power' is the only quality ascribed to them. We should note the consequence of this dehumanising construction of the 'enemy'. Any attempt to discuss differences, any attempt to introduce and maintain a cease-fire through consultation and accommodation, is ruled out of court. No chances may be taken, no openings for peace explored, if they involve a 'parley with an enemy'. No peace is acceptable except the peace which follows the abject surrender of the enemy.

At this stage of the 'call' care is taken to specify that both Roman Catholic and Protestant are the victims of the enemy's lust for power. And later, in discussing the third duty of reaffirming 'our principles' to 'our Roman Catholic fellow countrymen' the virtues of 'the heritage of Protestantism' ('civil and religious liberty') are extended to 'both Protestant and Roman Catholic'. However only Republican 'terror' is mentioned in this 'call'; Protestant paramilitaries and the British army are omitted. Moreover, in recounting Ulster's history as a history of betrayal the representation of the minority community in the power-sharing executive is referred to disparagingly, as follows: 'Republicans with 22 per cent of the vote must have 40 per cent of the seats in the new Executive.' With the effect that 'the violence escalated'. In this late reference to the Nationalist/Catholic community the prior careful distinction between the implacable Republican enemy and the Roman Catholic good neighbour is lost, as the minority community becomes an undifferentiated group of 'Republicans'.

In this construction of the Nationalist/Catholic other the rules of the dehumanising and persecutory positions are drawn upon. At first a split is made between those seeking the 'godless monster of a United Ireland' and those characterised as 'Roman Catholic fellow countrymen'. The former are construed via the dehumanising position, but what are we to make of the latter? Paisley creates a formal category of equality into which certain Roman Catholics may step. Perhaps he intends all such Roman Catholics other than members or committed supporters of political violence? It soon becomes clear that this is not the case as SDLP members and supporters, that is those associated with the most inclusivist of the major Nationalist/Catholic groupings, are reduced to the category 'Republican' and linked to the two themes of increased violence and unfair, undemocratic representation in the processes of government and administration. As we have seen in previous instances this construction of the 'good neighbour' Roman Catholic is iconic in form. I noted in chapter 4 that such iconic constructions of the 'good' Catholic are 'curiously devoid of content' and this is the case again here.[66] At the point that content is introduced the full implications of this reliance upon the persecutory position (for this aspect of the 'call') becomes apparent; the iconic positive construction turns to a persecutory negative construction embracing the Nationalist/Catholic community. No longer is the persecutory construction restricted to PIRA and its supporters, rather it is extended to include the most liberal or inclusivist members of the Nationalist/Catholic community. As soon as members of this community enter the sequence of political action, as soon as they act in ways which locate them in an actual position (thereby taking on content), viewed from the persecutory position they become a dangerous, untrustworthy other. Construed from within this position no interactions between Nationalists/Catholics and Unionists/Protestants could lead to peace; only unilateral surrender by the enemy, or divine Providence, can offer this. In this manner the fragility of Paisley's opening towards his 'fellow-countrymen' is revealed. Above we have already

[66] See p. 84 above.

seen how such constructions can feed back into a perverse cycle driving both communities towards exclusivist positions and policies.

If the construction of the Nationalist/Catholic other is persecutory in form, with a certain reliance upon the dehumanising position as well, what of the construction of Protestant subjectivity? Again we find a split, this time between the true Protestant and those, like William Arlow and his ilk, who have drunk the 'the heady wine of ecumenism'. The true Protestants of Ulster are understood as under attack from all sides. Their duty is to resist so as to preserve the traditions of their forefathers and thereby protect their freedom and their loved ones. This construction of the 'good' Protestant is clearly organised by the rules of the persecutory position, as is the construction of the 'bad' Protestant. Personified in the Rev. William Arlow, the 'bad' Protestant is construed as such because he treats with the enemy; indeed Arlow is akin to a latter-day Lundy in clerical garb. He is guilty of falsehood, he is an 'inebriated victim' of ecumenical and Republican propaganda. Because he has worked towards an inclusivist identity he must be repudiated. Arlow and others supporting negotiations are accused of 'vile treachery' and branded as 'traitors'.

In his call to the Protestants of Ulster in 1975 Paisley drew upon the persecutory position, with occasional reliance on the dehumanising position, to construct the subjectivities of Protestant and Catholic and to prescribe the proper form of relationship between the two communities. He constructed a split world in which the dominant affect is persecutory anxiety allied with feelings of righteousness, and he interpreted attempts at some form of cease-fire and negotiation as treachery. To the extent that such a construction was dominant within Unionism, especially within both Vanguard and the DUP, the possibility of changing the forms of subjectivity and intersubjectivity in Northern Ireland were severely limited.

BREAKING THE RULES FROM THE INSIDE

Terence O'Neill was always an unlikely leader of the Unionist community. Although born into one of the great old Ulster families he had been educated at Eton and had taken on the manner of an English gentleman. So out of tune with Ulster Unionism was he that upon his appointment as prime minister it was necessary for him to join, very belatedly, two significant Orange organisations: the Apprentice Boys of Derry and the Royal Black Preceptory. William

Craig, on the other hand, was one of Ulster's favourite sons. In place of O'Neill's stilted patrician manner Craig displayed an ability to move comfortably through all sectors of Ulster (Unionist) society. Craig was well connected at Stormont, where he was chief Unionist Party whip before succeeding to a ministry in 1963. He was often a keynote speaker at Twelfth of July demonstrations. At the same time he was well acquainted with Unionist workers' and paramilitary groupings. It was exactly this breadth of political range which suited him so well for his role as leader of Vanguard. But the question eventually arose as to how creative he could be in his leadership role. Could he break through to a new set of rules for subjectivity and intersubjectivity where O'Neill and others had faltered and fallen? Could he carry Unionism towards an inclusivist identity? Or would he suffer the same fate as O'Neill and, early in 1975, William Arlow. Would he too be treated as a Lundy if he moved too far?

In February 1975 William Craig told a Loyalist rally in Portrush that, 'It is only when Ulster men and women share the same allegiance that the conflict can end. We would like to see the minority give its allegiance to the country they live in and we are willing to consider ways and means of encouraging it.'[67] Interviewed by the *Irish Times* in June 1975, he was asked by Henry Kelly whether he or the UUUC would ever form a coalition government on the lines of the power-sharing Executive. Craig answered:

I can see that if we were to move towards a new status there might be a need for voluntary coalitions. Let us say for the sake of argument that in a future Parliament of Northern Ireland I was the leader of the majority party. Then certainly I would be looking round for members of other political parties to serve as members of a Government.[68]

In August and September of 1975, as one of the tripartite leaders of the UUUC coalition between Vanguard, the DUP and the Official

[67]   *Irish Times*, 'The Real Paisley Stands Up as Craig Dares to Move Forward', 13 September 1975, 8. In this article the author, Conor O'Clery, points out the unlikely character of this new initiative by Craig in the following terms: 'It was Craig who said in October, 1972, in a speech in London, that Loyalists might have to shoot to kill, an ominous warning of the gathering Protestant backlash. It was Craig who said as recently as May 1974, on [Irish Radio and Television network] that sectarian murders were understandable and excusable, pointing out that people who lived in the state of Northern Ireland must abide by the allegiance of the majority. Craig was also the Loyalist leader most actively identified with the rise of Loyalist paramilitary organisations. The UDA sprang from his early 1972 rallies, lining up in uniform for his inspection at mass gatherings culminating in the March '72 rally of 60,000 Loyalists in Belfast's Ormeau Park. To this day the Vanguard leader remains close to the UDA and the Ulster Army Council of paramilitary leaders.'

[68]   *Irish Times*, 13 September 1975, p. 8.

Unionist Party within the newly elected Constitutional Convention, Craig headed the three-person negotiating team for the UUUC in their consultations with the SDLP.[69] It was in this context that Craig developed, and courageously promoted, his new conception of a voluntary coalition government. This government, and its cabinet, would be modelled on the British War Cabinet in which the members of the major parties formed a voluntary coalition for the duration of the emergency. Hence, in Northern Ireland it would include SDLP members in cabinet along with members from the principal Unionist parties.This modest attempt to move the rules of Unionist ideology in an inclusivist direction was developed to meet British government requirements for some form of power-sharing and, thereby, to regain an Ulster parliament and government at Stormont in which Nationalists would sit in cabinet, for the duration of any emergency, by invitation of a Unionist prime minister. Conceived from within Vanguard, Craig's opening towards the voluntary inclusion of Nationalists was a bold move. If successful, it could have restored to Ulster its own regional parliament at Stormont. However, the proposal was firmly rejected by the UUUC, leading to Craig's resignation as Vanguard leader.[70]

Stories abound about the political calculations of Ian Paisley, Peter Robinson (DUP secretary at the time), Harry West (leader of the Official Unionist Party) and others.[71] No doubt these political actors were engaged in making strategic decisions in the interests of themselves and their parties. But beyond this it is clear from the various commentaries on these events that Craig's proposal seemed outlandish, either a profound mistake or an inexplicable betrayal.[72]

[69] Official Unionist Party had become the new name for the old Ulster Unionist Party. Subsequently it reverted to Ulster Unionist Party.

[70] In his letter of resignation Craig made the following points:

'Coalition government in accordance with British practice cannot be equated with the ill named concept of power-sharing as invented in 1973, which by law guarantees not only minority positions in the Executive but gives them real power. Any coalition government only comes into existence by agreement, an agreement which covers every aspect of government policy and such a government is at the end of the day a majority government with the Prime Minister hiring and firing so that government policy is not only conscientiously upheld but honestly implemented.

... 'I have, however, decided to resign my leadership of the Vanguard Convention Party having regard to the fact that only six Vanguard members supported me yesterday to delay the decision until the whole matter could be further investigated.' *Irish Times*, 10 September 1975.

[71] See Smyth, *Ian Paisley*, pp. 100–5.

[72] Ibid., pp. 101–3.

This was so, despite the fact that he received strong support from the *News Letter*, the principal newspaper of Unionist opinion, and that he could count on the loyalty of some members of the UDA.[73] Paisley had himself participated in some discussions regarding voluntary coalition, but eventually he had led the opposition to Craig's advocacy of this solution.[74] In full knowledge that the ground was moving from under him Craig, and Glen Barr, a leading member of the UDA, persisted with the attempt to move Unionism towards inclusivism.[75] As Craig said of these events at the time, when interviewed on BBC television:

'The SDLP undertook to look seriously at our proposals with a view to reaching agreement based on them and I would have thought the least we

[73] The *News Letter*, as reported in the *Irish Times*, responded to the situation as follows:

The *News Letter*, a strong supporter of the UUUC is emphatically backing the attitude of Mr. William Craig to power-sharing with the SDLP ... Its editorial headed 'Need for more bloody brains' – said: ... 'Lack of clarity of thought, if not actual lack of brains, seems to have been responsible for the present sad confusion in the ranks of the UUUC coalition, which has led to the resignation of Mr. William Craig from the leadership of the Vanguard Party. Mr. Craig contends that his proposal at the UUUC meeting on Monday – that the SDLP leaders could be admitted to a future cabinet at the discretion of an inevitably Unionist Prime Minister, to form a coalition to deal with an emergency, along the pattern that has been the case in the past at Westminster – is not in breach of the UUUC manifesto. The Rev. Ian Paisley had proposed a motion bluntly rejecting power-sharing with Republicans and an amendment was proposed and seconded at the meeting suggesting that Mr. Craig's scheme should be given a detailed examination. The amendment was defeated and those who demanded that the original motion be passed put the issue in thunderous 'black or white' terms: 'Are you for or against power-sharing at cabinet level?' Faced with the crudely stated choice, the meeting was stampeded into steam-rollering flat Mr. Craig's sensible plan which could have been a step towards bringing majority and minority closer in the province and isolating the terrorists. *Irish Times*, 11 September 1975, p. 5.

[74] See Smyth, *Ian Paisley*, pp. 101–2.

[75] See the *Ballymena Guardian*, 4 December 1975, p. 5, for the report of two follow-up speeches by Craig and Glen Barr to a local branch of Vanguard. In this retrospective view Glen Barr draws upon exclusivist rules to justify his support of the voluntary coalition scheme:

They were ... informed that the S.D.L.P would be prepared to accept the [voluntary coalition] document in its entirety, with the exception of one paragraph, and that was such a shift in the SDLP policy that we could not believe it. ... It was easy to shout 'No Surrender' and 'Not an Inch,' but while we have been looking after the inches we lost feet and yards. Their Area Boards had been 'taken over' by Republicans and we haven't got many inches left, but the SDLP were always able to close their ranks and to close any rift.'
... In the eyes of the world, Mr. Barr stated, the UUUC were bigots, but 'we have got to send our side of the story to the world at large.' The Loyalists had failed to do anything over the six years of the crisis, and 'if we bury our heads in the sand how do you think Westminster will give us devolved government?'
'There were those who said we will remain British at all costs, but did the British have nothing to say about it? Westminster was only looking for the day when she could cut off her links.

could do would be to facilitate them in exploring every aspect and every sort of situation that could arise out of our proposals.'

... Mr. Craig went on to say that he did not know if the SDLP would have given ground: 'and the tragedy is that I will never know because we have slammed the door on exploration, slammed it I think in a most unfair way. We have said to them, look, you're good enough to be the loyal Opposition and we're going to give you plenty of power as the loyal Opposition. But even if you became fully convinced that our policies are right, you're never going to be good enough in any emergency or in any set of circumstances to join in a widely based coalition.'

... 'if at the end of the day ... now there is a very big "if" here and I have no grounds for saying we would arrive at this situation ... but if at the end of the day the SDLP had said to us, "Look, we're prepared to give support to your proposals, we will help to get an unanimous report out of the Convention for the restoration of a Parliament of Northern Ireland, the restoration of majority rule in the province, but if we give you that help in order to inspire confidence and to help us out of the crisis that we are all in, would you be prepared to envisage for the first part on a purely voluntary agreement, a gentleman's agreement to have a widely based coalition", I certainly for one would be prepared to consider that.'[76]

Here we see Craig drawing upon the rules of the ambivalent position in his modest attempt to break the ideological rules in Northern Ireland. He failed to do so, at great cost to his own political career and the future of the Vanguard movement he had established, which rapidly declined in significance after his resignation from the leadership. The fate which Craig, his proposal and his movement met with is just one more example which highlights how deeply embedded exclusivist forms of Unionist ideology are in Northern Ireland. This example, like the several others we have seen in these last two chapters, makes it clear that ideology, understood as the field of subjectivity and intersubjectivity, is integral to both the way in which political reality is construed in Northern Ireland and, through the structuration process, just as integral to the ways in which political and social initiatives play themselves out in the on-going making of the history of Northern Ireland.

[76] *Irish Times*, 10 September 1975, p. 8. The Alliance Party also supported this proposal and drew upon the rules of the ambivalent position and the post-conventional-liberal mode of Unionist ideology to do so. See the *Irish Times*, 10 September 1975, p. 8 for the Alliance proposals.

Conclusion: the Framework Document and its discontents

> What momentum are you talking about? Nobody in Northern Ireland sees any momentum at all in terms of a peace process. All they see is the government making concession after concession to terrorists; they see the political concessions being made through the Framework Document; they see the IRA doing absolutely nothing by way of making any gesture in terms of setting out an agenda whereby it is going to stand down its organisation, where the killer gangs are going to be put down; or indeed where they are going to hand over any arms or ammunition, or explosives. They have done absolutely nothing. It is a one-way process of steady concessions being made to the IRA. That is not a peace process, that is a surrender process.
>
> (Peter Robinson, 2 April 1995, on BBC World Service)

As I write this final chapter Northern Ireland is in its eighth month of cease-fire. The killing has stopped and the politics has become more frenetic. How are the various political actors and groupings in Northern Ireland making sense of this new moment? Is there, at last, the real possibility of displacing exclusivist forms of identity and relations and instituting a new political imaginary?

At the end of August 1994, the IRA, after detailed negotiations with the British and Irish governments, and under the tutelage of Gerry Adams as leader of Sinn Fein and John Hume as leader of the SDLP, declared a cease-fire. This act, and its parallel accompaniment by Loyalist paramilitary groups six weeks later, has created in Northern Ireland a set of circumstances which is quite unique for the period since 1969. By now, April 1995, Northern Ireland has experienced a sustained period of peace within which a second major process has begun to play itself out. In late February 1995 the British and Irish governments, after lengthy negotiations which had their immediate origin in the Downing Street Declaration of late 1993, jointly released a 31 page *Framework Document* (*FD*) which, as the title suggests, offers a framework for the future governance of Northern Ireland and the form of its future affiliations with both Britain and Ireland. These circumstances, as has been readily recognised by many commentators, offer Northern Ireland a unique opportunity to re-order the pattern of community relations and establish a society which, finally, has escaped the disfiguring conflict, and the distorting patterns of relations, privilege and access, which have exercised such dominance over the conduct of everyday life. At the same time this possibility has cast Unionism into crisis. As in 1968, inclusivist forms of identity and inclusivist forms of political and social relations have been imagined by various groupings and the politics of institutionalising such forms has begun. Inevitably such moves have given rise to a resistance within Unionism; exclusivist Unionism feels itself threatened and is searching for ways to re-establish itself. The most potent symbolic object around which this political process is playing itself out is the *FD* itself.

THE FRAMEWORK DOCUMENT

In a 'joint declaration', launched in Northern Ireland on 22 February 1995, by their respective prime ministers, the governments of both the United Kingdom and the Republic of Ireland set out a common and agreed framework for a re-organisation of political life in Northern Ireland; 'a shared understanding reached between them on the parameters of a possible outcome to the Talks process'.[1] Paragraph 8 of this joint declaration conveys the scope of what is at stake:

Both Governments are aware that the approach in this document presents challenges to strongly held positions on all sides. However, a new beginning in relationships means addressing fundamental issues in a new way and inevitably requires significant movement from all sides. This document is not a rigid blueprint to be imposed but both Governments believe it sets out a realistic and balanced framework for agreement which could be achieved, with flexibility and goodwill on all sides, in comprehensive negotiations with the relevant political parties in Northern Ireland.

Paragraph 10 sets out certain 'guiding principles' which have been agreed upon by both governments. These are (i) self-determination; (ii) consent of the governed; (iii) 'that agreement must be pursued and established by exclusively democratic, peaceful means, without

[1]   *Framework Document*, paragraph 7. Reprinted in the *Irish Times*, 23 February 1995.

resort to violence or coercion'; and (iv) 'that any new political arrangements must be based on full respect for and protection and expression of, the rights and identities of both traditions in Ireland and even-handedly afford both communities in Northern Ireland parity of esteem and treatment, including equality of opportunity and advantage'.

Even by themselves, these two paragraphs establish that any new political arrangements which would satisfy the principles of the *FD* would inevitably involve a fundamental challenge to the exclusivist forms of both Unionism and Nationalism. This becomes even clearer as the document unfolds its proposed institutional arrangements and its proposed guarantees. Three institutional 'strands' are outlined. *First*, a set of structures within Northern Ireland. These structures have been given more elaborate specification in a separate document issued by the British government. They involve an assembly elected by proportional representation and a separate panel of three members, elected from within Northern Ireland, which would monitor and complement the Assembly.[2] *Secondly*, a set of North–South institutions charged with the following onerous objectives:

to enable representatives of democratic institutions, North and South, to enter into new, cooperative and constructive relationships, to promote agreement among the people of the island of Ireland; to carry out on a democratically accountable basis delegated executive, harmonising and consultative functions over a range of designated matters to be agreed; and to serve to acknowledge and reconcile the rights, identities and aspirations of the two major traditions.

The membership of this North–South body would be drawn from both the Northern Ireland Assembly and the Irish parliament. As part of the arrangement members of the Northern Ireland Assembly would be required to be available for service on the North–South body; they would have a 'right of duty' to serve. *Thirdly*, the so-called East–West structures linking Ireland and the UK in order 'to enhance the existing basis for cooperation between the two Governments, and to promote, support and underwrite the fair and effective operation of the new arrangements'.

These proposals for new political structures within Northern Ireland, between the two parts of Ireland and between the governments of the United Kingdom and the Republic of Ireland are

[2] 'Britain proposes new Northern Ireland assembly', *Reuters*, 22 February 1995.

complemented by a consideration of constitutional issues. Paragraph 17 states that 'it would be wrong to make any change in the status of Northern Ireland save with the consent of a majority of the people of Northern Ireland', thereby guaranteeing continued incorporation within the UK to any majority so desiring, for so long as it remains a majority. However, in a principled, if dispassionate, instance of even-handedness the paragraph continues by noting that if 'in future a majority of the people there wish for and formally consent to the establishment of a united Ireland, the two Governments will intro-duce and support legislation to give effect to that wish'. In paragraph 16 the Irish government accepts 'that the democratic right of self determination by the people of Ireland as a whole must be achieved and exercised with and subject to the agreement and consent of a majority of the people of Northern Ireland'. It also makes a commit-ment to changing Articles 2 and 3 of the Irish constitution in a manner which would 'fully reflect the principle of consent in Northern Ireland and demonstrably be such that no territorial claim of right to jurisdiction over Northern Ireland contrary to the will of a majority of its people is asserted'. Finally, in paragraph 55 the document states that both 'Governments intend that the outcome of these negotiations will be submitted for democratic ratification through referendums, North and South.'[3]

What are we to make of this set of joint proposals? Are they better viewed as either a trap or as an escape-hatch for Unionists? As Peter Robinson, deputy leader of the DUP, makes clear in the epigraph above, any reading of the *FD* in terms of exclusivist rules inevitably construes it as 'not a peace process, [but] a surrender process'. On the other hand an inclusivist reading, such as that by Siobhan Laird, a press officer for the Alliance party, construes the *FD*, and the process which generated it, as a guarantee that there is 'no threat to the legitimate rights of Unionists. There is, however, a challenge to Unionists to accept the equal rights of Nationalists.'[4] Such an acceptance would involve an inclusivist structuration of Unionist ideology; thereby creating the possibility of escape from the sectarian enmities of the past.

In a very interesting assessment of the *FD* one expert commen-tator, Padraig O'Malley, has suggested the following:

[3] All the above quotations are taken from the *Framework Document*, as reprinted in the *Irish Times*, 23 February 1995.

[4] S. Laird, 'Agreement threatens all', *Fortnight*, no. 338, April 1995, p. 17.

The remarkable thing is that, in the end, the IRA has settled for so little. Almost every proposal in the joint Framework Document has been on the table or discussed in one form or another during the last 15 years ... The Unionists have blinkered themselves if they cannot see that they are being given a veto not only in the matter of the constitutional status of Northern Ireland but in virtually every other structure of governance which the document proposes. Indeed, the document is replete with an almost obsequious acquiescence to the need for the consent of the Unionists at every stage ... [It] 'wraps the unionists' constitutional status in ironclad guarantees}..

What would be the benefits to Unionists? ... [P]eace, an end to what they regard as a war of genocide against their people, a new parliament for Northern Ireland, and a copperfastened, guarantee of their constitutional status. In short, if Unionists are willing to accept a North–South body with executive powers ... the [Irish] Government will amend its constitution to drop its territorial claim to Northern Ireland. Negotiations necessarily imply compromise, and on this basis the Framework Document puts in place the parameters of a non zero sum game. Both sides can be winners, if only they are prepared to give some. Without a willingness to compromise on many important and deeply felt issues on the part of both Unionists and Nationalists, the process will go nowhere, setting the stage for civil strife to boil over into civil war. It is not just a matter of the seed withering on the vine; the seed itself will never get sown.[5]

In my opinion this is a very acute analysis of the character of the *FD*. I would extend the claim by suggesting that the *FD* is itself a principal repository and carrier of inclusivist rules for the patterning of identities and relations in Northern Ireland. It amounts to a politically negotiated attempt by the two sovereign governments to reimagine the pattern of relations in Northern Ireland and establish an inclusivist framework within which the particulars of new forms of identity and novel forms of relationship can start to develop. For Unionists this entails two linked possibilities. First, the opportunity to secure, indefinitely, an inclusivist Unionist identity at the cost of discarding exclusivist Unionism. As O'Malley puts this, Unionists have an opportunity to begin playing 'a non zero sum game'. But, of course, in order to be able to do so they need the capacity to read the *FD* for what it offers; i.e. they need to construe it from outside the rules of exclusivist Unionism; hardly an easy option given the deep layering of such exclusivist rules into the practices and institutions of social and political life. Second, as just implied, Unionists may have

[5] P. O'Malley, 'North Needs Its DeKlerks and Mandelas to Move Centre Stage', *Irish Times*, 13 March 1995 (reparagraphed for convenience of presentation).

so much invested in exclusivism, and the exclusivist rules themselves
may be so deeply entrenched, that such an 'outside' reading is
difficult to sustain; indeed is an affront to commonsense and the
established exclusivist ethic. In this case the structuration of Unionist
ideology will tend to consolidate around exclusivist forms of commonsense understanding.

As we have seen throughout this study, it is a mistake to ignore the
internal differentiation within Unionism. Unionist ideology is never
entirely exclusivist or inclusivist. Rather these two broad forms of the
ideology, and the more particular sets of rules which they subsume,
contest to establish themselves as the predominant form. Characteristically in Northern Ireland, this conflict has produced a preponder-
ance of exclusivist forms which have achieved near hegemony in the
structuration of politics and everyday life. But at each moment
inclusivist forms have also been in play, no outcomes have been
automatic and inevitable. What we are seeing in the contemporary
period is yet another conflict within Unionism to establish whether
inclusivist or exclusivist forms will become predominant. This time,
however, the field within which Unionism is operating is more
constrained in scope than ever before. This constraint arises, principally, from the whole set of intergovernmental relations between
Ireland and the UK which have consolidated around the *FD* process.
It also arises from the new international respectability afforded to
Sinn Fein and the constraints which this status imposes upon any
tendency to, again, advocate recourse to 'the bullet' as well as 'the
ballot-box'. Similar processes also have occurred within the Unionist
community. Exclusivism and inclusivism coexist as before, but now
the inclusivist aspects of Unionism are operating in a quite transformed environment. The very fact of a sustained cease-fire is itself a
major change. Beyond this, Direct Rule, intergovernmental cooperation, changes within both the SDLP and Sinn Fein; all these have
created a context within which inclusivist rules have become the
common currency; even when only half-heartedly embraced.[6] In

---

[6]   Sinn Fein is another party in which inclusivist rules hold only a fragile purchase, for the
      moment. The peace process itself has virtually locked the Sinn Fein leadership into a
      position whereby they must draw upon a public discourse of inclusivism in their relations
      with other parties and groupings. This condition has provided an opportunity for a more
      thorough-going transformation of the rules of ideology through which the party construes
      its relations with Unionists, Britain and the Republic. However, whether such inclusivist
      rules will reach into the commonsense assumptions of the party and its supporters is an
      open issue. Its outcome will depend, in large part, upon whether Unionists can themselves
      make such a transition.

such a context the inclusivist forms of Unionism have a renewed opportunity to establish their predominance within the Unionist community, for the very reason that they offer a way forward, an escape hatch rather than a trap. Whether they will be seen as such, whether they will be adopted as the predominant form of Unionist commonsense; these are the issues around which the future of Northern Ireland will be determined.

REACTIONS TO THE FRAMEWORK DOCUMENT

A few weeks prior to its official release a partial draft of the *FD* was leaked to *The Times* newspaper. It generated such fury within the two major Unionist parties, the UUP and the DUP, that the British prime minister, John Major, hurriedly arranged a televised broadcast in an attempt to allay Unionist anxiety and suspicion. In this broadcast Major granted that the *FD* would propose a North–South body but stressed that 'nothing is going to be imposed in Northern Ireland', that any 'North–South bodies must be accountable to the people of Northern Ireland' and that such bodies 'will not be run by London, and they cannot and will not be overridden by the British and Irish governments'.[7] Within Unionism these reassurances met with a mixed reception. Both the DUP and the UUP rejected them in hostile terms. Paisley announced: 'You can't expect any self-respecting Unionist to sit down at a table if that is going to be on the agenda', Molyneaux, then leader of the UUP, stated that 'People in Northern Ireland have already made up their minds, and don't like what they see', and David Trimble, an Ulster Unionist MP at Westminster (and, since September 1995, the new leader of the UUP), announced that if 'the Government endorse this, there is no question of being able to maintain any relationship'.[8] The reaction from two fringe Loyalist groupings with strong links to the two principal Loyalist paramilitary groups, the Ulster Defence Association (UDA) and the Ulster Volunteer Force (UVF), was more measured. Speaking for the Ulster Democratic Party, closely linked to the UDA, John White criticised 'kneejerk' reactions by the UUP and DUP and suggested that their response to the leaked document was 'creating the wrong impression in the Loyalist community and intensifying fears. They don't seem to be

---

[7]   Alan Wheatley, 'Major pleads for trust on N Ireland peace plan', *Reuters*, 1 February 1995.
[8]   P. Vallely, 'Low-Key Theme to Historic Day', *Independent*, 23 February 1995.

trying to give the peace process a chance.' David Ervine, of the
Progressive Unionist Party, closely linked to the UVF, favoured
publication of the *FD* despite his rejection of 'grandiose' plans for
cross-border bodies. His rationale was that although 'We may
never resolve the implacable differences in Northern Ireland ... I
think we can transform the circumstances in which the argument
takes place.'[9]

The leaking of a partial draft of the *FD* gave both the UUP and
the DUP a head start in preparation of their response to the final
documents. Indeed in a scene which might well have been drawn
from Alice's experiences 'through the looking-glass', both parties
promulgated their response to the *FD* prior to its actual release. In
its pre-emptive response, 'A Practical Approach to Problem Solving
in Northern Ireland', the UUP invoked 'the fundamental principles
of democracy' and went on to advocate the creation of a Northern
Ireland Interim Assembly which would play the pivotal role in
determining the character and extent of any relations with the
Republic of Ireland. In effect this proposal amounted to advocacy of
a return to an exclusivist governmental institution in which Unionists would hold all the cards. Viewed from within an exclusivist
perspective such a proposal is the obvious and proper way to
proceed. Viewed from outside such a perspective, however, it
amounts to an attempt to foreclose any possibility for a re-working
of identities and relations in Northern Ireland which might prove
acceptable to both traditions. Hence it is a nice irony that the UUP
response should have pre-dated the document to which it was
intended as an answer.

One feature of the *FD* attracted special scorn from the UUP: its
advocacy of referenda in both Northern Ireland and the Republic as
the final moment in the ratification of any new arrangements
generated from the process of all-party talks. Instead of regarding
this as a further guarantee of the Unionist veto over unacceptable
arrangements, the UUP saw it as a ploy by the British government to
divide the Unionist community from its political leadership. 'It
would now appear that the government believes it can create a
divide between the greater number of people in Northern Ireland
and the Unionist leadership, and hopes to use a referendum to
deliver Northern Ireland's affairs into the hands of all Ireland

[9]   N. Watt, 'Fringe Loyalists Attack "Kneejerk" Reaction to Leak', *The Times*, 3 February
1995.

political institutions.'[10] Of course it is the case that one of the many possibilities opened up by the referendum process is exactly the possibility of achieving majority support for proposals with which one or both of the principal Unionist parties is unhappy. However the other, more likely, possibilities include achieving majority support for a position advocated by one or both of the principal Unionist parties. As it stands the *FD* can guarantee nothing about outcomes from inter-party discussions. The political process is inevitably contingent. It is this contingency and the possibility of inclusivist outcomes from inter-party talks to which this UUP 'Approach' raises objections. These objections would appear to arise from a reading of the current political process through a lens provided by the rules of exclusivist Unionism. Of course, insofar as this is the case it is likely to produce a systematic distortion in any inter-party discussions with parties drawing upon inclusivist rules and to lead to a complete stalemate, and the probable breakdown of the negotiation process, in talks with parties from the other tradition drawing upon exclusivist rules.

The DUP response was broadly similar in kind.[11] Paisley branded the *FD* a 'nefarious conspiracy' and claimed that the British and Irish governments were 'planning the eventual betrayal and dismantling of the Union'. In a statement uncannily reminiscient of William Craig's exclusivist reading, in 1968, of the Government of Ireland Act of 1920,[12] Paisley continued: 'It (the *FD*) is setting out the only conditions whereby we can have an assembly, and what sort of assembly we are going to have, and what will be the restriction of that assembly, *so it is a blatant interference in Northern Ireland's right to govern itself*.'[13] Again, as with the UUP, this would appear to be an exclusivist reading of the *FD*. However, given the evidence I have discussed, such a judgement remains an impression, although one with a basis in the analysis of Unionist ideology already developed in this study. In particular it is important to note that disagreement with the *FD* is not, *per se*, exclusivist; such disagreement *could* proceed from an inclusivist perspective. It is the form which any such rejection takes, and the

---

[10] 'A Practical Approach to Problem Solving in Northern Ireland', published by the Ulster Unionist Party and reproduced in the *Irish Times*, 22 February 1995.

[11] For details see Gerry Moriarty, 'DUP Issues Alternative to Framework Document', *Irish Times*, 21 February 1995.

[12] See the discussion of this in chapter 8, p. 169 above.

[13] Moriarty, 'DUP Issues Alternative to Framework Document'.

consequent implications for intergroup relations, which are of critical interest in this regard. To explore this further I now want to focus on two significant Unionist figures: Peter Robinson of the DUP and John Taylor of the UUP.

Peter Robinson, the deputy leader of the DUP, responded to the *FD* in the following vein:

The people I represent, more than any others, deserve peace and stability. They are the most wronged, persecuted and vilified people in the civilised world. For a quarter of a century, they have refused to bow to terrorism and many have paid for it with their life's blood. They have been bombed and shot at, bullied and blackmailed, yet even in their darkest hour, they held on to their cherished membership of the British family.

Being British, for them, was no nominal condition. Their citizenship was under attack, but that danger only caused them to cling more tightly to their Britishness. A dagger wielded by the hand of a friend is the cruellest cut of all and they now see, once again, a Tory Prime Minister betraying loyal Ulster.

The process is clear. It is to bring about a United Ireland, incrementally and by stealth. This week's published Framework Document offers no Union-strengthening option. It is entirely a nationalist agenda for bringing about a united Ireland. We are told rejection of this proposal could end the peace process. As if we, who have been the victims of violence, would be responsible for the terrorists starting up again because we refuse to surrender.

Politicians have a duty to talk, but it would be an irresponsible politician who would sit down at a negotiating table if the agenda excluded any outcome that would be satisfactory to those he represents. It would be an even more foolish politician who would sit down at a negotiating table knowing that the other negotiators had previously pledged themselves to a predetermined outcome.

For the Unionist community of Northern Ireland, this document confirms their worst fears – that they are no longer wanted and that their Government no longer has any selfish, strategic or economic interest in them.

I do not point an accusing finger at Gerry Adams, John Hume or John Bruton. They are acting out their republican role. Just as a dog barks and a pig grunts, I expect nothing else from them, but when I hear John Major proclaim that he is a Unionist while taking an axe to the root of the Union, I find it hard to come to terms with such nauseating hypocrisy. Mr Major's framework is for an all-Ireland structure with executive power, which will be a precursor to a united Ireland.

Mr Major knows the principle behind this proposal well – it is based on the European modus operandi ... Just as in the EU, two territories are brought together and in a number of practical, functional ways, they are treated as one. They are told that it is for economic reasons or for better co-operation, but the truth is that it is to bring about a political union.[14]

This is an eloquent statement concerning the current position of the Unionist community, as construed according to exclusivist forms. The rules of both the persecutory position and the affiliative-corporate mode of Unionist ideology are at play in organising this response to the challenge contained within the *FD*. Robinson draws on the rules of the persecutory position to construct a split world in which his people (the people I represent) are uniquely entitled (more than any others) to 'peace and stability'. Instead, however, they have been continually assaulted and murdered ('shot at, bullied and blackmailed; paid ... with their life's blood') and have become 'the most wronged, persecuted and vilified people'. Throughout this ordeal they have clung ever 'more tightly to their Britishness'. Now, once again, they have been betrayed by 'the hand of a friend', this time by the Conservative prime minister, John Major. His treachery (a dagger wielded by the hand of a friend) is a gross betrayal. Robinson implies (although he does not state this explicitly) that Major is akin to Lundy, the infamous Mayor of Derry. Major is worse than Adams, Hume or Bruton because he is a hypocrite who proclaims 'he is a Unionist while taking an axe to the root of the Union'. They, on the other hand, are mere ciphers of their 'republican role'; ('Just as a dog barks and a pig grunts, I expect nothing else from them'). In this split world the affective structure also contains feelings of abandonment; Unionists 'are no longer wanted', not even for interests which are 'selfish, strategic or economic'.

The discussion of Major also highlights the affiliative-corporate character of this construction of the *FD*. His authority as prime minister is repudiated because of his failure to subscribe to an affiliative-corporate construction of the proper forms of identity and intergroup relations in Northern Ireland. Because he is part of a process which is attempting transformation, because he regards himself as a Unionist without agreeing to the exclusivist construction of what this entails, he is cast beyond the pale.

The dismal outcome from such constructions is provided quite explicitly by Robinson in his discussion of talking and negotiating. A politician's 'duty to talk' is extinguished by the presumption that everything has already been decided and stitched up, so to speak.

[14] P. Robinson, 'Dagger In A Friend's Hand', *Independent*, 24 February 1995.

However we have already seen that this is not a necessary reading of the *FD*; indeed an argument has been made that the *FD* has much to offer Unionism, if only Unionism can see it for what it, mainly, is; more pointedly, for what it could become with enthusiastic Unionist engagement. However the effect of construing the *FD* through exclusivist forms is exactly as this example indicates. Robinson talks about the exclusion of 'any outcome that would be satisfactory to those he represents' and about a 'predetermined outcome' to any talks. The feelings of persecution, betrayal and abandonment and the evaluation of what is 'satisfactory' in terms of the affiliative-corporate mode have produced a refusal to entertain inclusivist forms for the organisation of identities and relations in Northern Ireland. Talks on such grounds are forbidden because they challenge the established commonsense assumptions of the dominant form of Unionism. The effect of such a reading is to promote further a form of Unionist commonsense which trades in presupposition, which is locked into a vicious cycle in which all opportunities for change are discounted and disabled and in which compromise is seen as weakness and treachery. The previous sections of this study have documented in some detail the characteristic effects of such exclusivist readings of events.

Given the extent of DUP commitment to exclusivist forms, and given the absence within its ideology of any genuine scope for inclusivism, attention inevitably turns to the UUP as the potential agent of transformation within established Unionism. The UUP has always been a container of both inclusivist and exclusivist forms of Unionism, but throughout the history of Northern Ireland exclusivist forms have always become predominant within the party at critical moments. Terence O'Neill in the 1960s, and Brian Faulkner at the time of the power-sharing executive in 1974, were, in their different ways, leaders of the UUP who, in attempting to make a difference, precipitated a resurgence of exclusivism. In the current circumstances, due to various factors, such as intergovernmental cooperation and its consequences, such a resurgent exclusivism is somewhat less likely to re-establish itself as the predominant Unionist reality principle. Inclusivism has become the common currency in terms of which all parties are expected to conduct the business of politics. At the same time it is clear enough that inclusivist forms have only a loose purchase on intragroup readings of contemporary events. In the changed circumstances of the current moment it has become pragmatic for predominantly exclusivist groupings from both communities to, at least, affect an inclusivist façade.[15] Whether such pragmatism will win out, whether it can be sustained through lengthy and inevitably difficult negotiations, whether it can lead on to a genuine re-working of the core assumptions of hitherto predominantly exclusivist groupings, be these DUP, UUP, Sinn Fein or, at times, the SDLP, or whether, yet again, exclusivist forms will reassert their hegemony within Unionism and Nationalism; these are the critical issues which will determine the future of Northern Ireland.

IMAGINING A UNIONIST FUTURE: JOHN TAYLOR AND THE UUP

As we have seen, the *FD* has been rejected by both the DUP and the UUP. These rejections have, in the main, been conceived and couched in exclusivist forms. As such they are inevitably part of the problem rather than part of the solution. However within the UUP an unlikely figure, John Taylor, has emerged as the carrier of what, at least for the moment, I will term pragmatic Unionism. Taylor's rejection of the *FD* has been sharp and clear, as will be illustrated below. At the same time he has refused to resort to the bunker and the certitudes of the traditional forms of exclusivism. Instead he has taken a striking political initiative by visiting the Republic of Ireland and presenting a series of speeches in which he has set out both strong Unionist claims and some pragmatic propositions for cooperation. Writing in the *Irish Times* Taylor greeted the *FD* as follows:

The government's proposals represent an unconditional surrender to the IRA and a denial of democratic control to the majority within Northern Ireland. They are designed to create all Ireland bodies with executive powers and to bring about harmonisation of all policies within the island of Ireland until there is an eventual acceptance, i.e. consent, for a united Ireland and the departure of Northern Ireland from the United Kingdom.

The British government states that it wants a democratically elected assembly in Northern Ireland which will reflect the wishes of the electorate and be straightforward to operate. But the Framework Document proposes,

---

[15] Indeed a figure such as Peter Robinson can be understood as someone who finds such affectation repugnant. The purpose of this study is not to question the integrity of such a position and it is not to in any way denigrate the obvious courage and commitment of such a political figure. Its intention, from this perspective, is to point to the vicious consequences of a politics of exclusivist identities in which major groupings from both communities are unable to imagine and help to institute a novel set of identities and relations which move beyond the disfiguring certainties of exclusivism.

instead, a complex institutional arrangement which has so many inter-locking mechanisms that it would collapse from gridlock. It would also deny the will of the greater number of people in Northern Ireland to support and enhance the Union between Great Britain and Northern Ireland.[16]

If these are the common-place Unionist objections, Taylor's will-ingness to engage with the Republic is more novel. As part of his, eventually unsuccessful, attempt to challenge Molyneaux for the leadership of the UUP he gave talks in both Northern Ireland and the Republic. Speaking in Belfast to the annual conference of the Friends of the Union early in April he argued that Unionists must 'take risks' and make their ideology attractive 'to people of all religions and of none'.[17] As part of promoting Unionism, in a context where 'the British government no longer supported the Union', he urged the following:

We must promote Unionism in Britain in a manner which appeals and gains support. We must internationalise the message of the Union in the US and Europe by, for example, developing support groups within the USA and joining the European Democratic Union. *And we must not hesitate to talk to our neighbours in the South to build a new island of Ireland within which two states co-operate as neighbours.*[18]

In the Republic Taylor has been engaged in what one commentator has termed a 'charm offensive of speeches and articles, subtly distinguishing "cross-border" (acceptable) from "all-Ireland" (anathema) institutions, and putting himself about in the Irish Times and cities across the island as the *verligte* voice of Unionism.'[19] Two aspects of Taylor's new position are of particular significance. On several occasions Taylor has said something like the following: 'The onus is upon Unionists to convince the SDLP and the Dublin Government of our willingness to co-operate and to normalise relations based upon democratic will and the resolve of the people in the two parts of the island.'[20] He has also commented favourably upon the many changes in the Republic over the past several years, noting 'the creation of a pluralist society free from church control'.[21]

---

[16] John Taylor, 'Proposed Assembly Will Not Reflect Unionist Concerns', *Irish Times*, 9 March 1995.

[17] S. Breen, 'Taylor Says Unionists Must Attempt To Make Ideology Attractive', *Irish Times*, 3 April 1995.

[18] Ibid.

[19] N. Biggar, 'Taylor-Made', *Fortnight*, no. 338, April 1995, p. 16.

[20] M. Holland, 'Challenge of Making Historic Transition for Taylor', *Irish Times*, 30 March 1995.

[21] M. M. Tynan, 'Framework Document Seen As Conditional Surrender By Taylor', *Irish Times*, 28 March 1995.

For someone once seriously wounded by the Official IRA, for a Unionist politician who strenuously opposed both O'Neill and Faulkner, these recent initiatives by Taylor are both brave and significant. Construed from within an exclusivist position, they are quite radical both in their opening towards Dublin and Sinn Fein and in their preparedness to put the past behind. However, whether they could sustain the weight of future negotiations, whether they could provide a fulcrum upon which a more developed Unionist inclusivism could be swung into practice, these are difficult issues to determine.

The example of John Taylor makes it clear that Unionism, as at all moments of its past, contains a capacity for a pragmatic orientation to future negotiations and relations in and about Northern Ireland. Taylor is one figure, and no doubt there are several others, who is prepared to draw cautiously upon inclusivist forms of Unionist ideology to reimagine intergroup relations within Northern Ireland and relations with the Republic. In so doing he and others open up the possibility for Unionism to be more securely incorporated into the emerging inclusivist vision of future relations and identities. However it is not clear whether or not this opening will be sufficient for an eventual re-working of the basic rules of Unionist ideology. Clearly, in so far as such a re-working is possible it will only be so, in the short to medium term, under the guise of pragmatism. In other words, the principal chance to re-work Unionist commonsense from within Unionism will not arise from some overnight conversion to inclusivism but rather from the complex balance of opportunity and vulnerability which the prevailing circumstances entail. In these circumstances of peace, intergovernmental agreement, etc., the fact that pragmatism now speaks only in an inclusivist idiom is of critical significance. This feature of contemporary pragmatism provides a fundamental support for inclusivist tendencies within the various political groupings; it provides the opportunity for inclusivist forms to begin to re-work commonsense assumptions. Can they succeed?

It is not possible to offer any definitive answer to such a question. However, what my analysis does highlight is the likelihood that the outcome of this conflict within Unionism, and more particularly within the UUP, will determine the future of Northern Ireland. My analysis throughout this study has indicated that such has always been the case. However, in all previous instances the hegemony of exclusivist Unionism, the parallel exclusivism of major nationalist groupings and the absence of an authoritative inclusivist idiom as the lingua franca of interparty talks proved fatal for a re-working of identities and relations. This time things have changed, although not utterly.

Almost paradoxically, the very process of moving towards a consolidation of peace through re-formed political arrangements, re-imagined identities and re-worked forms of relationship is also the very process likely to produce political conflict and its inherent dangers. Indeed, here lies the rub. Interparty discussions with any chance of a successful outcome necessarily presuppose at least a pragmatic acceptance of inclusivist rules as the lingua franca of political negotiation. But if this acceptance remains a mere façade then the very progress of the talks is likely to uncover systematic distortions in the pattern of communication between the parties and to exacerbate interparty conflict. If, on the other hand, the pragmatic acceptance of inclusivism begins to work itself into the core unconscious rules for the structuration of Unionism or Nationalism and to institutionalise itself within particular parties such as Sinn Fein, the DUP or the UUP, then it will inevitably experience resistance from within, thereby uncovering systematic distortions in the pattern of communication within the party and exacerbating intraparty conflict. To walk the wire between these various tendencies without overbalancing is a very demanding task for any political circus!

These are the dangers inherent in attempting to implement a new political order. There is a distinct possibility that the same vicious cycle which has played itself out so destructively in Northern Ireland over the past twenty-five years will do so yet again and that very similar processes to those I have specified with regard to the period from 1962 until 1975 will recur. If so I would expect to see an unfolding process of polarisation within the Unionist community, and between Unionists and Nationalists, with first the DUP and, subsequently, part of the UUP withdrawing from negotiations and attempting to re-groove Unionist ideology in entirely exclusivist forms. Such circumstances would inevitably involve renewed political activity on the streets of Northern Ireland and the high likelihood of renewed paramilitary activity. Parallel movement within Nationalist ideology, and especially within Sinn Fein, would also be likely. For Unionists the world would have become an entirely treacherous place, the presumptions at the core of exclusivist constructions would have become self-fulfilling prophecies. In such a situation a movement akin to the Vanguard movement of the 1970s, one which would attempt to integrate religious and secular exclusivism and to establish ideological hegemony in Northern Ireland, would be likely to emerge.

The hope for avoiding such a dread recurrence lies in the novelty of the current situation, a novelty which has been produced through the difficult, and often courageous, work of various political actors and agencies. Between them, although not always in concert, the British and Irish governments, the SDLP, Alliance, Sinn Fein, the UUP and even the DUP, along with the United States government and the European Community; all of these corporate actors have, to varying extents, contributed to establishing the authority of an inclusivist lingua franca for the conduct of political life in Northern Ireland. At the moment this lingua franca is, as it were, a foreign tongue for the principal Unionist groupings. They fear it and they resent it, even though they may occasionally condescend to use it. However, in the case of John Taylor, to take him merely as an example, we may be seeing the emergence within the UUP, the principal Unionist party, of an inclusivist Unionism which has the capacity to carry pragmatism beyond itself and into the unknown of a future beyond the politics of exclusivist identity.

CONCLUSION

Both in Northern Ireland and elsewhere, we live in a world in which it is essential to take ideologies and identities seriously. Such has been the broad claim of this study. The first five chapters have developed a novel theory and method for the analysis of ideology, identity and intersubjectivity. I have argued that, in the contemporary world, such a theory and method is more necessary than ever. In chapters 7 and 8 I have carried this theory and method to the analysis of a particular ideological formation by exploring the structuration of Unionist ideology over the critical period from 1962 until 1975. These chapters have observed the re-production of exclusivist identities and patterns of relationship in Northern Ireland through a political process which, while contingent upon political action, has been played out within an ideological field in which exclusivist forms held a massive predominance. In order to develop such an analysis I have, first of all, identified a variety of unconscious rules of Unionist ideology, rules which are drawn upon in the making of subjectivity and history. Second, I have explored the ways in which these different rules for the construction of subjectivity and intersubjectivity constitute the forms through which, and about which, intra-Unionist ideological conflict is fought out. From this perspective the political conflict within Unionism is, first and last, an ideological conflict. This does not mean that class processes, material interests, religious beliefs or political advantage are not part of this conflict. What it does mean is that these and other interests are organised through ideology and fought over within ideology; which is to say within the field of subjectivity and intersubjectivity.

In this concluding chapter I have tried to develop, rather gingerly, some of the principal implications of my approach for the analysis of contemporary events in Northern Ireland. These events involve a concerted attempt to re-order political identities and relations. Hence I have tried to analyse the internal dynamics of the political and ideological conflict which has been set in motion by such a bold attempt. I have done so as it is starkly evident that the processes involved in changing the rules need to be understood as inevitably and irreducibly ideological and because I believe that the failure to take this ideological feature into account is likely to lead to significant misunderstandings of both the ongoing process of change and the inevitable conflicts and reversals which will be encountered. The current attempt to make a difference in Northern Ireland has a long way to go before inclusivist forms of identity and relations will have any real opportunity to institutionalise themselves. In a world rapidly experiencing globalisation and diverse social and cultural transformations, this attempt at re-imagining and re-working political identities and relations will carry lessons for all of us.

Select bibliography

Althusser, L. 'Ideology and the Ideological State Apparatuses' in *Lenin and Philosophy*. New York and London: Monthly Review Press, 1971.

Barton, B. *Brookeborough: The Making of a Prime Minister*. Belfast: Institute of Irish Studies, The Queen's University of Belfast, 1988.

Bew, P., Gibbon, P. and Patterson, H. *The State in Northern Ireland: 1921–1972*. Manchester: Manchester University Press, 1979.

Billig, M. *Ideology and Social Psychology*. Oxford: Blackwell, 1982.

Bruce, S. *God Save Ulster!: The Religion and Politics of Paisleyism*. Oxford: Oxford University Press, 1989.

The Red Hand: Protestant Paramilitaries in Northern Ireland. Oxford: Oxford University Press, 1992.

Buckland, P. *Irish Unionism 1885–1923: A Documentary History*, Belfast: Her Majesty's Stationery Office, 1973.

Burke, K. *A Grammar of Motives*. New York: Prentice Hall, 1945.

Burton, F. *The Politics of Legitimacy*. London: Routledge, 1978.

Cash, J. 'Ideology and Affect: The Case of Northern Ireland'. *Political Psychology*, 10:4 (1989), 703–24.

Colby, A., Gibbs, J., Kohlberg, L., Speicher-Dubin, B., and Candee, D. *Standard Form Scoring Manual*. Cambridge, MA: Centre for Moral Education, Harvard University, 1979.

Darby, J. *Conflict in Northern Ireland: The Development of a Polarized Community*. Dublin: Gill & Macmillan, 1976.

Davies, A. F. *Skills, Outlooks and Passions: A Psychoanalytic Contribution to the Study of Politics*. Cambridge University Press, 1980.

Farrell, M. *Northern Ireland: The Orange State*. London: Pluto Press, 1980.

Fromm, E. 'The Method and Function of an Analytic Social Psychology' in A. Arato and E. Gebhardt, eds., *The Essential Frankfurt School Reader*.

Geertz, C. 'Ideology as a Cultural System' in *The Interpretation of Cultures*. New York: Basic Books, 1973.

Giddens, A. *The Constitution of Society*. Cambridge: Polity Press, 1984.

Social Theory and Modern Sociology. Cambridge: Polity Press, 1987.

Gramsci, A. *Selections from Prison Notebooks*. Translated by Q. Hoare and G. Nowell Smith. London, Lawrence and Wishart, 1971.

Greenberg, S. *Race and State in Capitalist Development.* New Haven and London: Yale University Press, 1980.

Legitimating the Illegitimate: State, Markets and Resistance in South Africa. Berkeley: University of California Press, 1987.

Habermas, J. *Knowledge and Human Interests.* Translated by J. Shapiro. Boston: Beacon Press, 1971.

Legitimation Crisis. Translated by T. McCarthy. Boston: Beacon Press, 1975.

Hall, S., Critcher, C., Clarke, J., and Roberts, B. *Policing the Crisis: Mugging, the State and Law and Order.* London: Macmillan, 1978.

Held, D. *Introduction to Critical Theory.* London: Hutchinson, 1980.

Hepburn, A. C., ed., *The Conflict of Nationality in Modern Ireland.* London: Edward Arnold, 1980.

Jacques, E. 'Social Systems as Defense Against Persecutory and Depressive Anxiety', in M. Klein, P. Heimann and R. Money-Kyrle, eds., *New Directions in Psycho-analysis.* London: Tavistock Publications, 1955.

Janis, I. and Mann, L. *Decision-Making: A Psychological Analysis of Conflict, Choice, and Commitment.* New York: Free Press, 1977.

Kohlberg, L. 'From Is to Ought' in T. Mishel, ed., *Cognitive Development and Epistemology.* New York: Academic Press, 1971.

Lacan, J. *Ecrits: A Selection.* Translated by A. Sheridan. London: Tavistock, 1977.

McAllister, I. *The Northern Ireland Social Democratic and Labour Party: Political Opposition in a Divided Society.* London: Macmillan Press, 1977.

McLellan, D. *Ideology.* Bristol: Open University Press, 1986.

Menzies, I. 'A Case-Study in the Functioning of Social Systems as a Defence Against Anxiety', in A. D. Colman and W. H. Bexton, eds., *Group Relations Reader.* California: A. K. Rice Institute, 1975.

Nelson, S. *Ulster's Uncertain Defenders: Loyalists and the Northern Ireland Conflict.* Belfast: Appletree Press, 1984.

O'Malley, P. *The Uncivil Wars: Ireland Today.* Belfast: Blackstaff Press, 1983.

O'Neill, T. *The Autobiography of Terence O'Neill: Prime Minister of Northern Ireland 1963–1969.* London: Hart-Davis, 1972.

Parkin, F. *Marxism and Class Theory.* London: Tavistock, 1979.

Purdie, B. *Politics in the Streets.* Belfast: Blackstaff Press, 1990.

Saul, J. *The State and Revolution in Eastern Africa.* New York: Monthly Review Press, 1986.

Saul J. and Gelb, S. *The Crisis in South Africa.* New York and London: Monthly Review Press, 1981.

Segal, H. *Introduction to the Work of Melanie Klein.* London: Hogarth Press, 1979.

Smith, A. D. *The Ethnic Revival in the Modern World.* Cambridge University Press, 1981.

Smyth, C. *Ian Paisley: Voice of Protestant Ulster.* Edinburgh: Scottish Academic Press, 1987.

Stewart, A. T. Q. *The Narrow Ground: Aspects of Ulster 1609–1969*. London: Faber & Faber, 1977.

Thompson, J. B. *Ideology and Modern Culture: Critical Social Theory in the Era of Mass Communication*. Cambridge: Polity Press, 1990.

Studies in the Theory of Ideology. Cambridge: Polity Press, 1984.

Wright, F. 'Protestant Ideology and Politics in Ulster'. *European Journal of Sociology*, 14:2 (1972), 213–80.

Index to Identity, Ideology and Conflict

Index

Unionist politics, basic rules of structuration 63

Unionists 130, 160, 185–6
  and British connection 104, 105, 157
  reaction to Bloody Sunday killings 165–6
  see also Protestant/Unionist community

United Ireland, fear of 128

United Ulster Unionist Coalition 152, 199–200

United Ulster Unionist Council 130

utilitarianism 189

UUP *see* Ulster Unionist Party

UUUC *see* United Ulster Unionist Coalition

Vanguard movement 152, 153, 169–70, 171–7, 186–7, 199

see also Craig; Loyalists
Vanguard Unionist Party 153

violence 152–4, 159–60, 161–2, 171

voluntarism 52

voluntary coalition government 200, 201–2

vulnerability, and vigilance 14

welfare state legislation, Northern Ireland 126–7

Westminster 126–7, 153, 168, 174, 176
  see also British government

White, John 209–10

Whitelaw, William 153, 172, 173, 174

Wilson, Harold 161

working class solidarity 19, 132–3

Wright, Frank 188, 189